CLOU
HOTEL

by
JULIAN HANSHAW

Top Shelf PRODUCTIONS

Cloud Hotel © 2018 Julian Hanshaw.

Published by Top Shelf Productions, PO Box 1282, Marietta, GA 30061-1282, USA.
Top Shelf Productions is an imprint of IDW Publishing, a division of Idea and Design Works, LLC.
Offices: 2765 Truxtun Road, San Diego, CA 92106. Top Shelf Productions ®, the Top Shelf logo,
Idea and Design Works ®, and the IDW logo are registered trademarks of Idea and Design Works, LLC.
All Rights Reserved. With the exception of small excerpts of artwork used for review purposes, none
of the contents of this publication may be reprinted without the permission of IDW Publishing.
IDW Publishing does not read or accept unsolicited submissions of ideas, stories or artwork.

Editor-in-Chief: Chris Staros.

Edited by Chris Staros and Leigh Walton.

Designed by Julian Hanshaw and Gilberto Lazcano.

Printed in Korea.

ISBN: 978-4-60309-425-2   22 21 20 19 18   5 4 3 2 1

Visit our online catalog at topshelfcomix.com.

When I was a boy, my family and I were coming back from seeing my nan in Cheltenham. It was a Sunday evening, 26th October 1980, and we were just leaving the A41 into Tring in our white Maxi when we all saw an unusual light in the night sky. As we drove closer, it did not move away, and we eventually drove directly underneath it.

We all excitedly got out of the car to view the large, rectangular object that was hovering about 100 metres above us and covered a large part of the sky.
There was no noise coming from the object, which had a large dome on the underside. I couldn't see the top of the craft. It was very bright, and a light shone down around us and the car.

We all watched it for a few minutes before it shot upwards, silently, until it was just a white speck in the night sky. Then it vanished completely.

This story was inspired by that night.

Julian Hanshaw

1st March

1981

Wilstone Reservoir
Hertfordshire
England

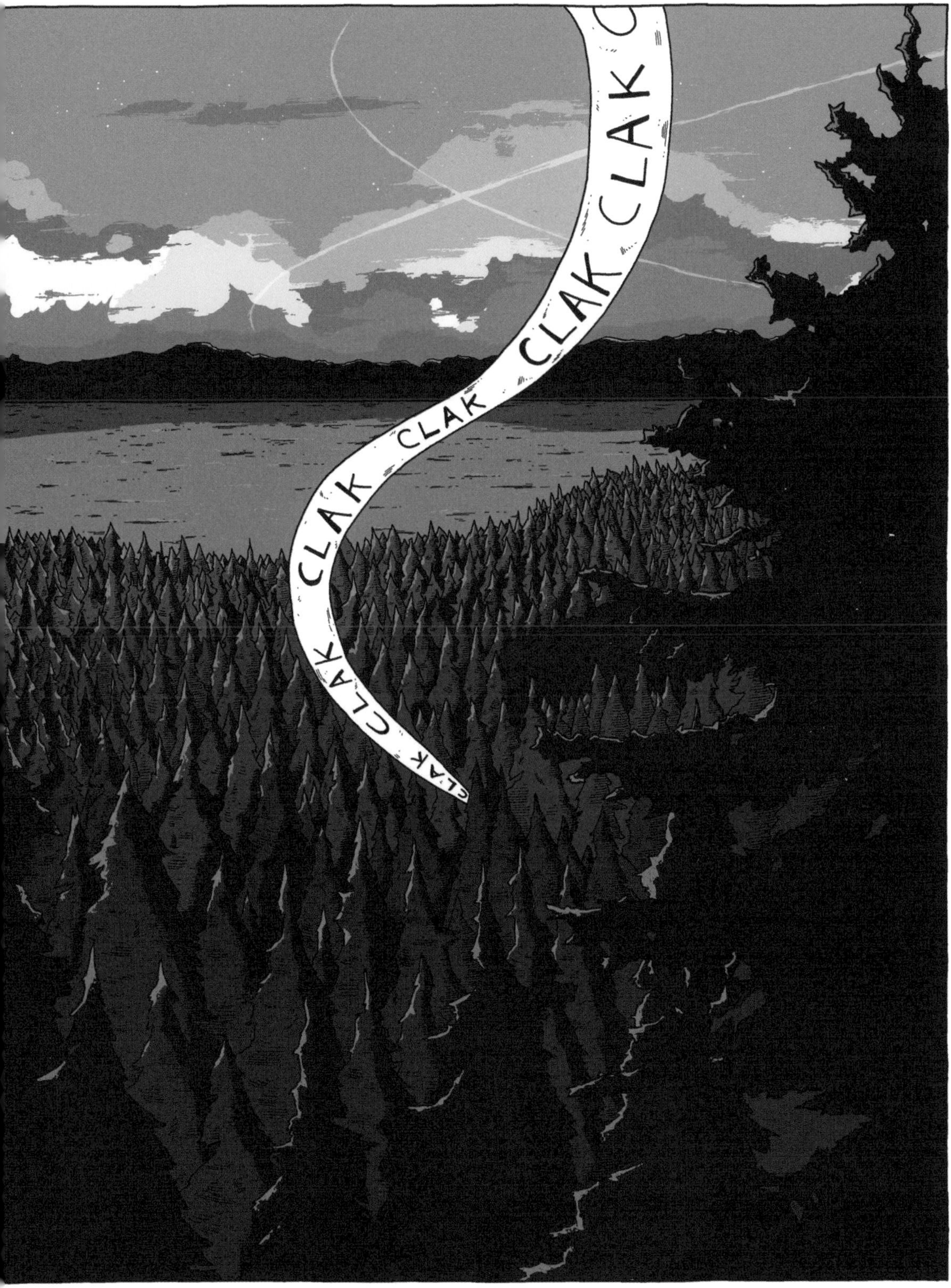
CLAK CLAK CLAK CLAK CLAK CLAK CLAK

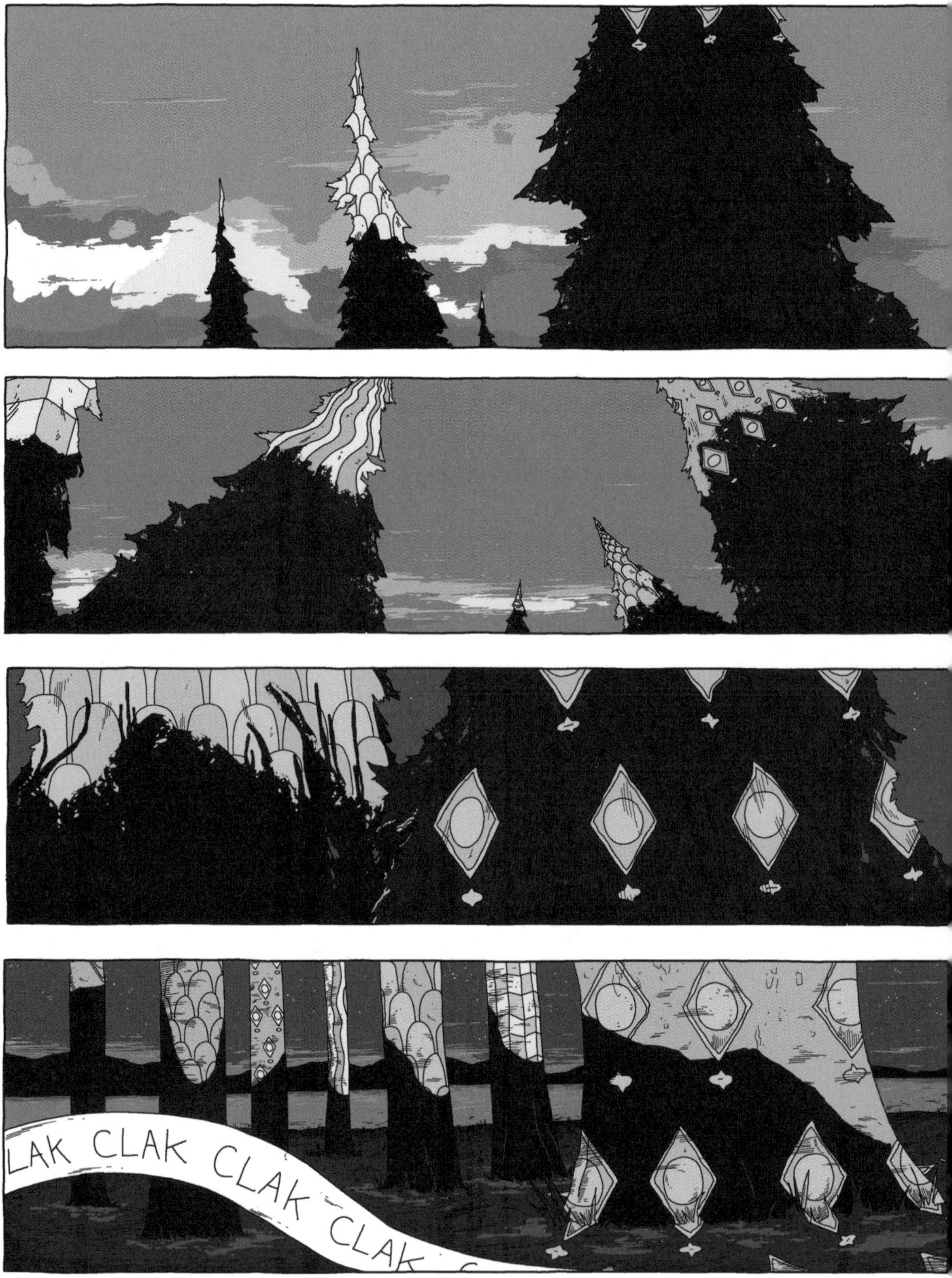
LAK CLAK CLAK CLAK CLAK

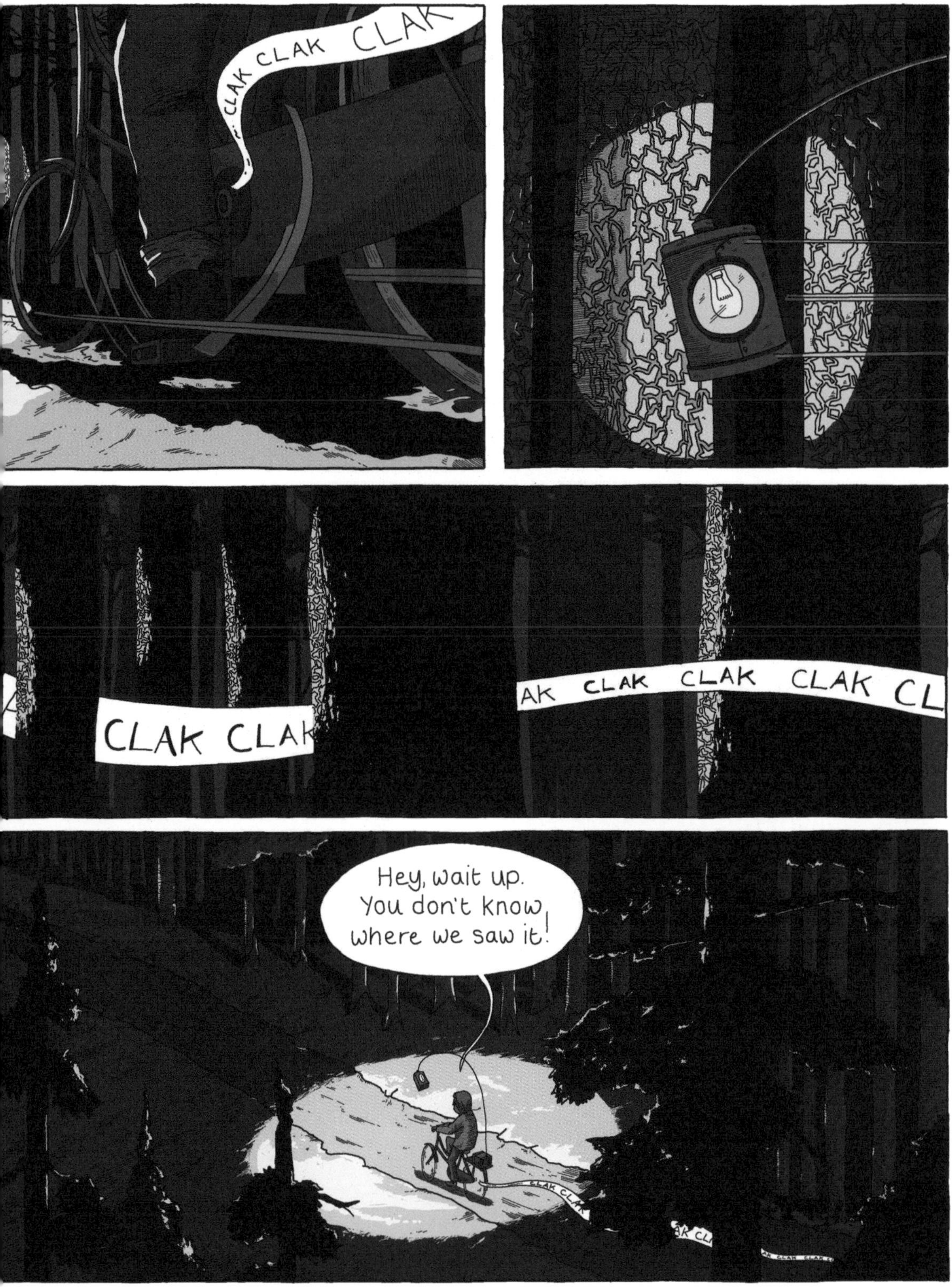
CLAK CLAK CLAK
CLAK CLAK
AK CLAK CLAK CLAK CL
Hey, wait up. You don't know where we saw it!
CLAK CLAK

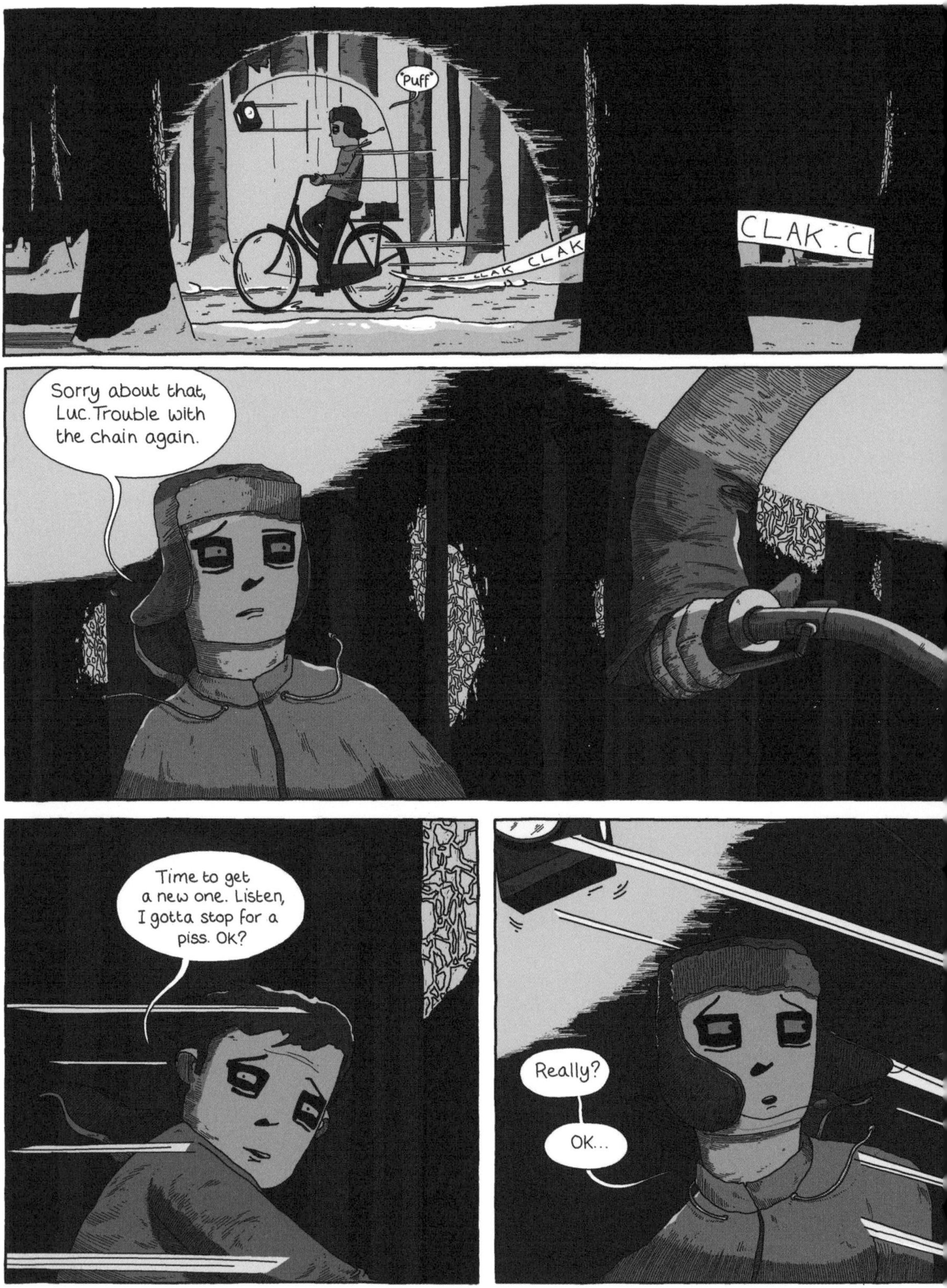
puff
CLAK CLAK
CLAK CLAK
CLAK · CL
Sorry about that, Luc. Trouble with the chain again.
Time to get a new one. Listen, I gotta stop for a piss. OK?
Really?
OK...

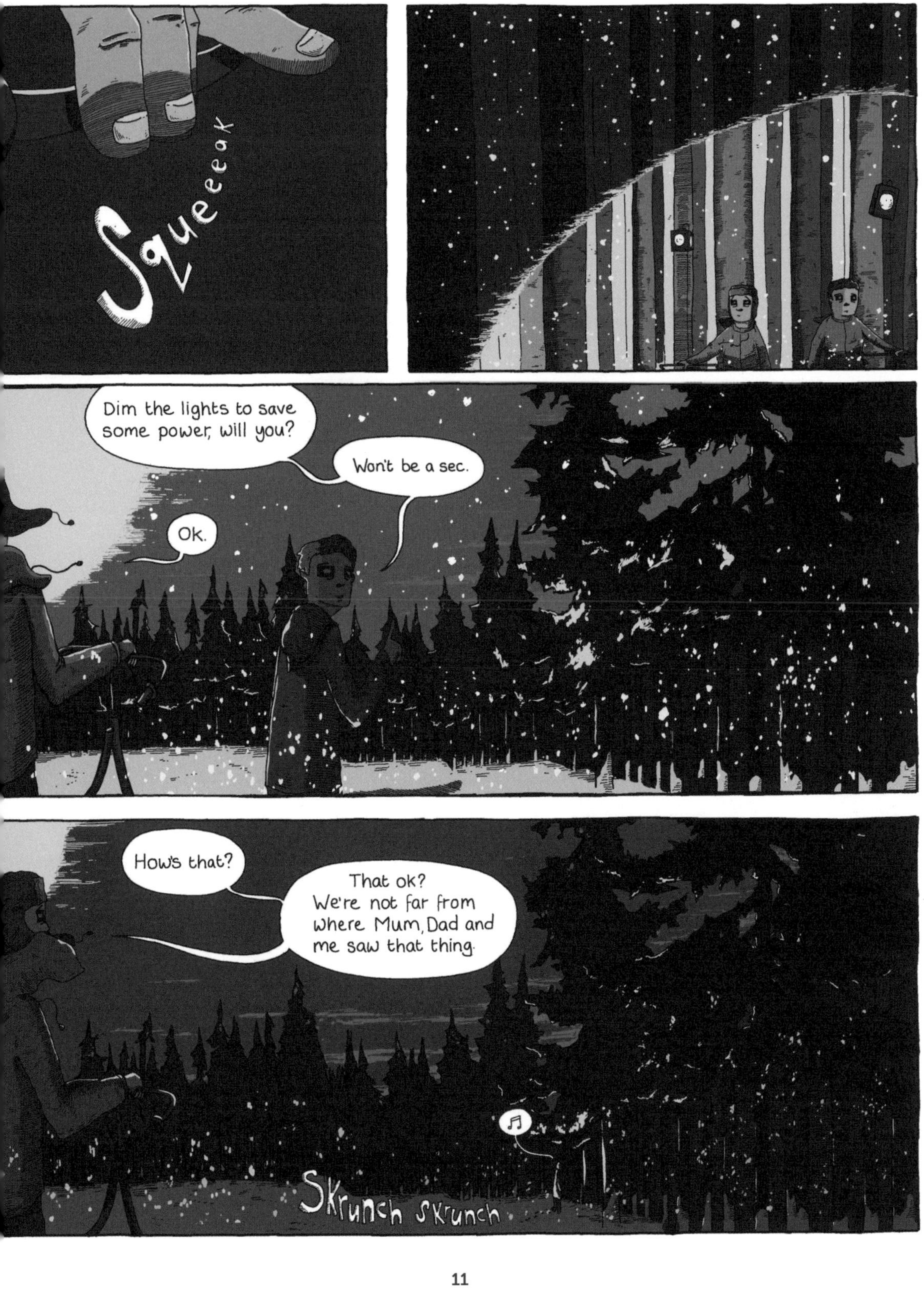
Squeeeeak
Dim the lights to save some power, will you?
Won't be a sec.
Ok.
How's that?
That ok? We're not far from where Mum, Dad and me saw that thing.
♫
Skrunch skrunch

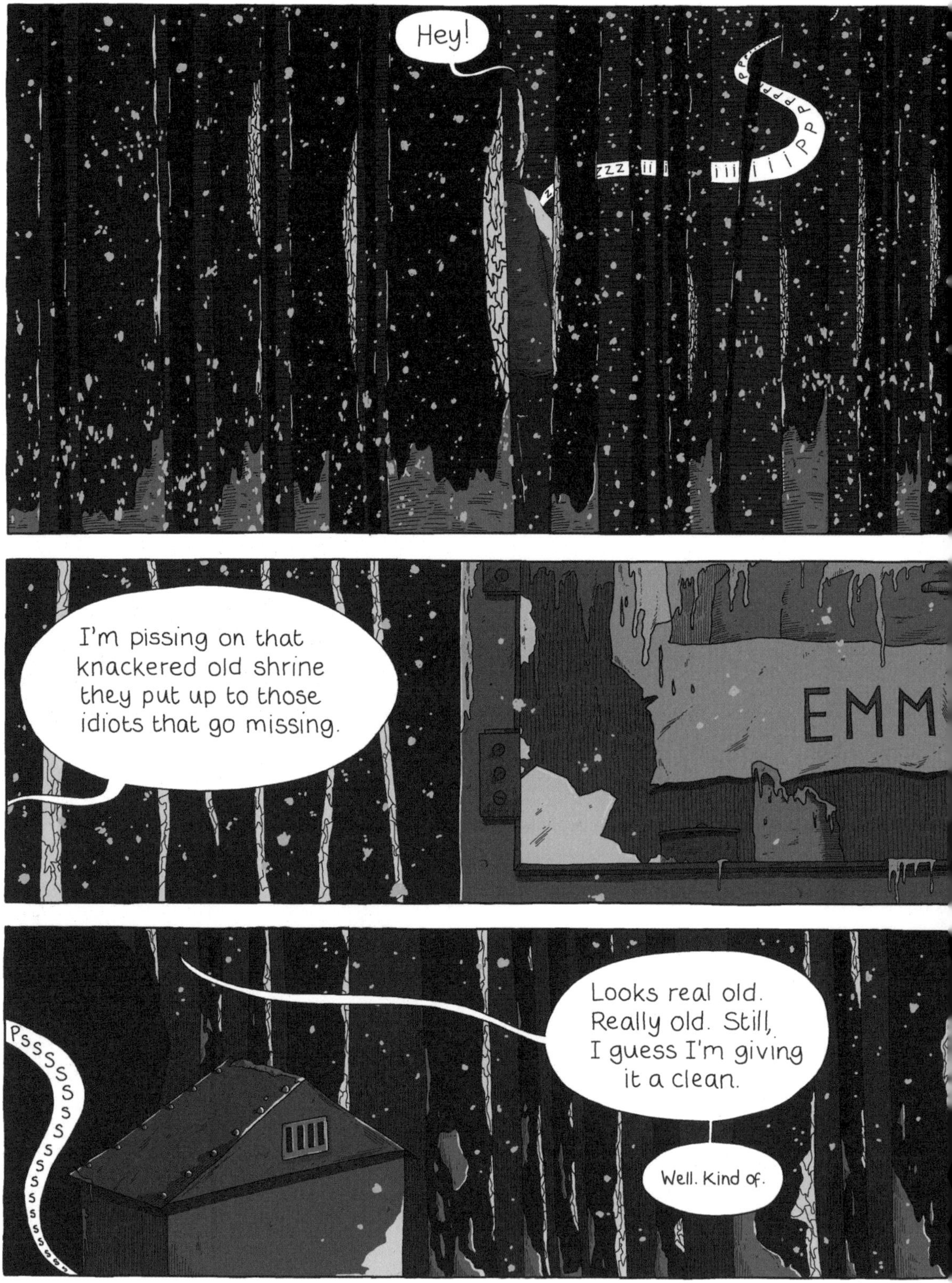
Hey!
I'm pissing on that knackered old shrine they put up to those idiots that go missing.
EMM
Psssssssssssss
Looks real old. Really old. Still, I guess I'm giving it a clean.
Well. Kind of.

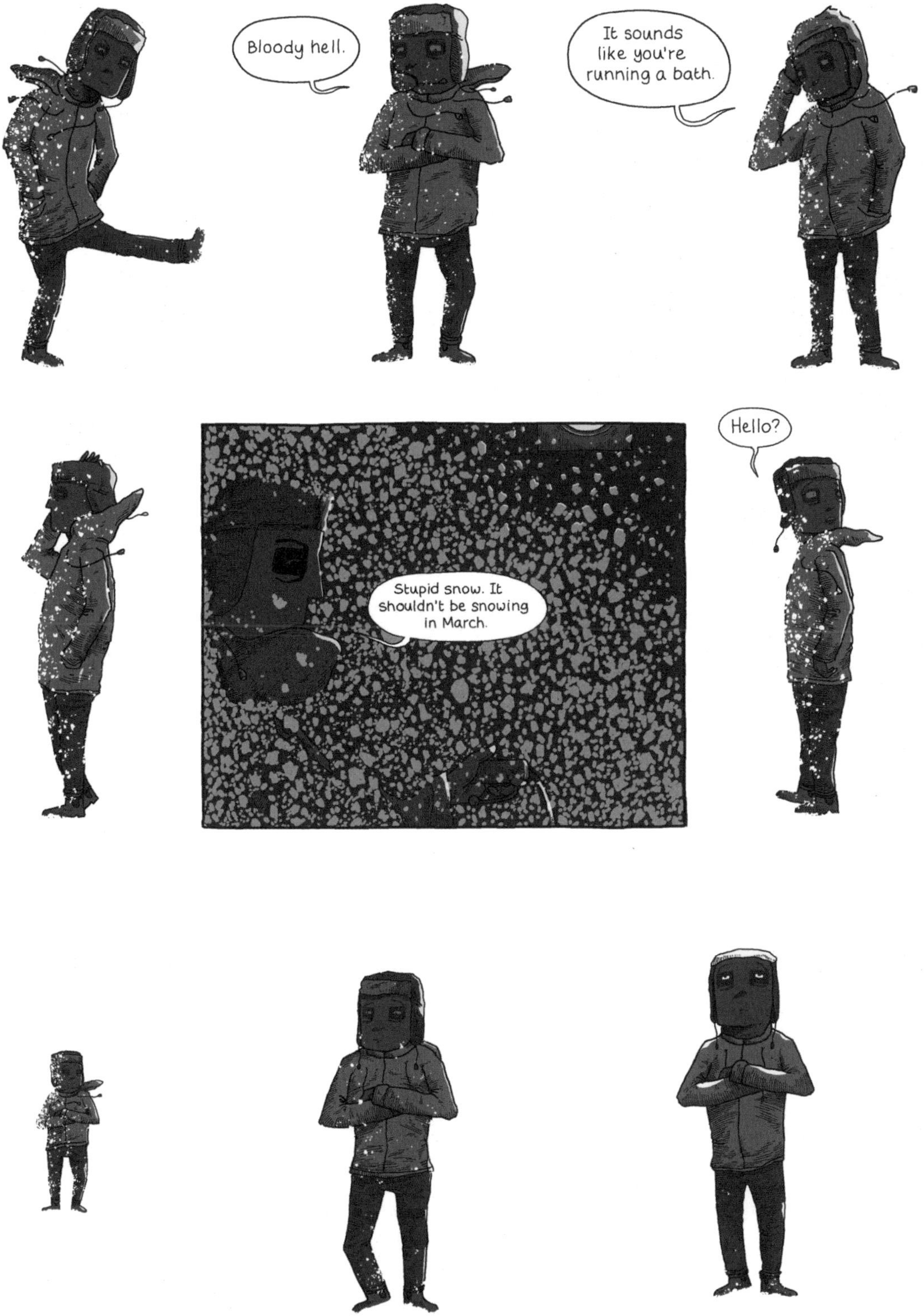
Bloody hell.
It sounds like you're running a bath.
Stupid snow. It shouldn't be snowing in March.
Hello?

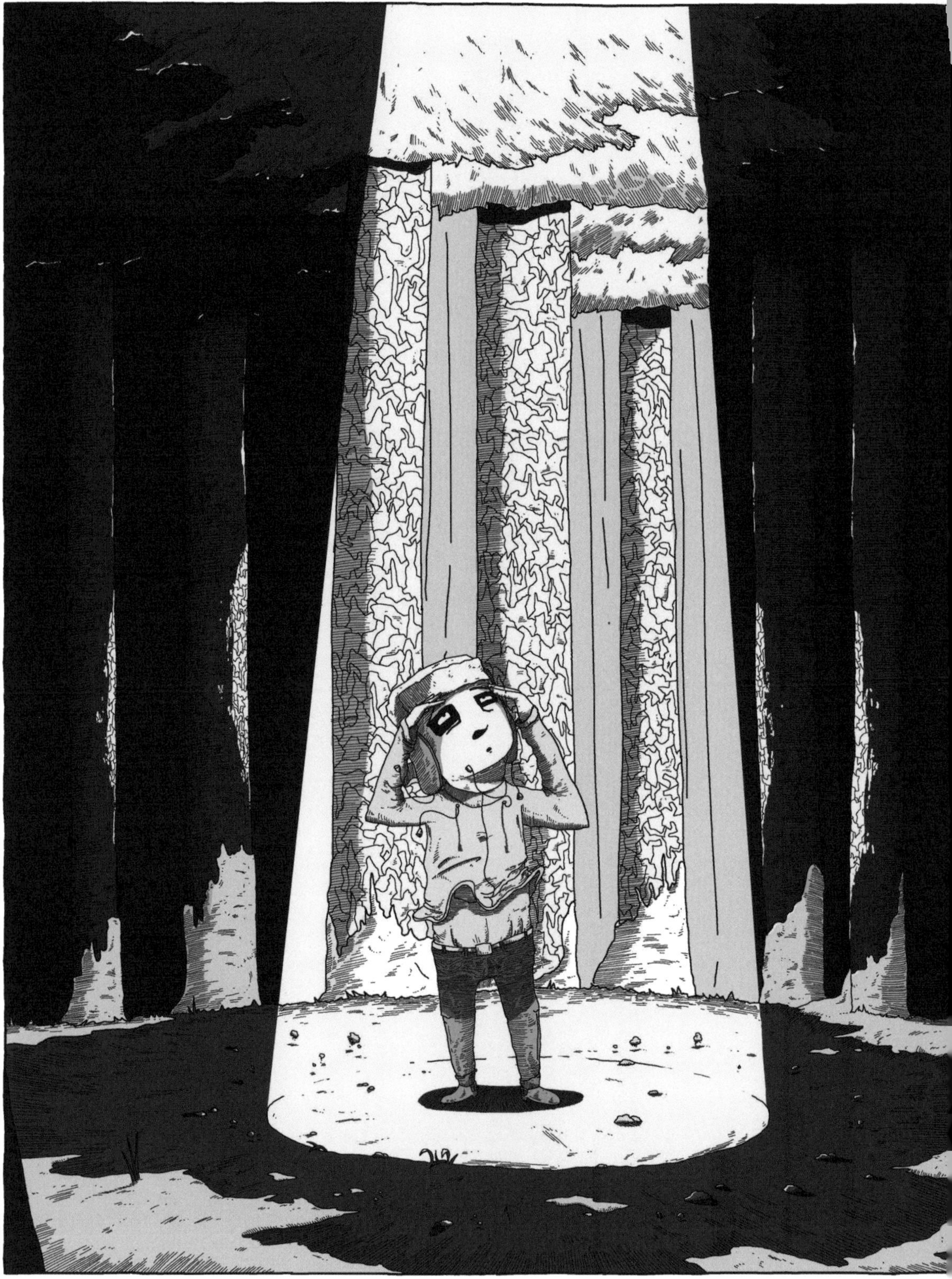

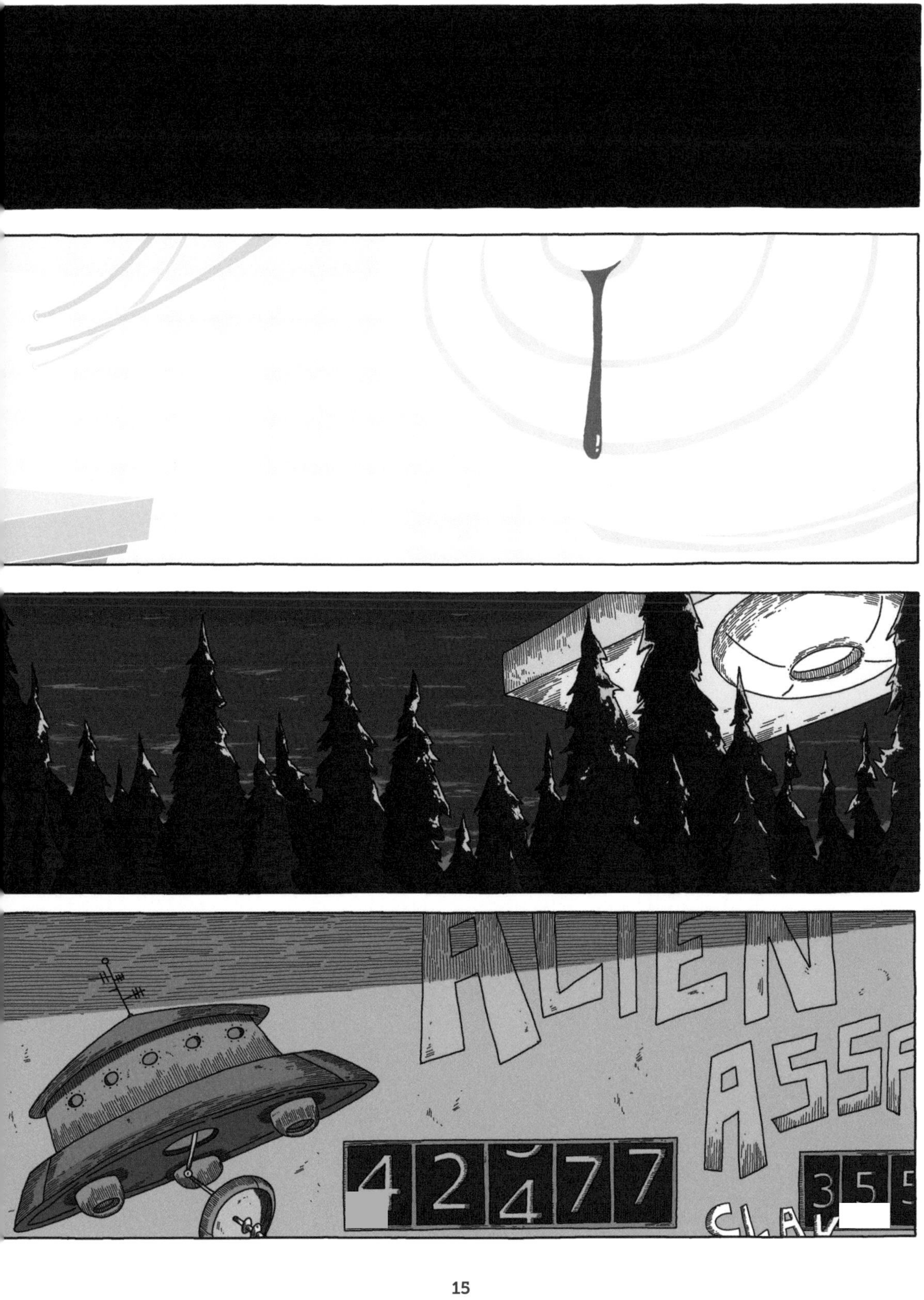
ALIEN
42477
CLAK

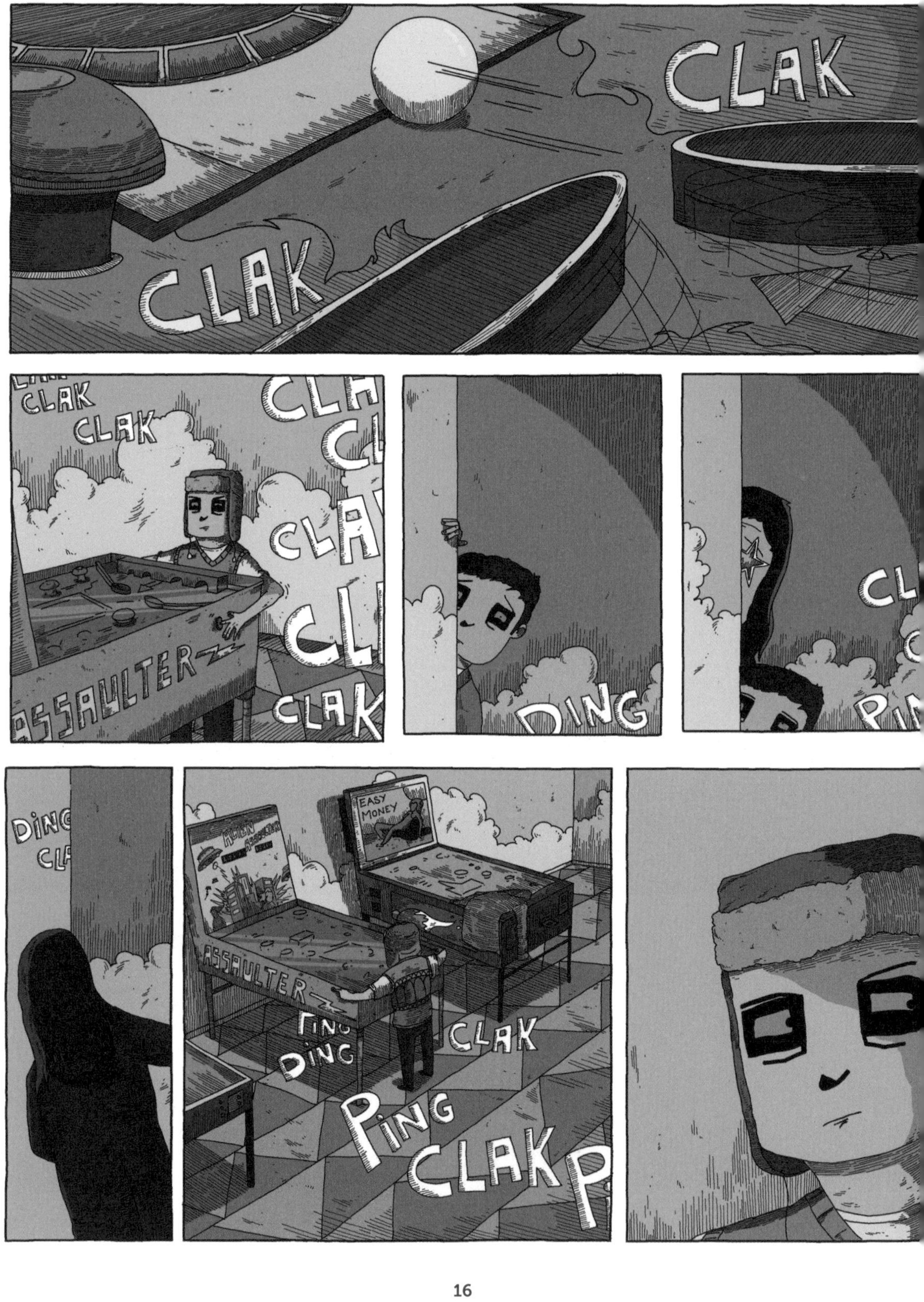
CLAK
CLAK
CLAK
CLAK
ASSAULTER
CLAK
DING
DING
EASY MONEY
ASSAULTER
DING
CLAK
PING
CLAK

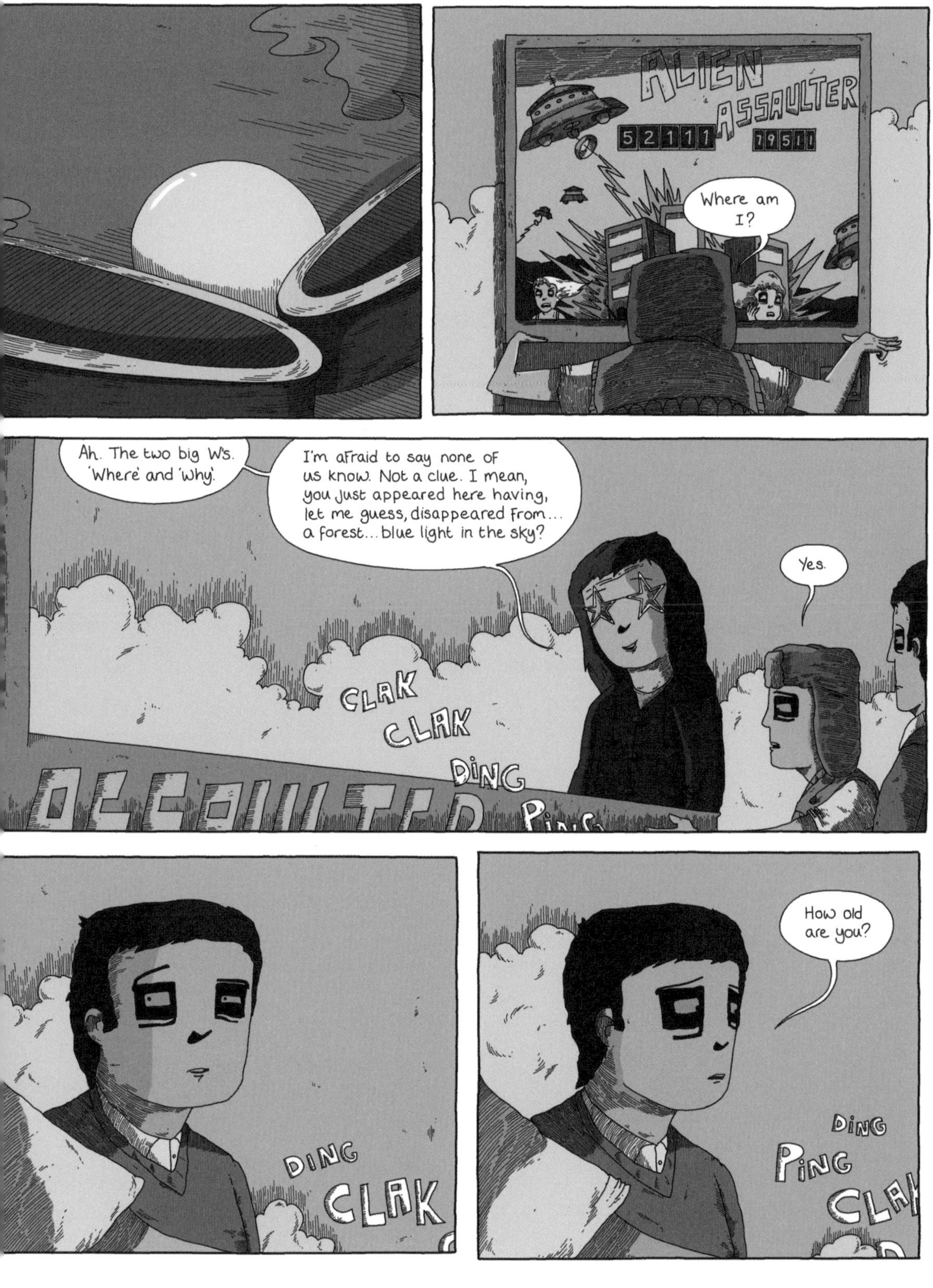
ALIEN ASSAULTER
52111
79511
Where am I?
Ah. The two big W's. 'Where' and 'Why'.
I'm afraid to say none of us know. Not a clue. I mean, you just appeared here having, let me guess, disappeared from... a forest... blue light in the sky?
CLAK
CLAK
DING
Yes.
DING
CLAK
How old are you?
DING
PING

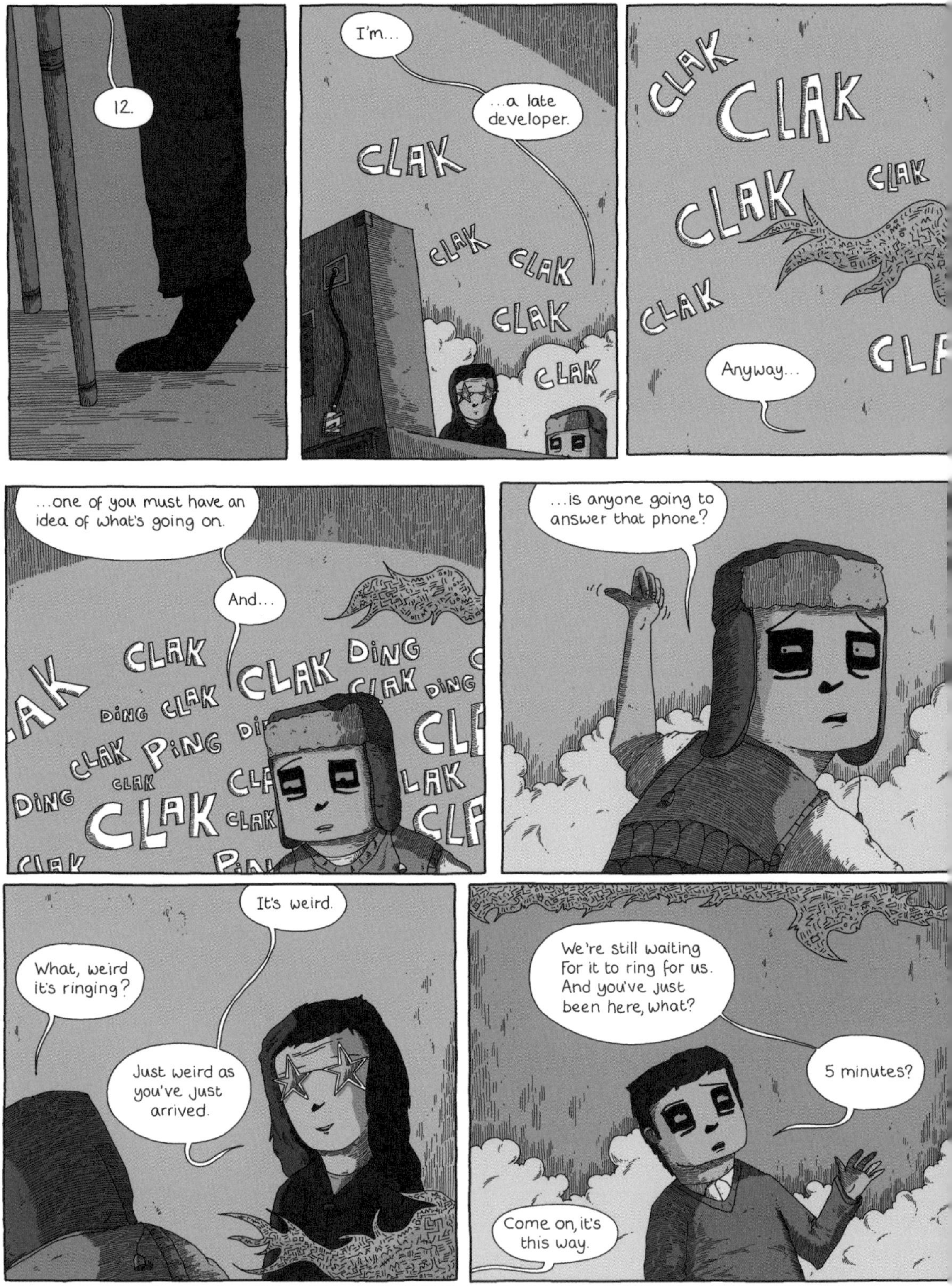

12.
I'm...
...a late developer.
CLAK
CLAK
CLAK
CLAK
CLAK
CLAK
CLAK
CLAK
CLAK
CLAK
Anyway...
...one of you must have an idea of what's going on.
And...
CLAK
CLAK
DING
CLAK
DING
CLAK
PING
DING
CLAK
CLAK
...is anyone going to answer that phone?
What, weird it's ringing?
It's weird.
Just weird as you've just arrived.
We're still waiting for it to ring for us. And you've just been here, what?
5 minutes?
Come on, it's this way.

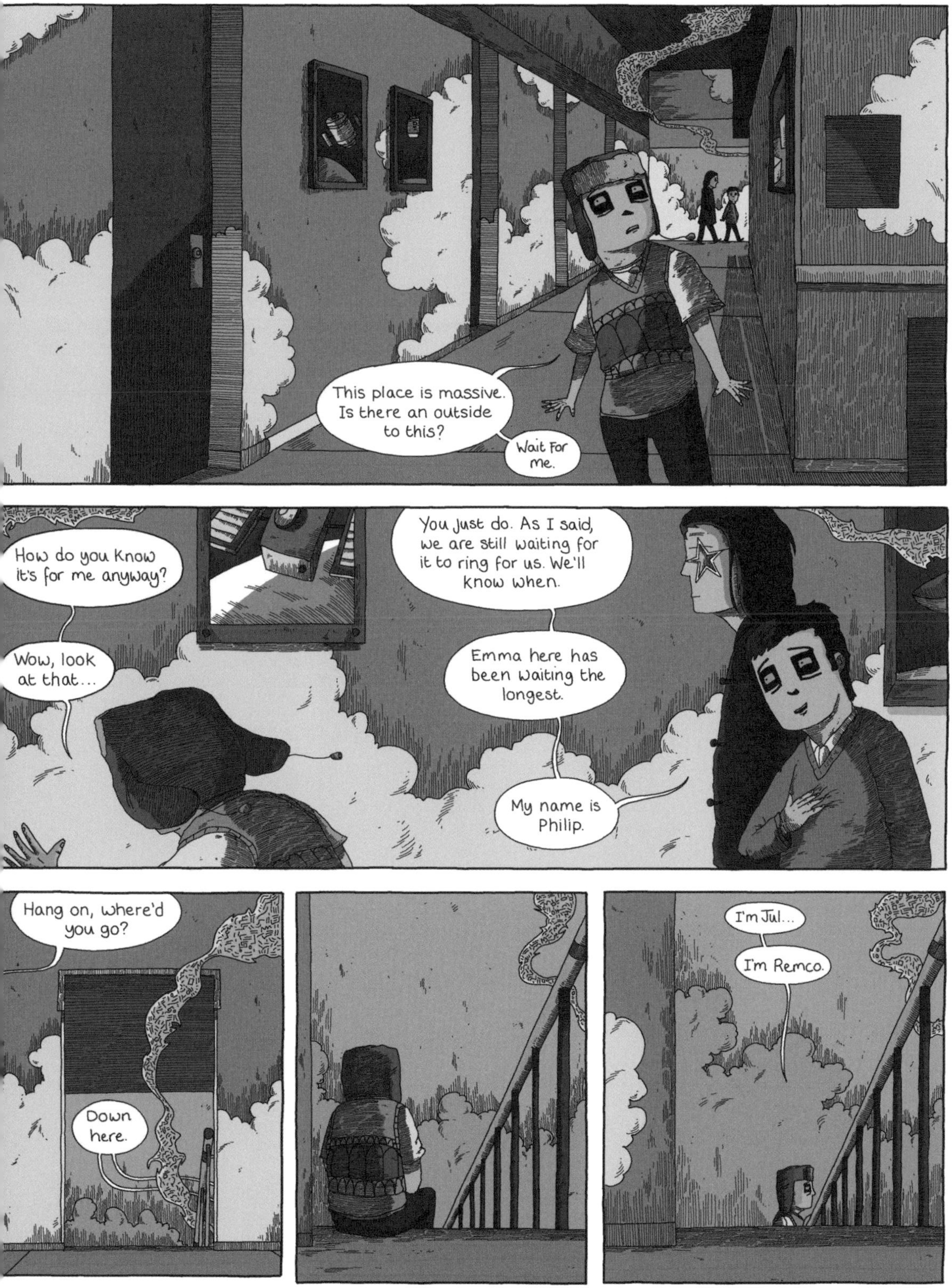
This place is massive. Is there an outside to this?
Wait for me.
How do you know it's for me anyway?
Wow, look at that...
You just do. As I said, we are still waiting for it to ring for us. We'll know when.
Emma here has been waiting the longest.
My name is Philip.
Hang on, where'd you go?
Down here.
I'm Jul...
I'm Remco.

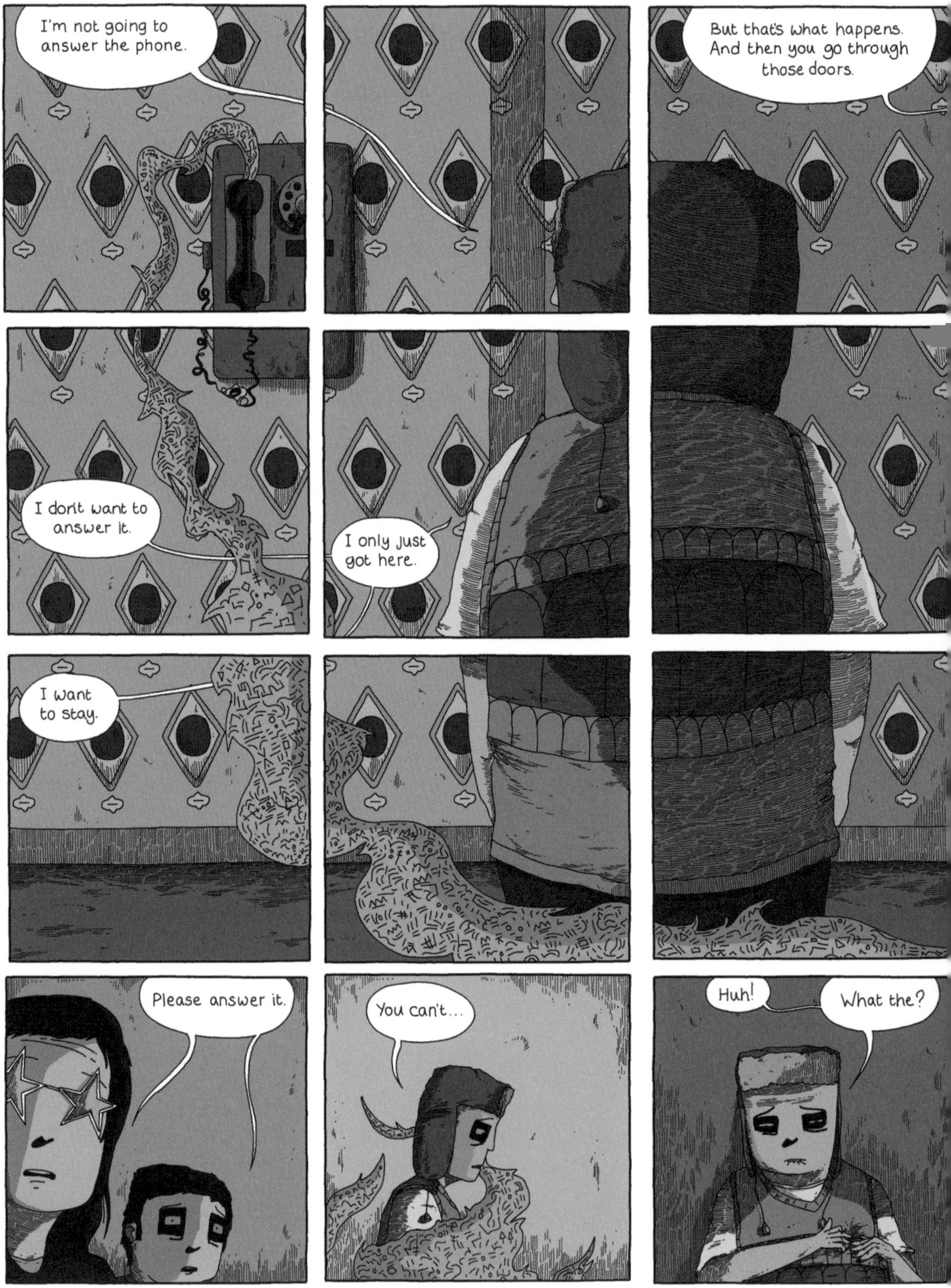
I'm not going to answer the phone.
But that's what happens. And then you go through those doors.
I don't want to answer it.
I only just got here.
I want to stay.
Please answer it.
You can't...
Huh!
What the?

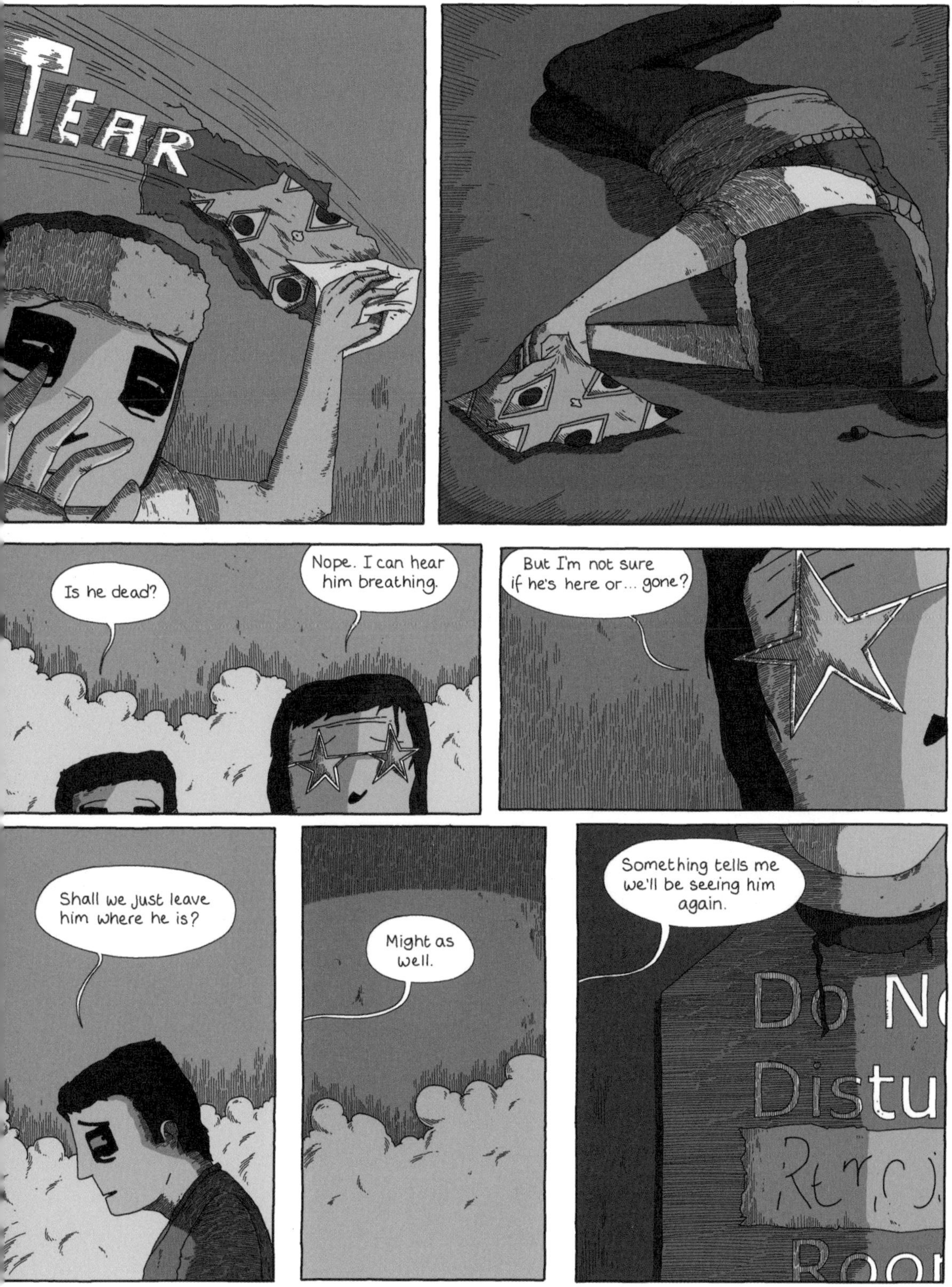
TEAR
Is he dead?
Nope. I can hear him breathing.
But I'm not sure if he's here or... gone?
Shall we just leave him where he is?
Might as well.
Something tells me we'll be seeing him again.
Do N
Distu
Roo

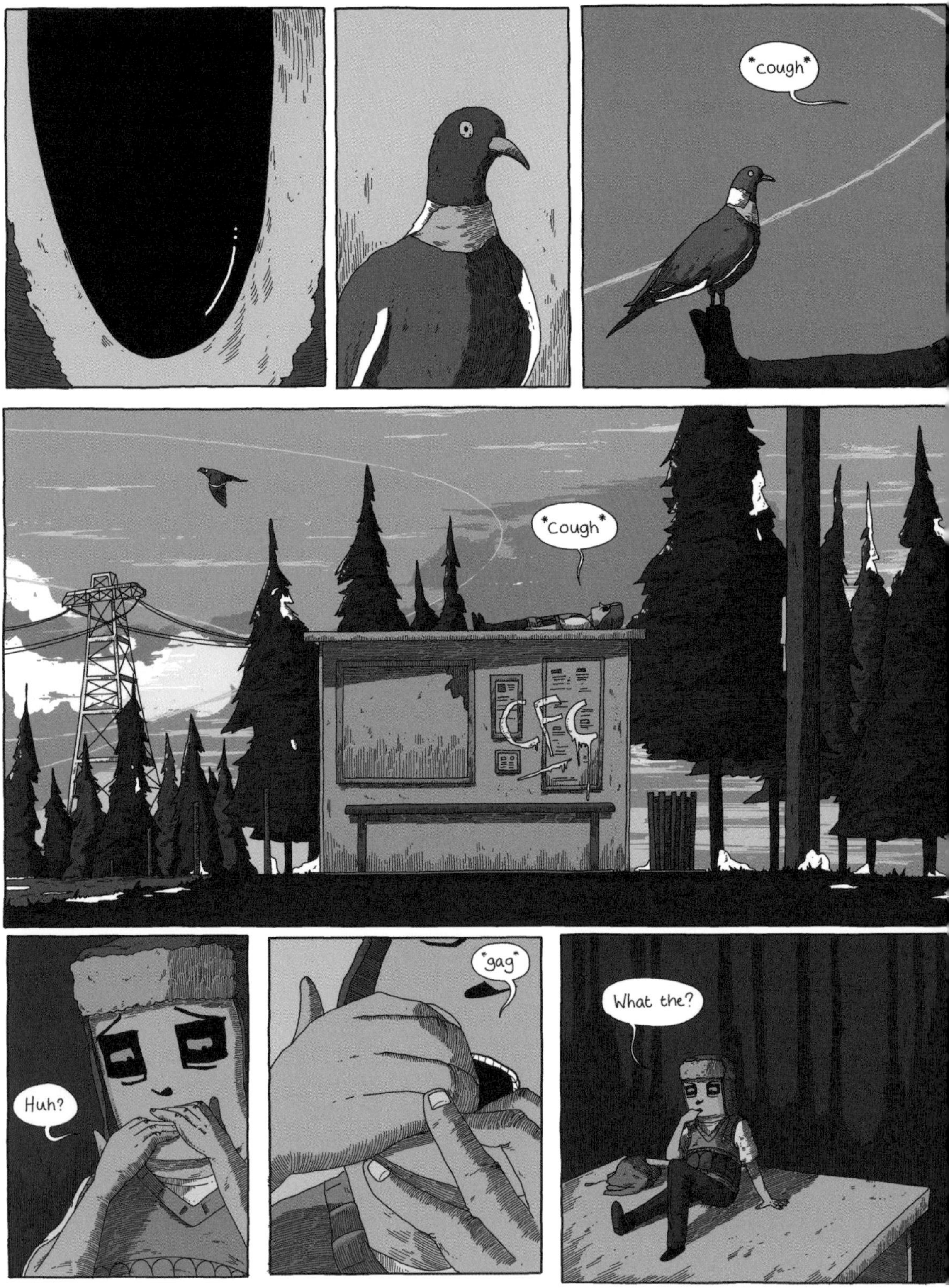
cough
cough
CFC
Huh?
gag
What the?

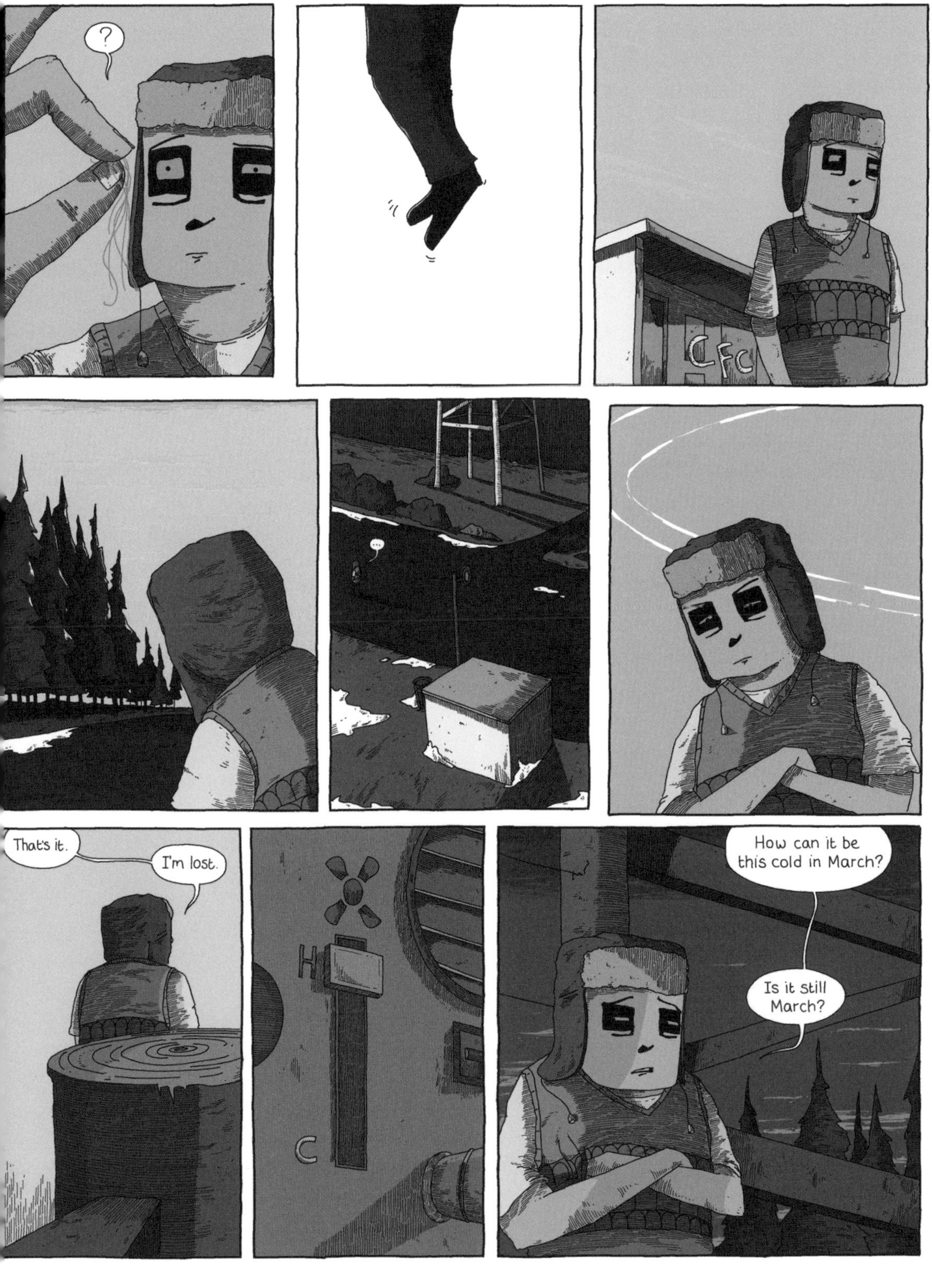
?
CFC
...
That's it.
I'm lost.
H
C
How can it be this cold in March?
Is it still March?

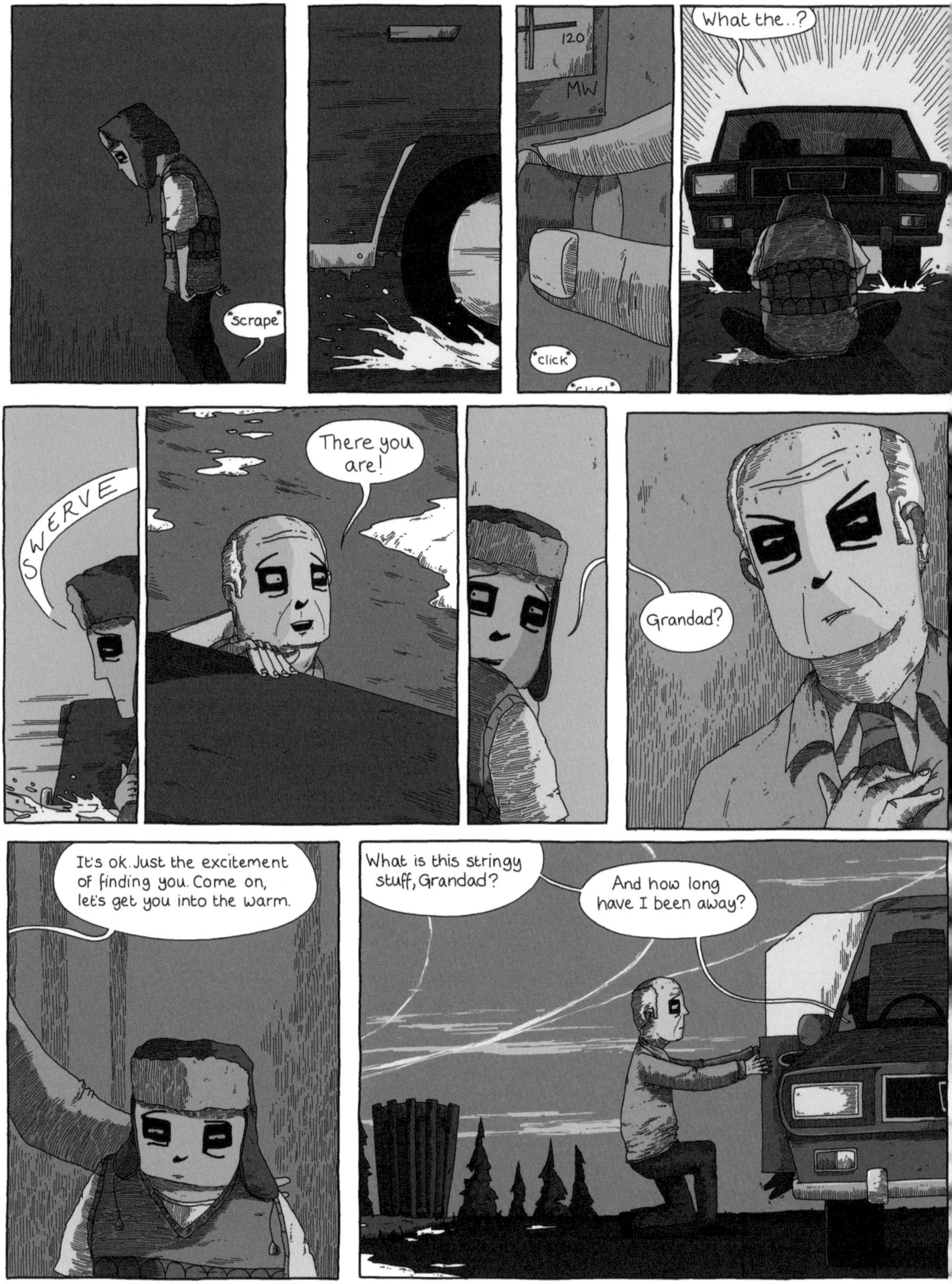
scrape
120
MW
click
What the..?
SWERVE
There you are!
Grandad?
It's ok. Just the excitement of finding you. Come on, let's get you into the warm.
What is this stringy stuff, Grandad?
And how long have I been away?

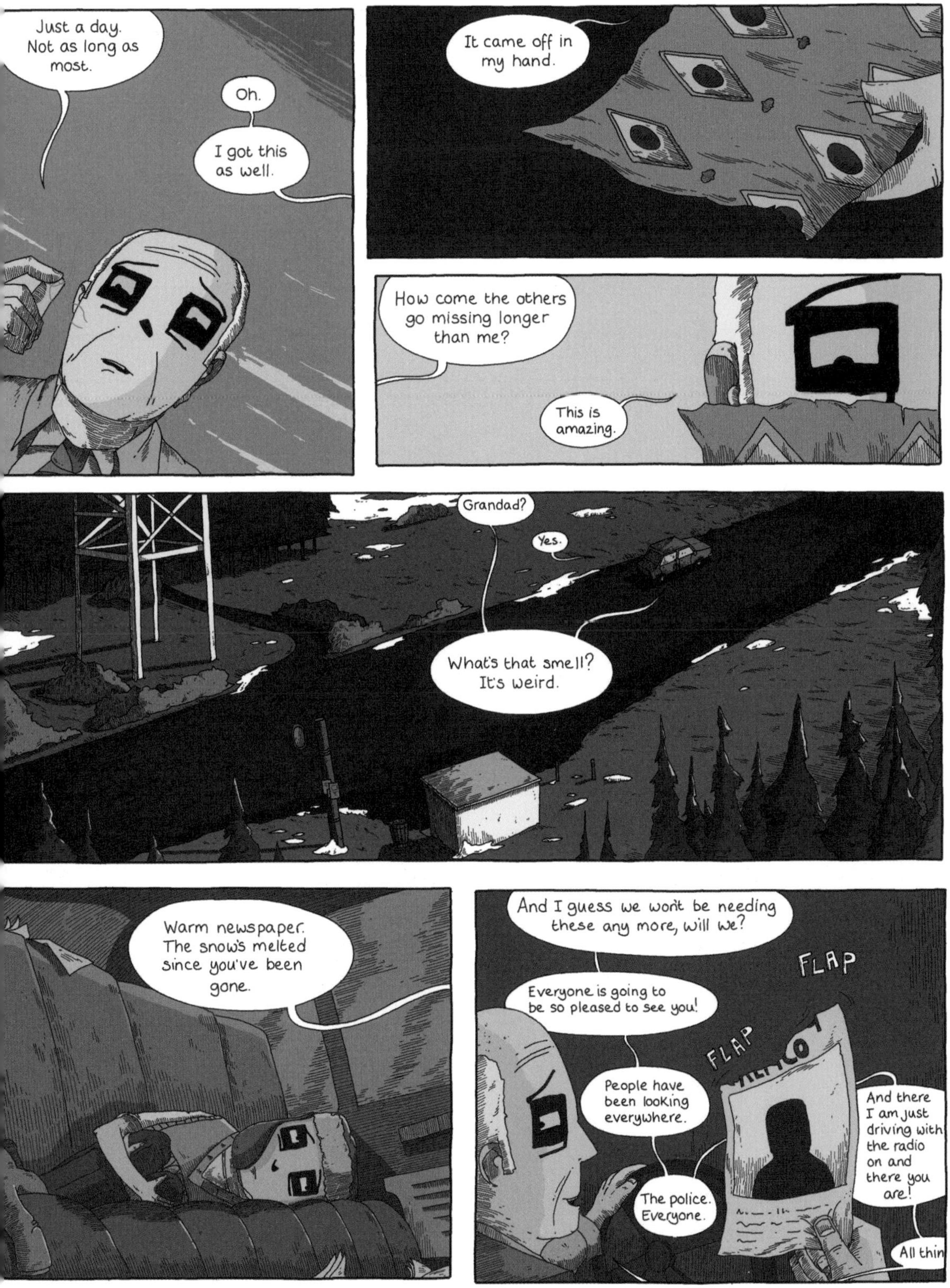
Just a day. Not as long as most.
Oh.
I got this as well.
It came off in my hand.
How come the others go missing longer than me?
This is amazing.
Grandad?
Yes.
What's that smell? It's weird.
Warm newspaper. The snow's melted since you've been gone.
And I guess we won't be needing these any more, will we?
FLAP
Everyone is going to be so pleased to see you!
FLAP
People have been looking everywhere.
The police. Everyone.
And there I am just driving with the radio on and there you are!
All thin

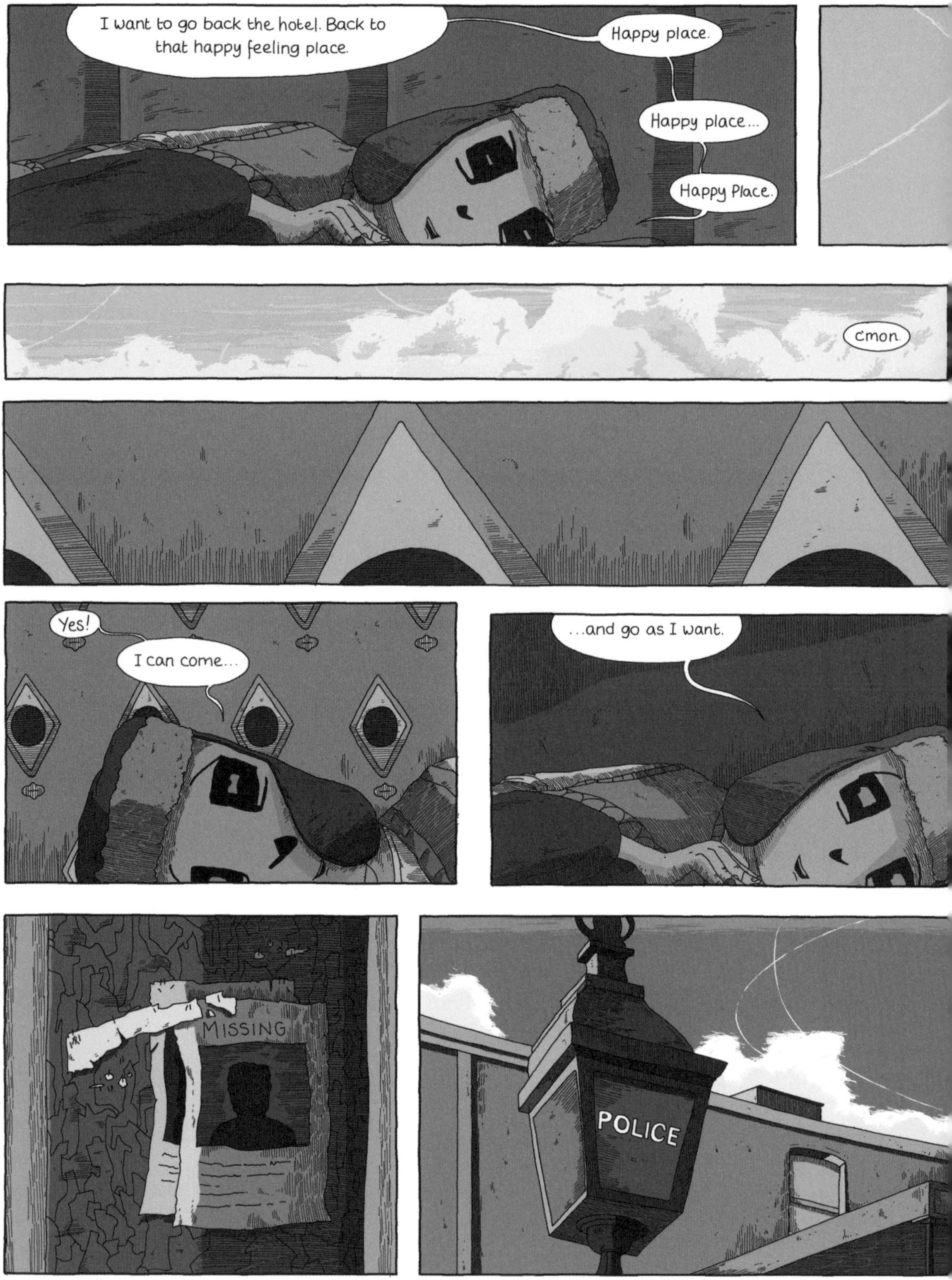

I want to go back the hotel. Back to that happy feeling place.
Happy place.
Happy place...
Happy Place.
c'mon.
Yes!
I can come...
...and go as I want.
MISSING
POLICE

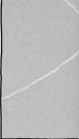

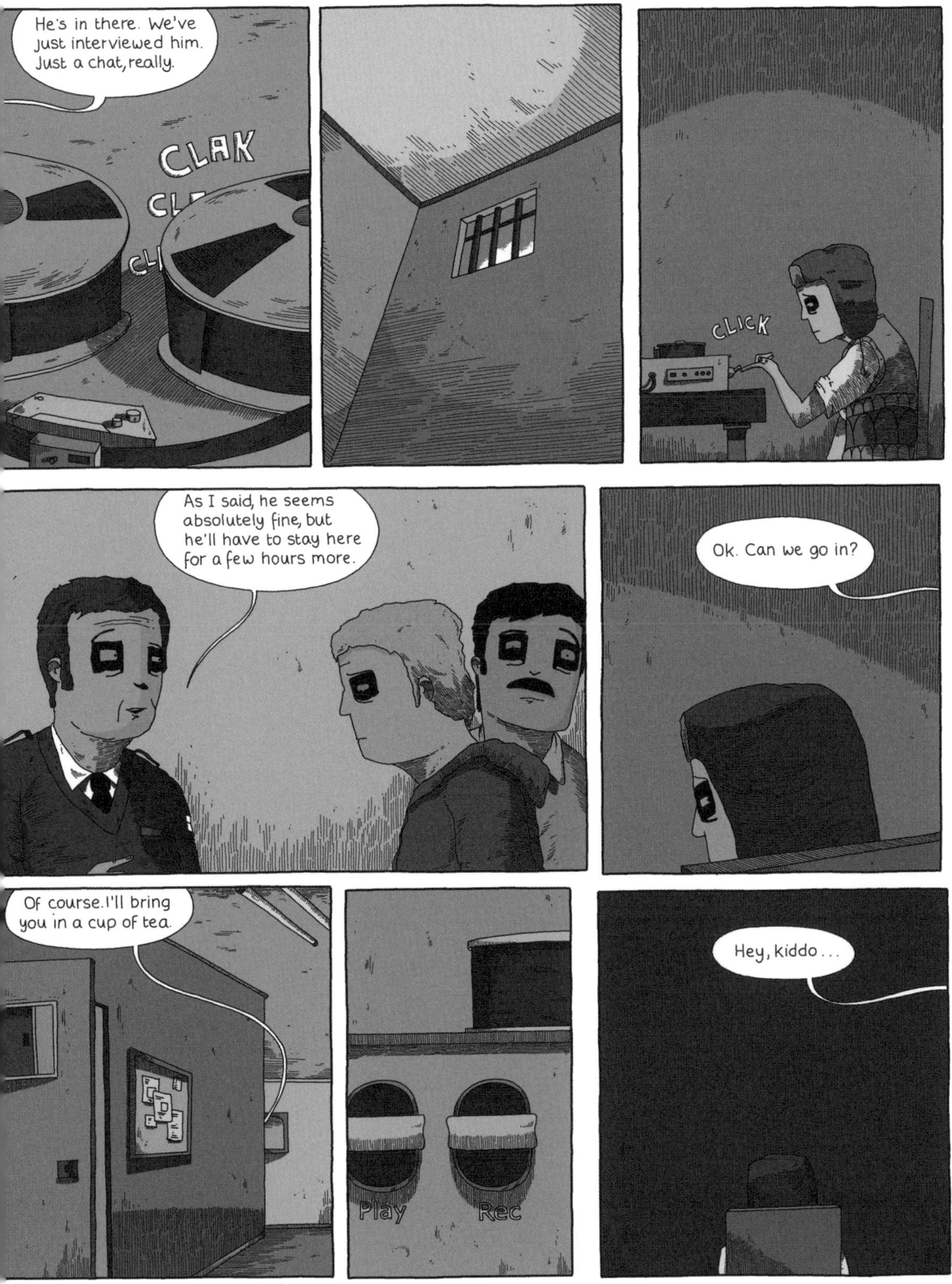
He's in there. We've just interviewed him. Just a chat, really.
CLAK
CLICK
As I said, he seems absolutely fine, but he'll have to stay here for a few hours more.
Ok. Can we go in?
Of course. I'll bring you in a cup of tea.
Play
Rec
Hey, kiddo...

21st April

1981

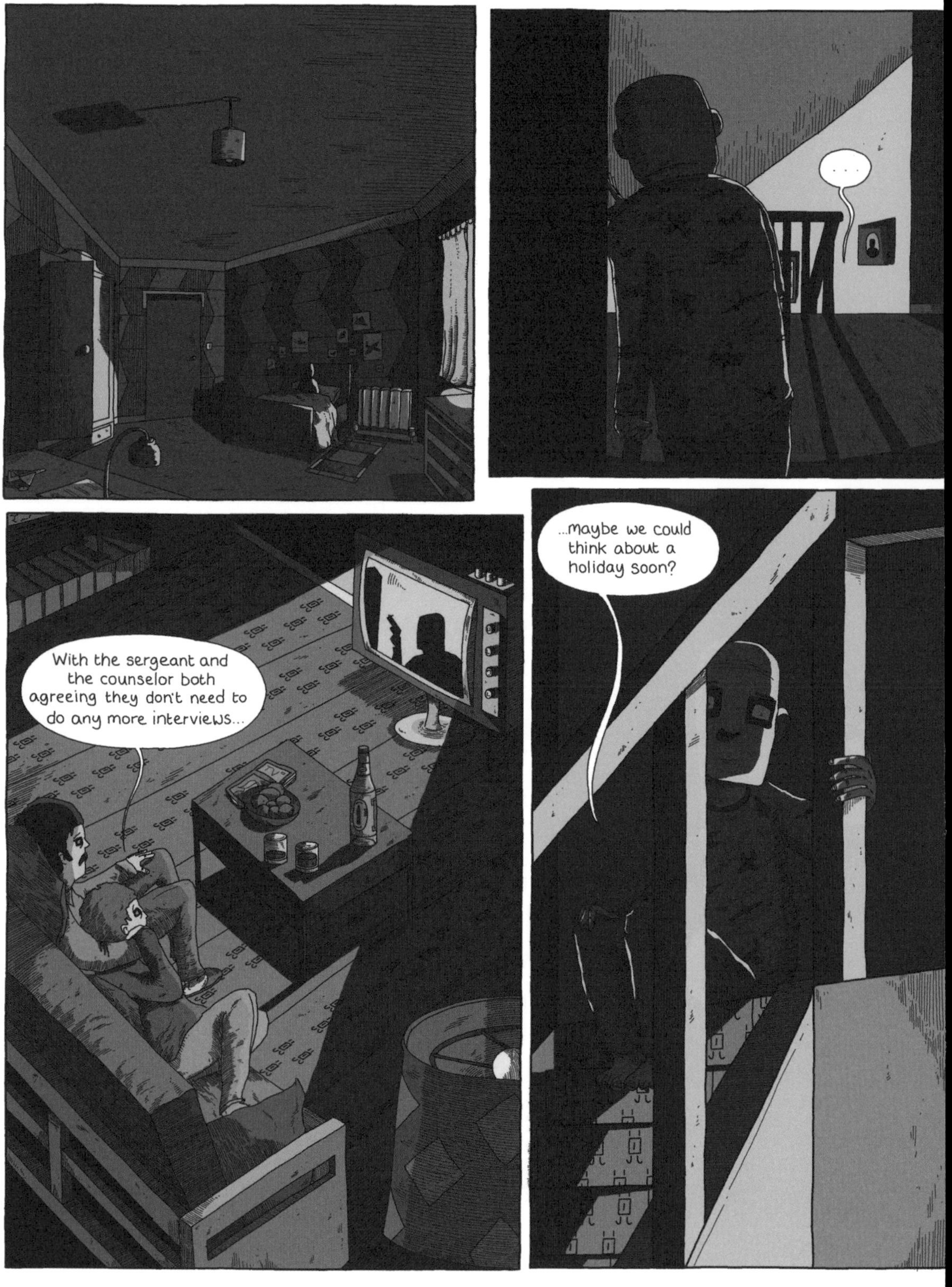
. . .
With the sergeant and the counselor both agreeing they don't need to do any more interviews...
...maybe we could think about a holiday soon?

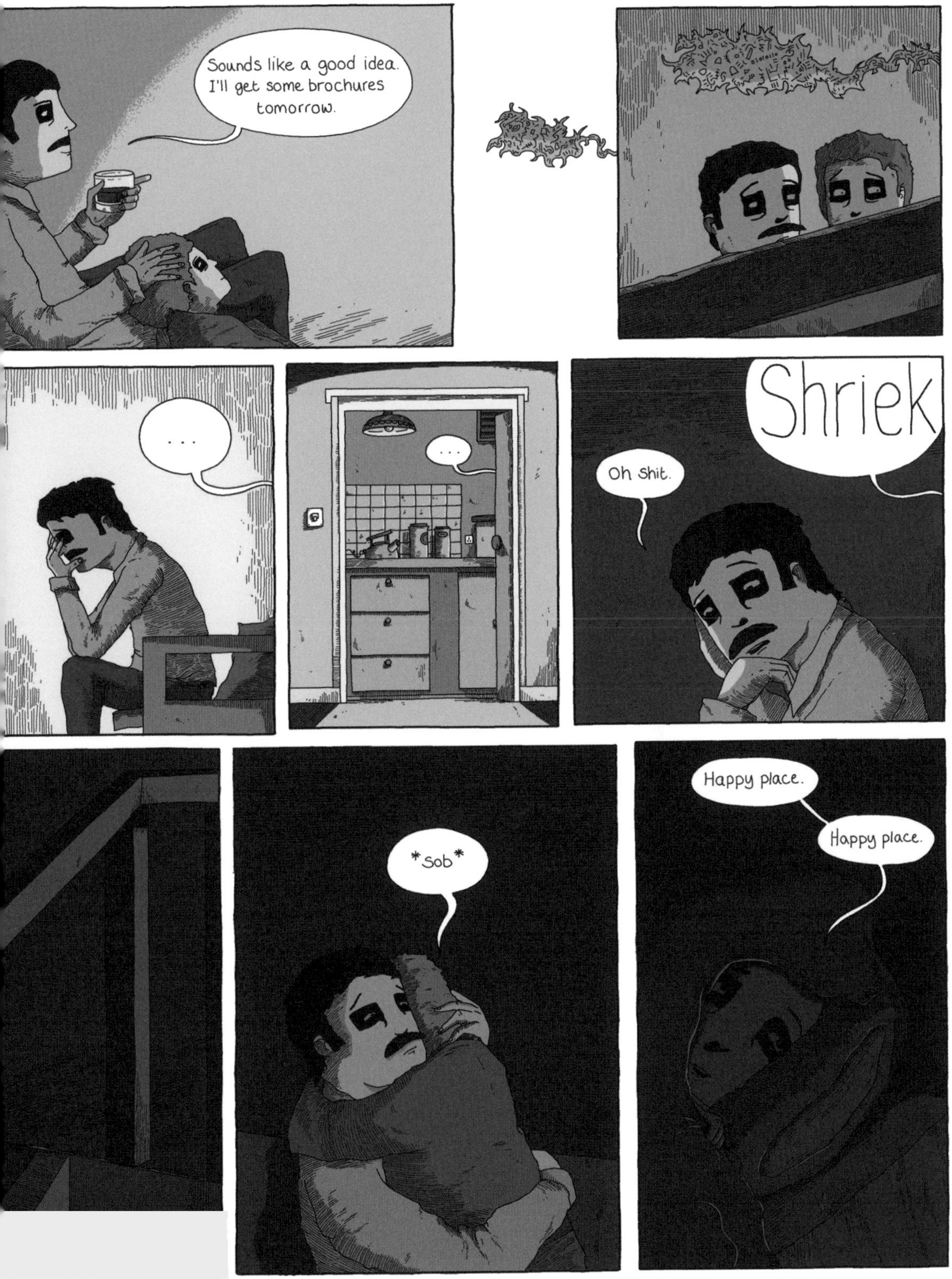
Sounds like a good idea. I'll get some brochures tomorrow.
...
...
Shriek
Oh shit.
Sob
Happy place.
Happy place.

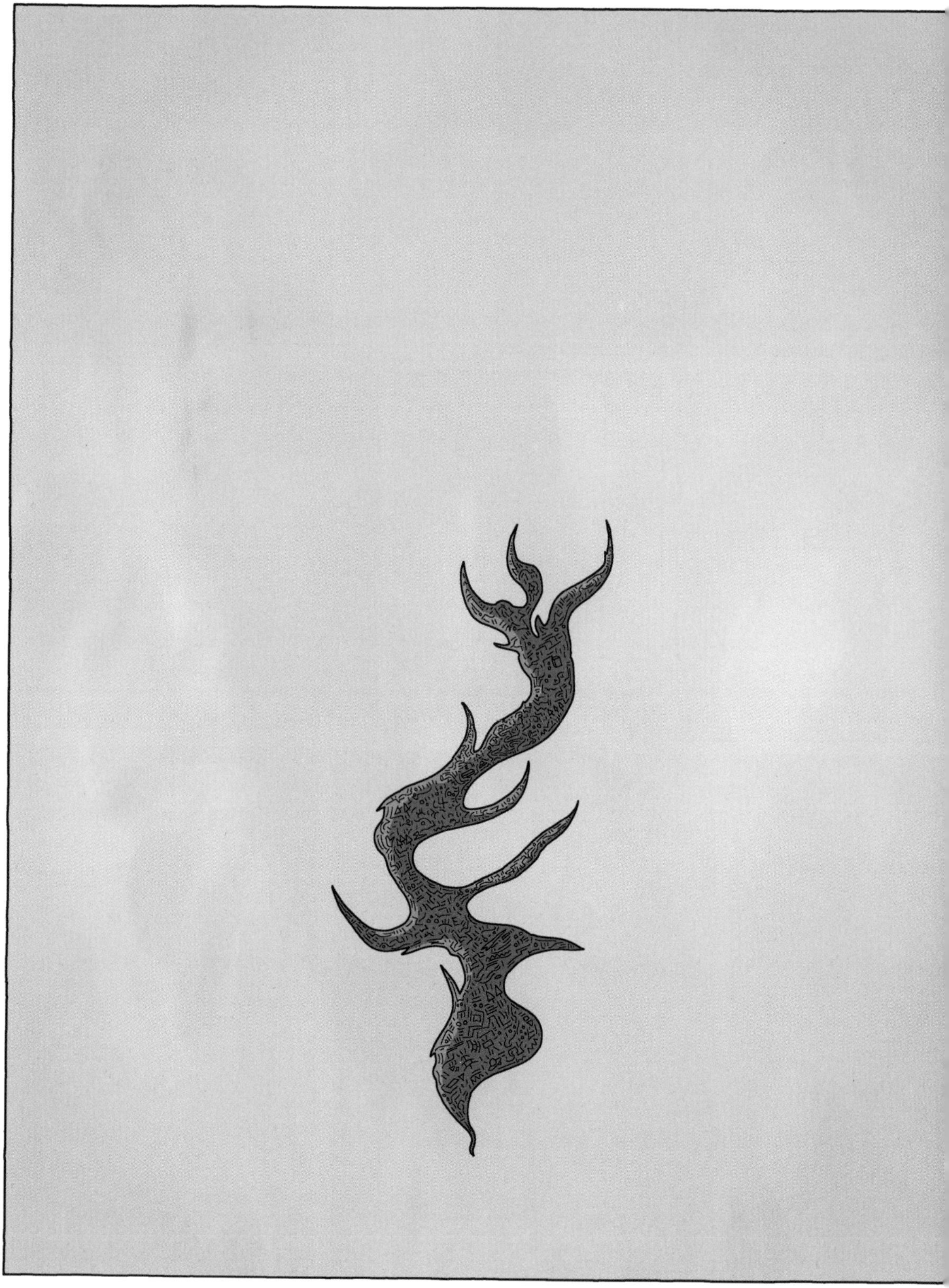

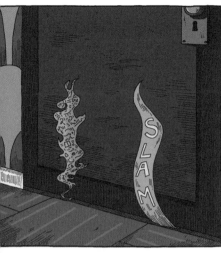

I hate that phone. But it's good to be back.

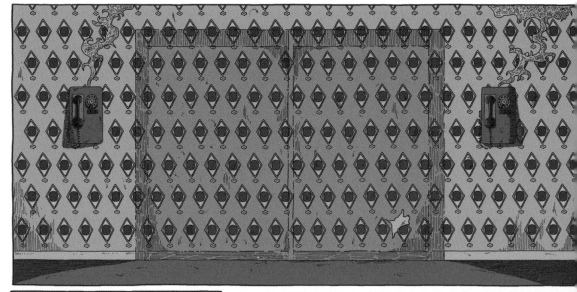

Yes.

Ok.

CLICK

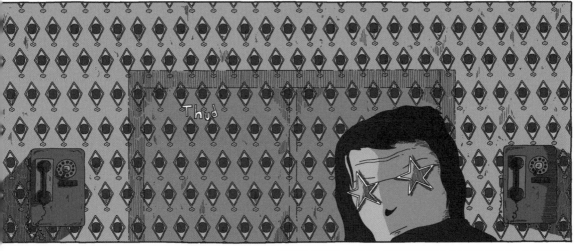

Thud

FLAP

Well, that's that, then. Just Emma and me in this place.

Which could be ok.

I guess.

But I'm not going through that door. That's for sure.

THHWAP

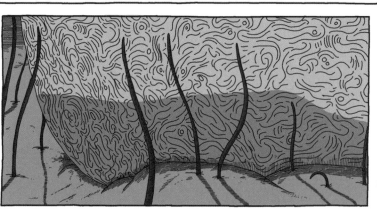

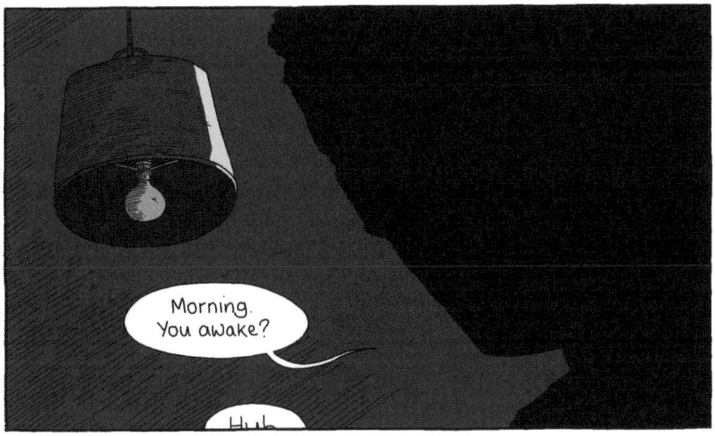
Morning.
You awake?

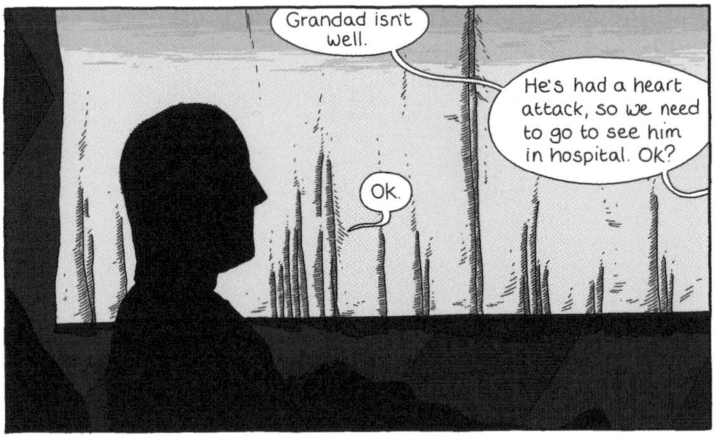
Grandad isn't well.
He's had a heart attack, so we need to go to see him in hospital. Ok?
Ok.

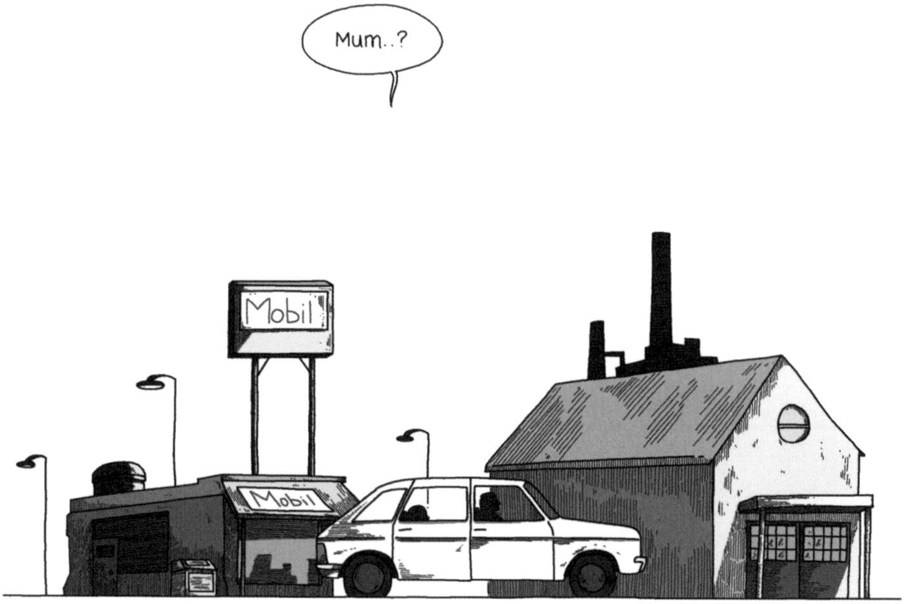
Mum..?
Mobil
Mobil

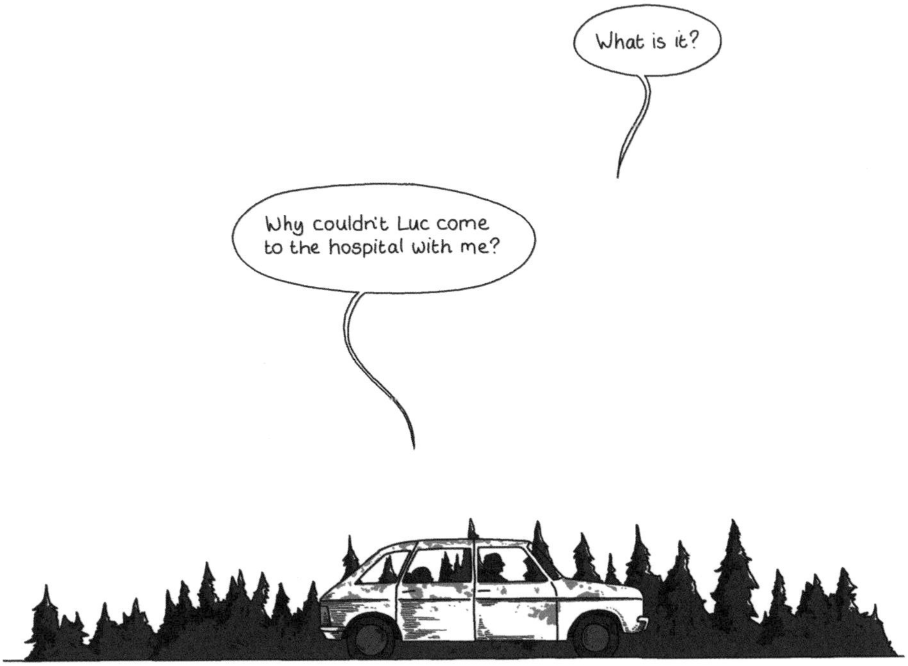
What is it?
Why couldn't Luc come to the hospital with me?

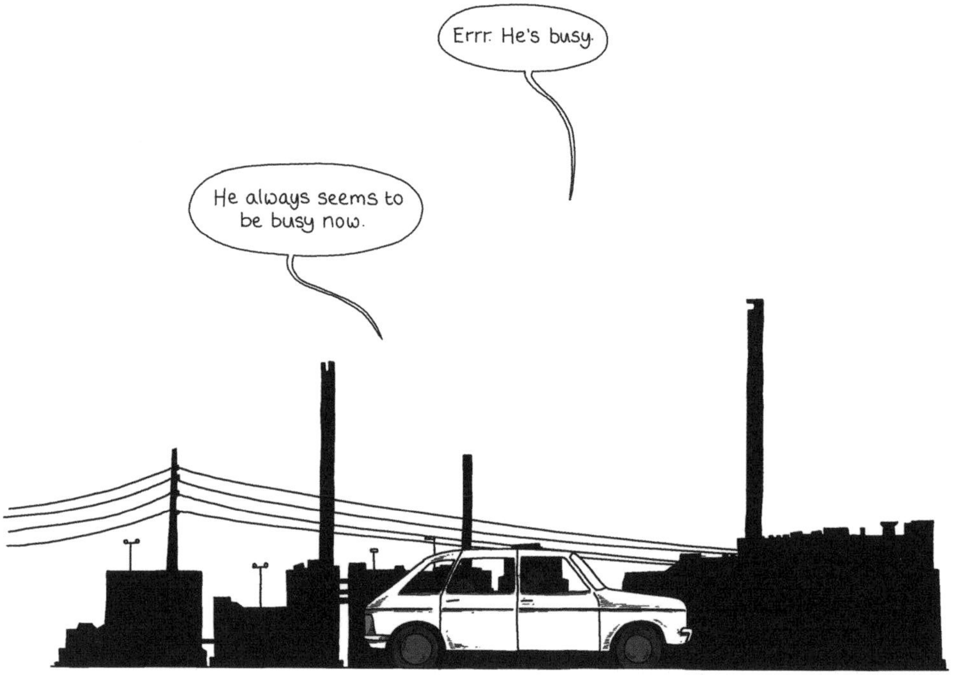
Errr. He's busy.
He always seems to be busy now.

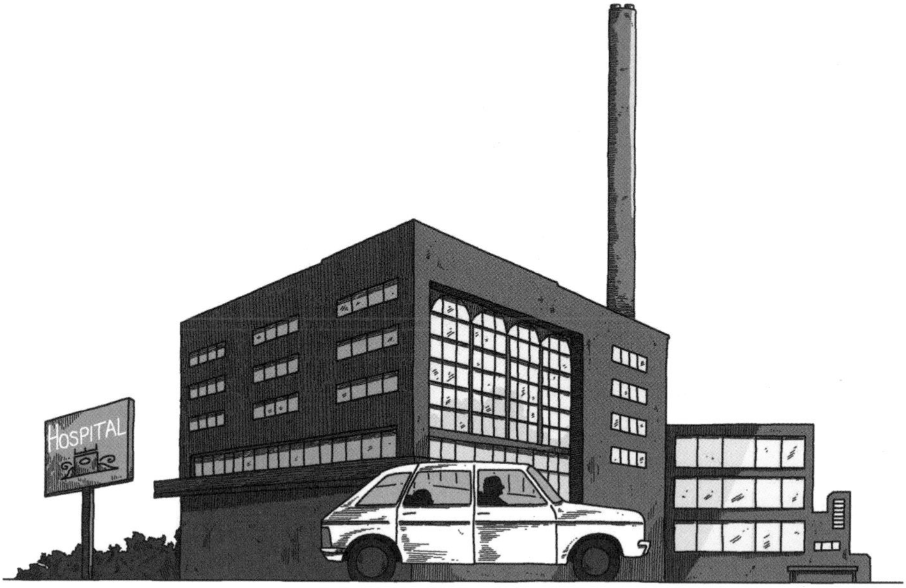
HOSPITAL

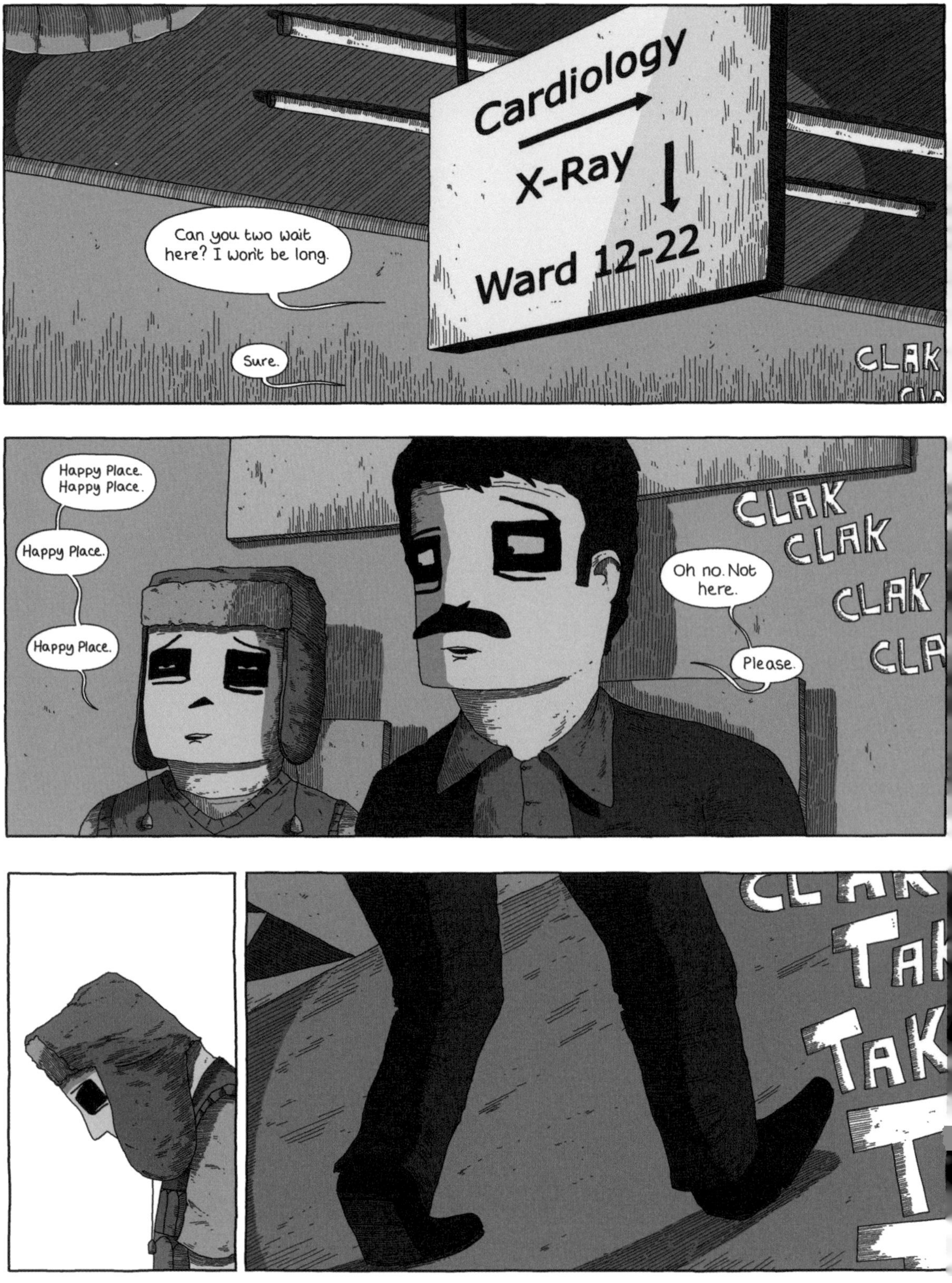

Cardiology
X-Ray
Ward 12-22
Can you two wait here? I won't be long.
Sure.
CLAK
Happy Place. Happy Place.
Happy Place.
Happy Place.
CLAK
CLAK
CLAK
Oh no. Not here.
Please.

Tak

Tak

Tak

That was a good nap.

Glad to hear it.

You haven't seen that small kid in the green jumper, have you?

Philip? No. Can't say I have.

Huh.

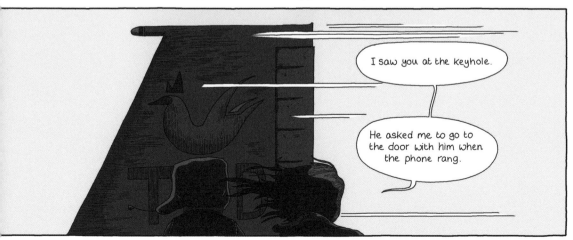

I saw you at the keyhole.

He asked me to go to the door with him when the phone rang.

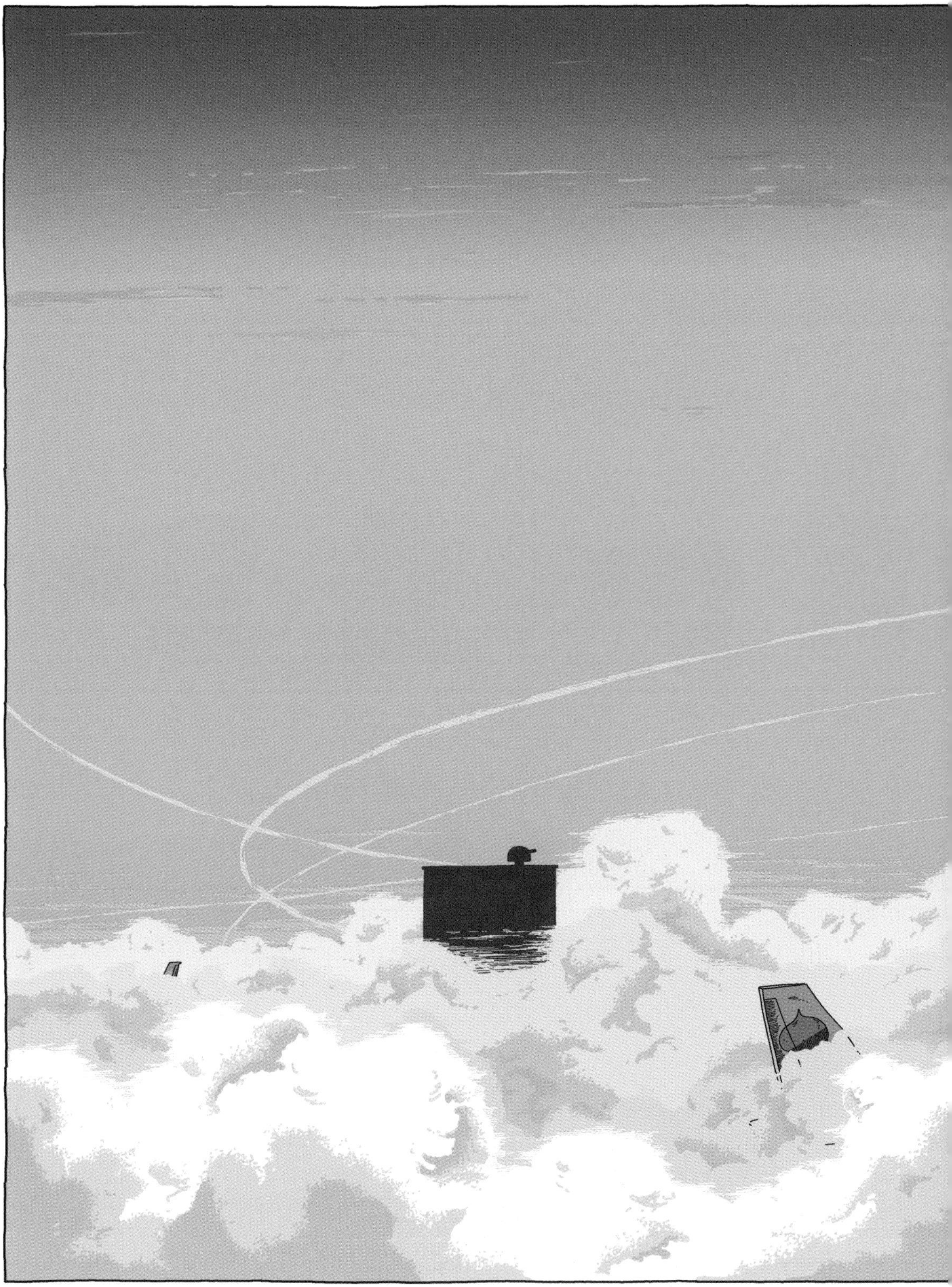

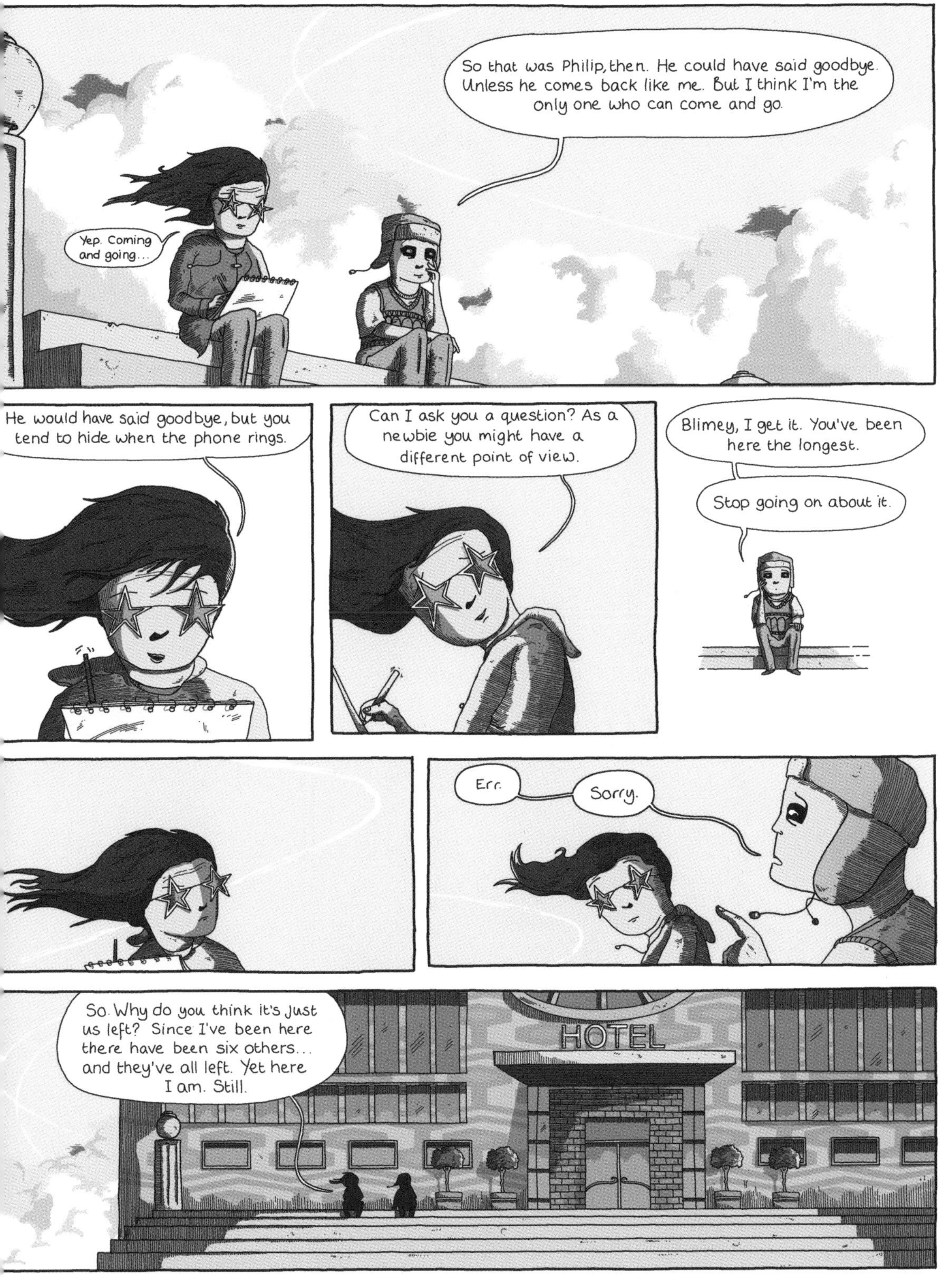

So that was Philip, then. He could have said goodbye. Unless he comes back like me. But I think I'm the only one who can come and go.
Yep. Coming and going...
He would have said goodbye, but you tend to hide when the phone rings.
Can I ask you a question? As a newbie you might have a different point of view.
Blimey, I get it. You've been here the longest.
Stop going on about it.
Err.
Sorry.
So. Why do you think it's just us left? Since I've been here there have been six others... and they've all left. Yet here I am. Still.
HOTEL

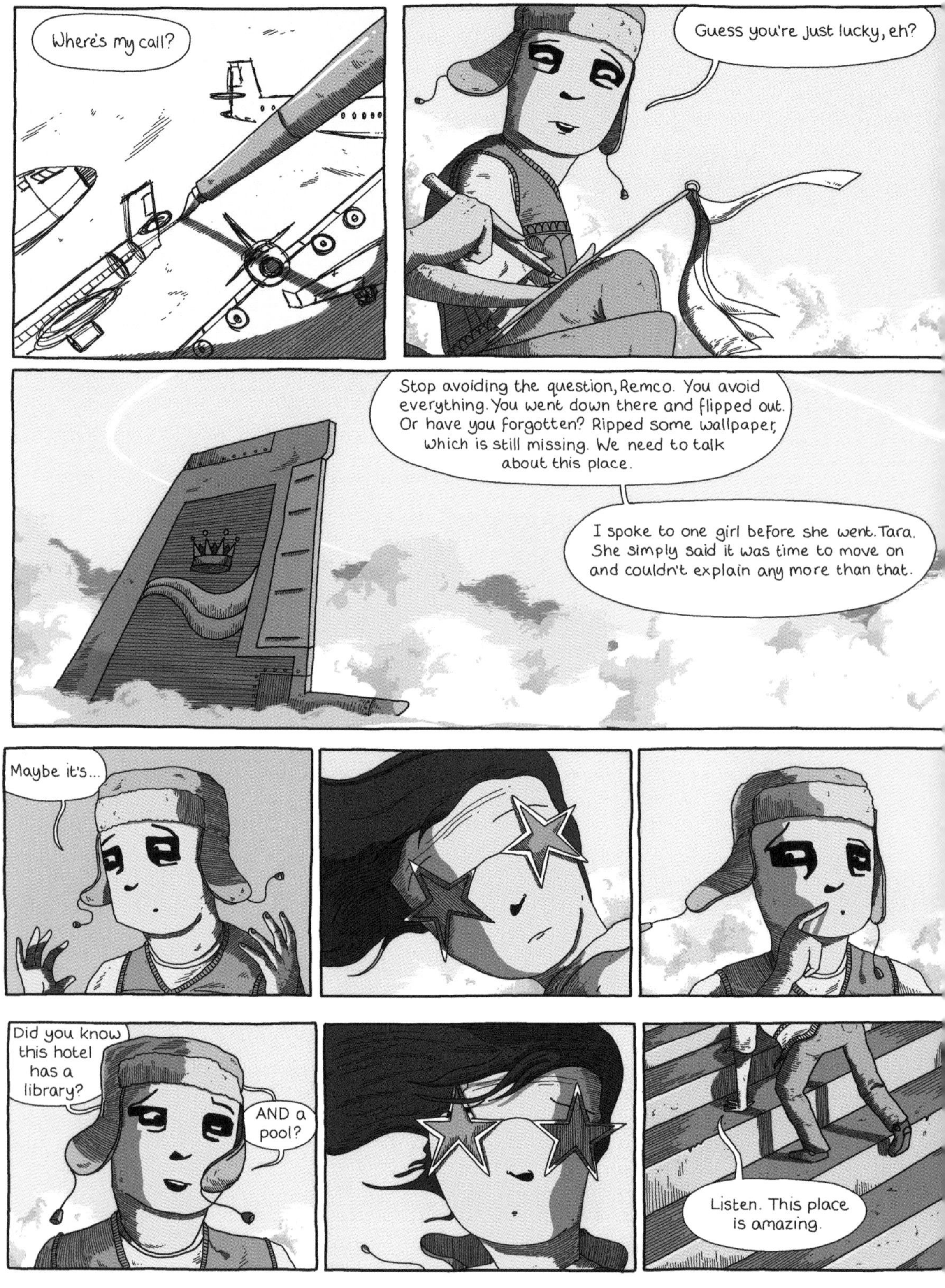

Where's my call?
Guess you're just lucky, eh?
Stop avoiding the question, Remco. You avoid everything. You went down there and flipped out. Or have you forgotten? Ripped some wallpaper, which is still missing. We need to talk about this place.
I spoke to one girl before she went. Tara. She simply said it was time to move on and couldn't explain any more than that.
Maybe it's...
Did you know this hotel has a library?
AND a pool?
Listen. This place is amazing.

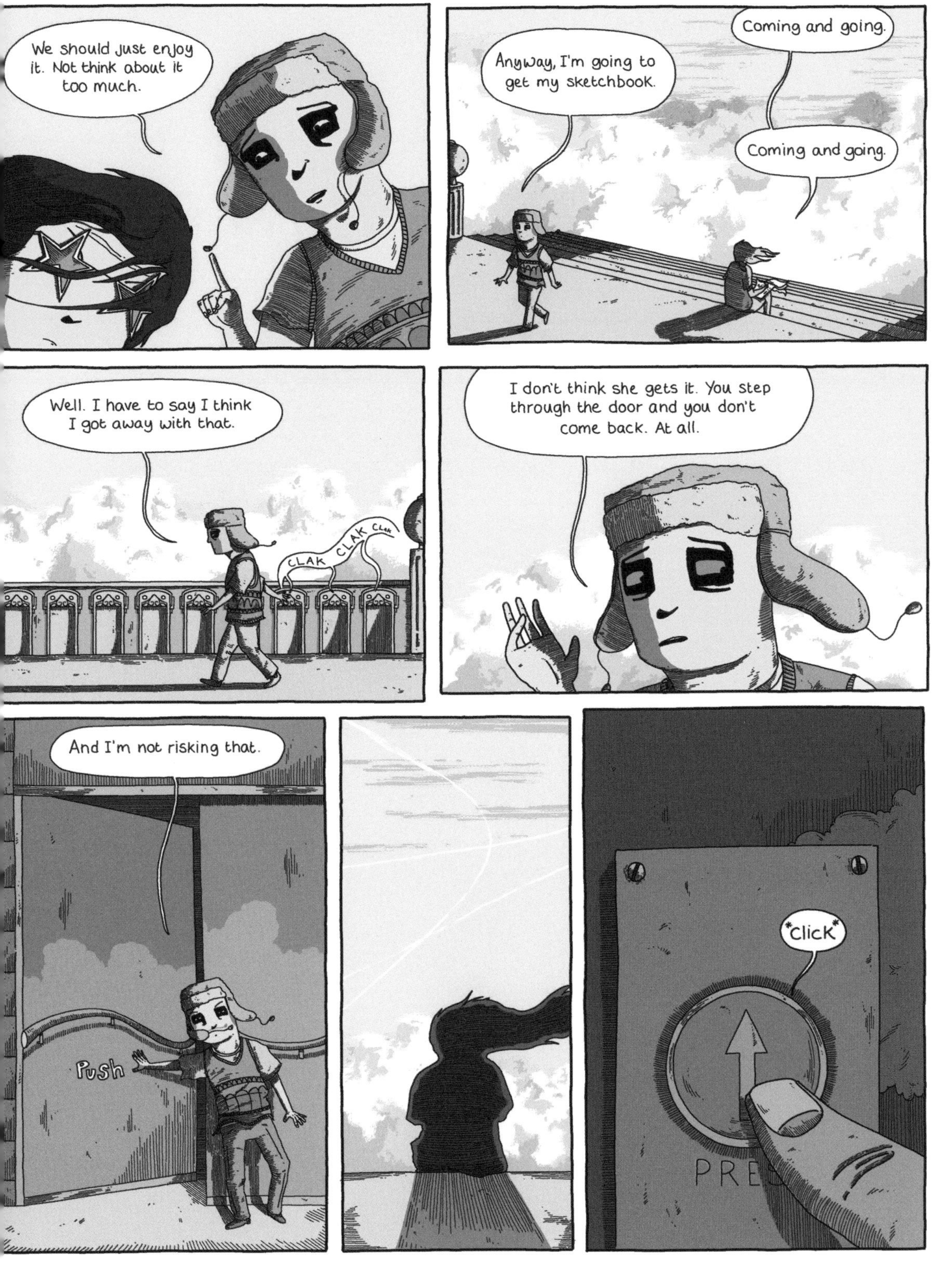
We should just enjoy it. Not think about it too much.
Anyway, I'm going to get my sketchbook.
Coming and going.
Coming and going.
Well. I have to say I think I got away with that.
CLAK CLAK CLAK
I don't think she gets it. You step through the door and you don't come back. At all.
And I'm not risking that.
Push
Click
PRES

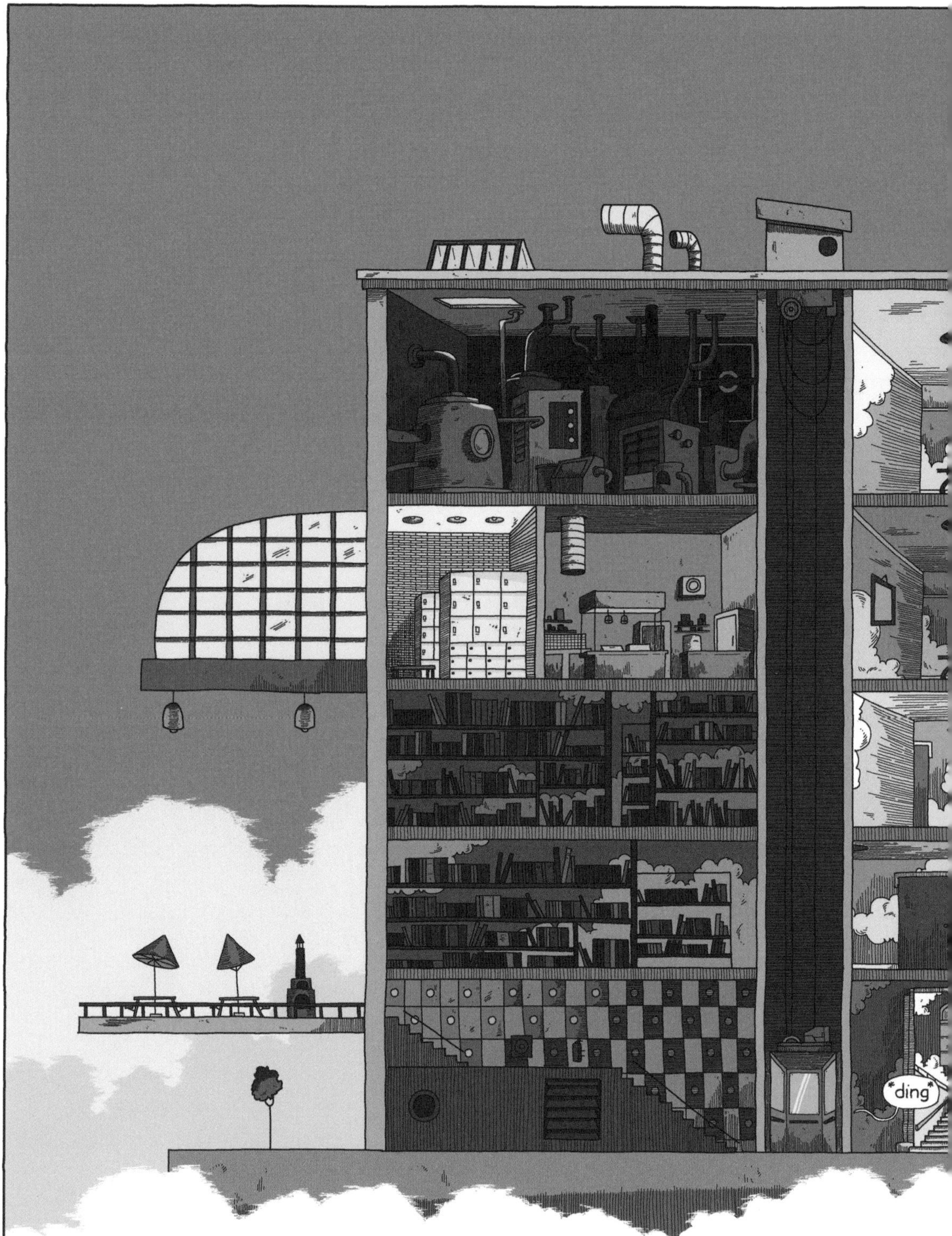
ding

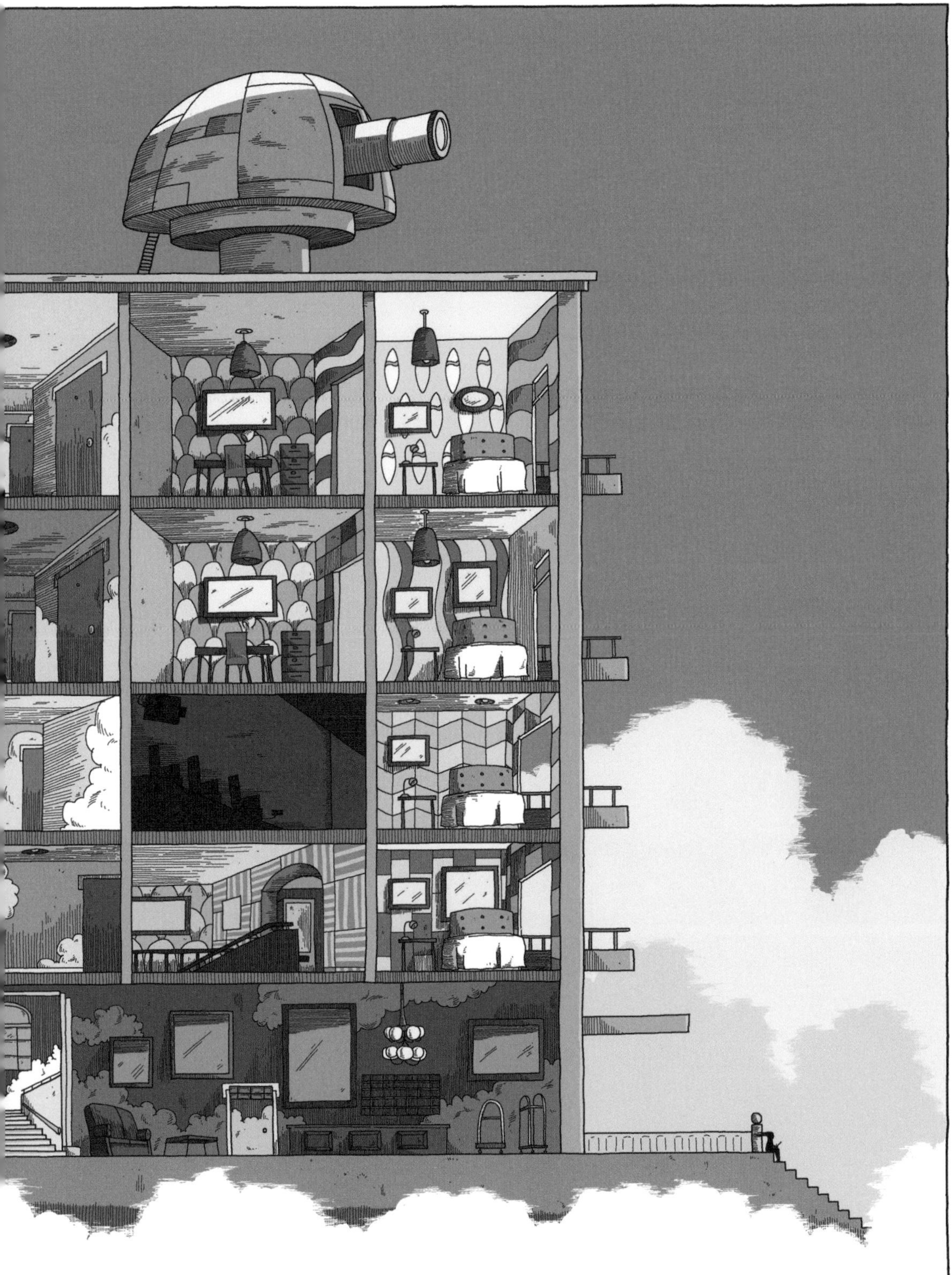

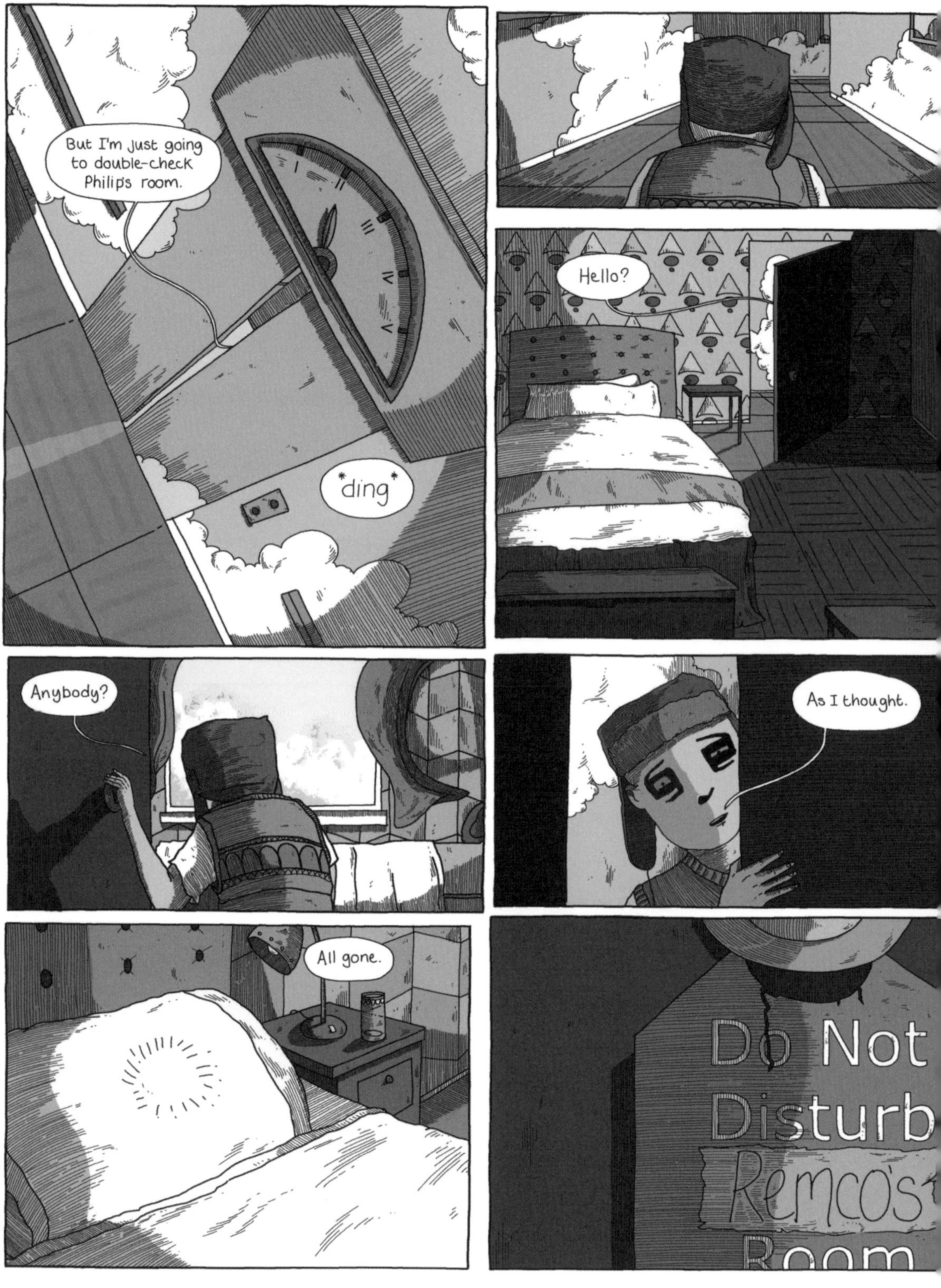

But I'm just going to double-check Philip's room.
ding
Hello?
Anybody?
As I thought.
All gone.
Do Not Disturb
Remco's
Room

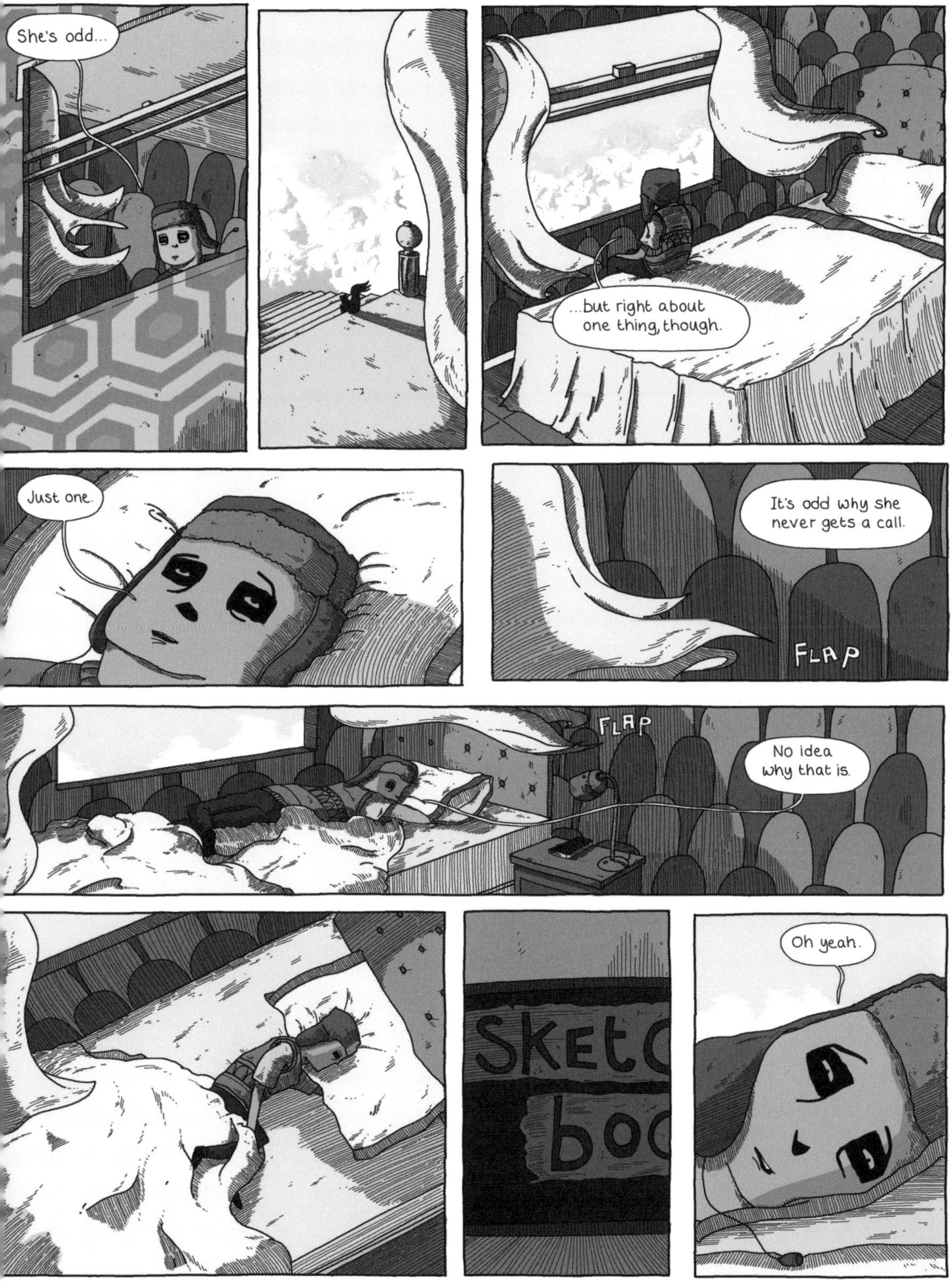

She's odd...
...but right about one thing, though.
Just one.
It's odd why she never gets a call.
FLAP
FLAP
No idea why that is.
Sketc
boo
Oh yeah.

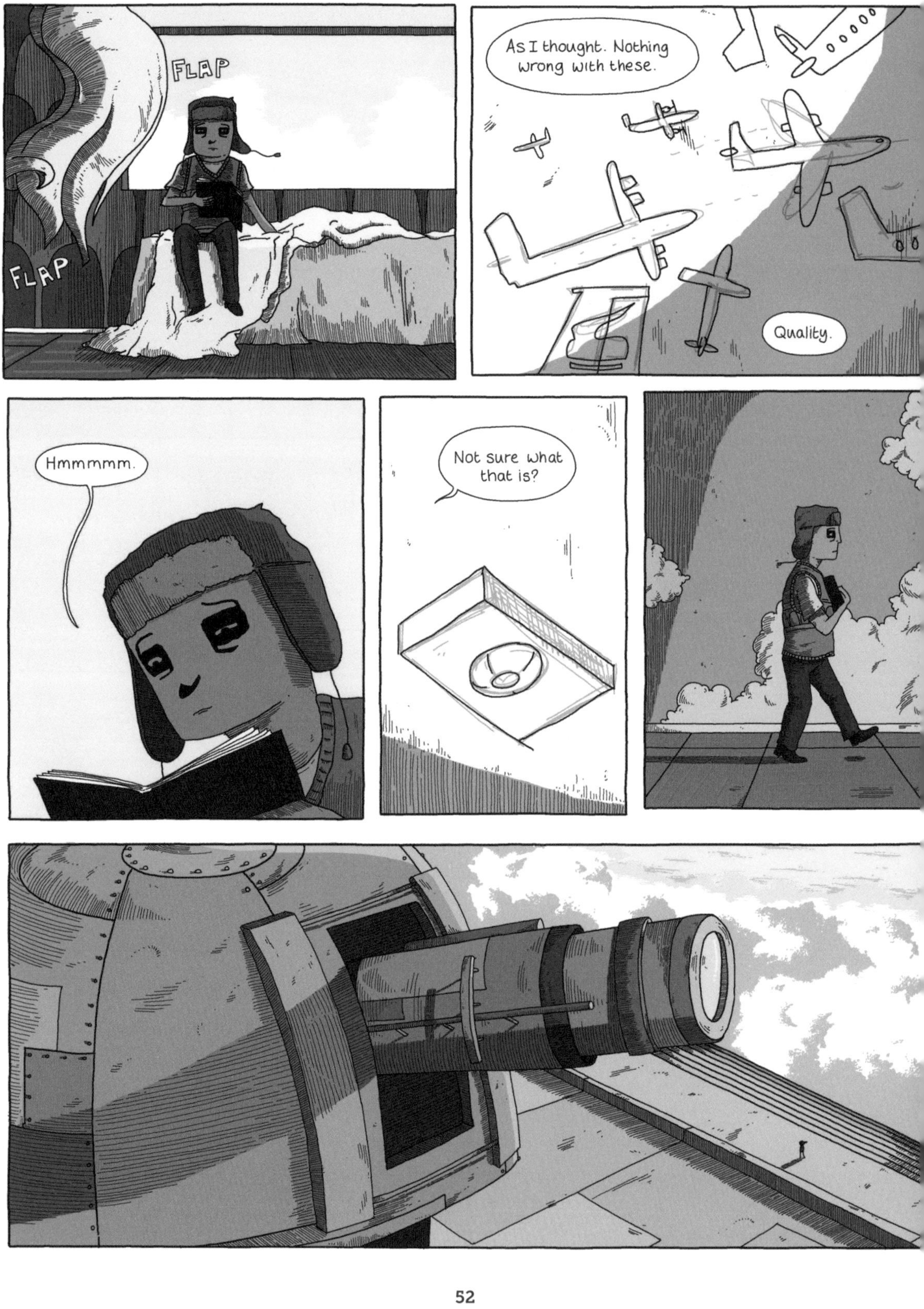
FLAP
FLAP
As I thought. Nothing wrong with these.
Quality.
Hmmmmm.
Not sure what that is?

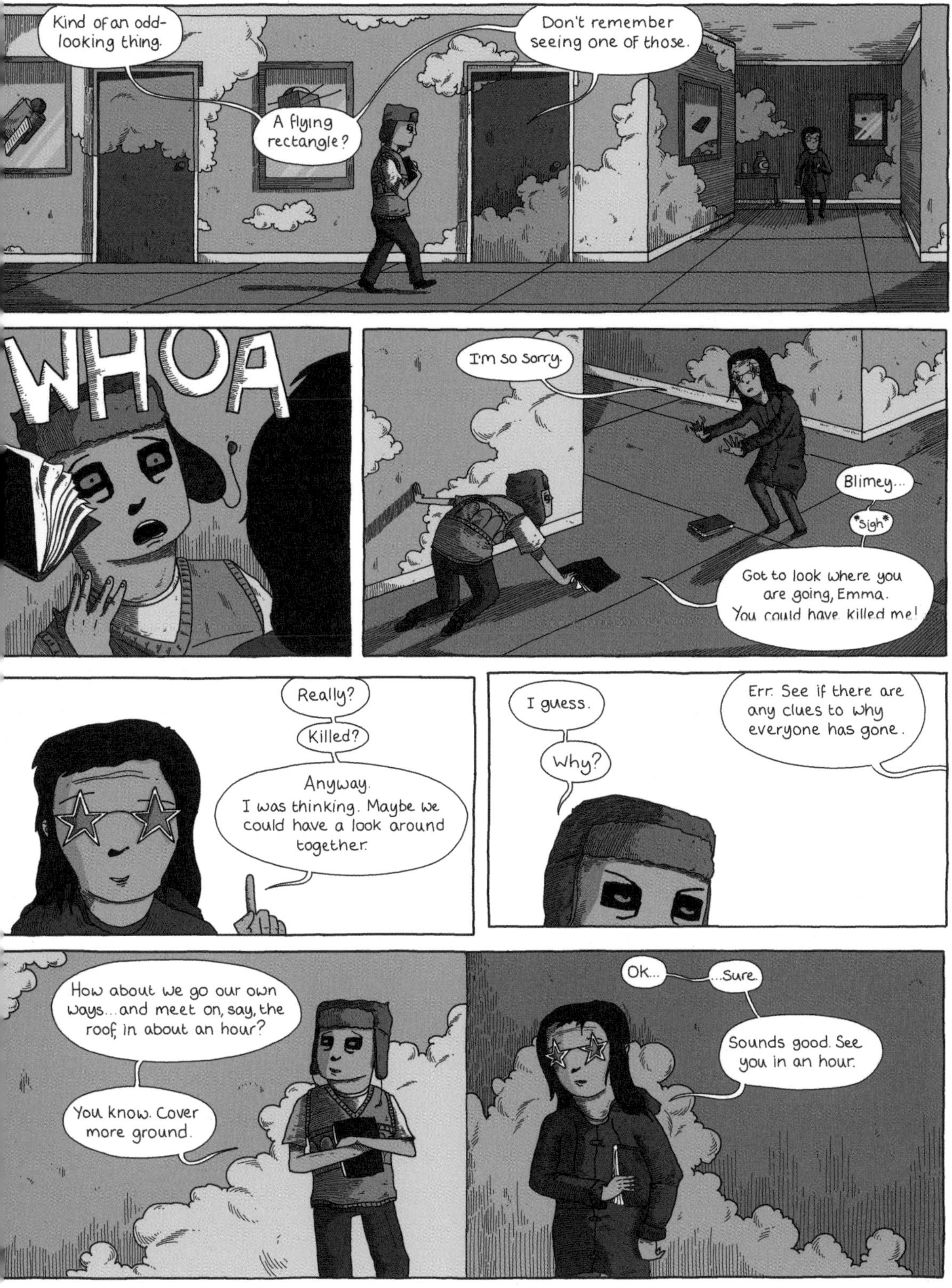
Kind of an odd-looking thing.
A flying rectangle?
Don't remember seeing one of those.
WHOA
I'm so sorry.
Blimey...
sigh
Got to look where you are going, Emma. You could have killed me!
Really?
Killed?
Anyway. I was thinking. Maybe we could have a look around together.
I guess.
Why?
Err. See if there are any clues to why everyone has gone.
How about we go our own ways... and meet on, say, the roof, in about an hour?
You know. Cover more ground.
Ok...
...Sure.
Sounds good. See you in an hour.

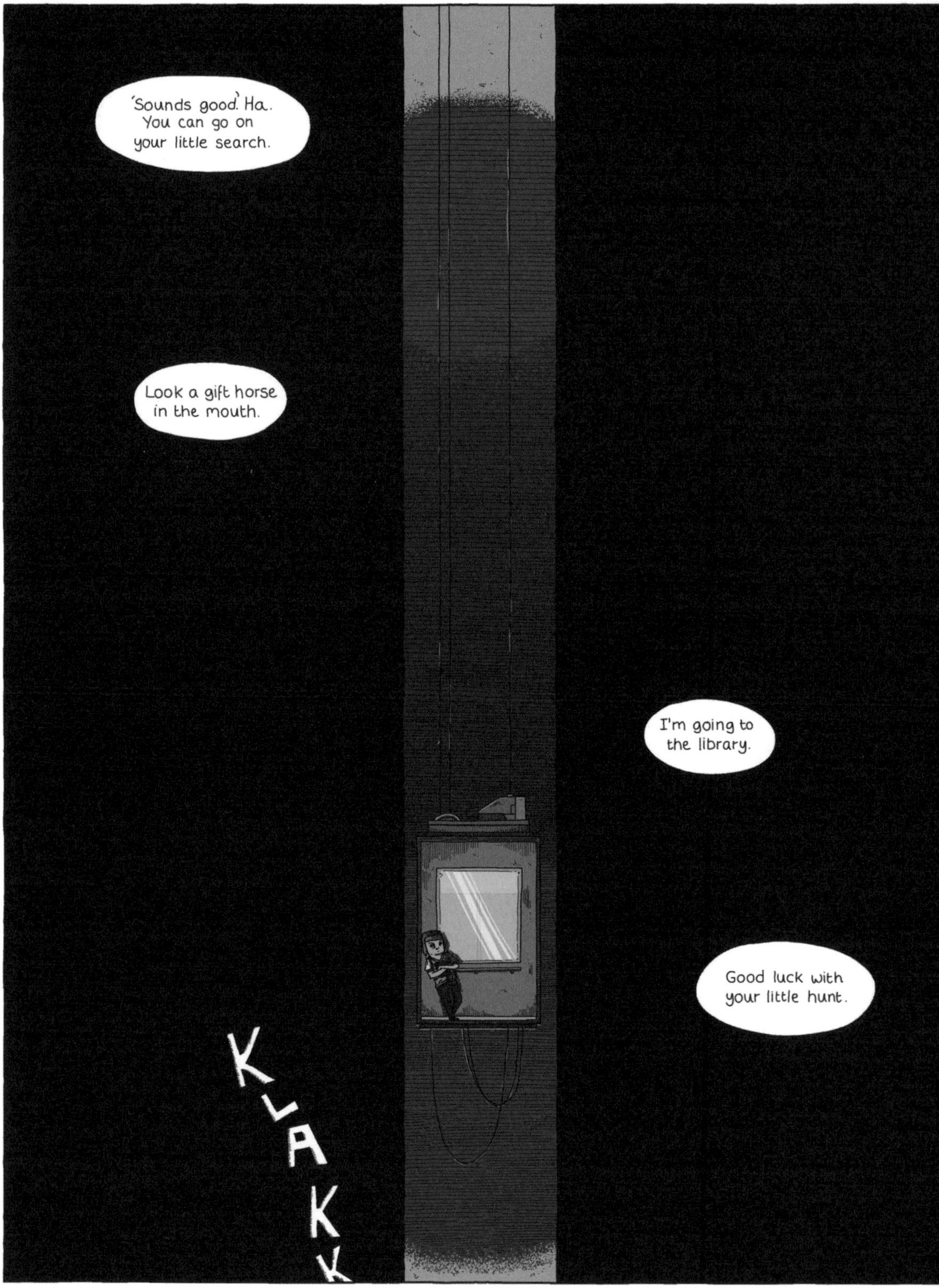
'Sounds good.' Ha. You can go on your little search.
Look a gift horse in the mouth.
I'm going to the library.
Good luck with your little hunt.
KLAKK

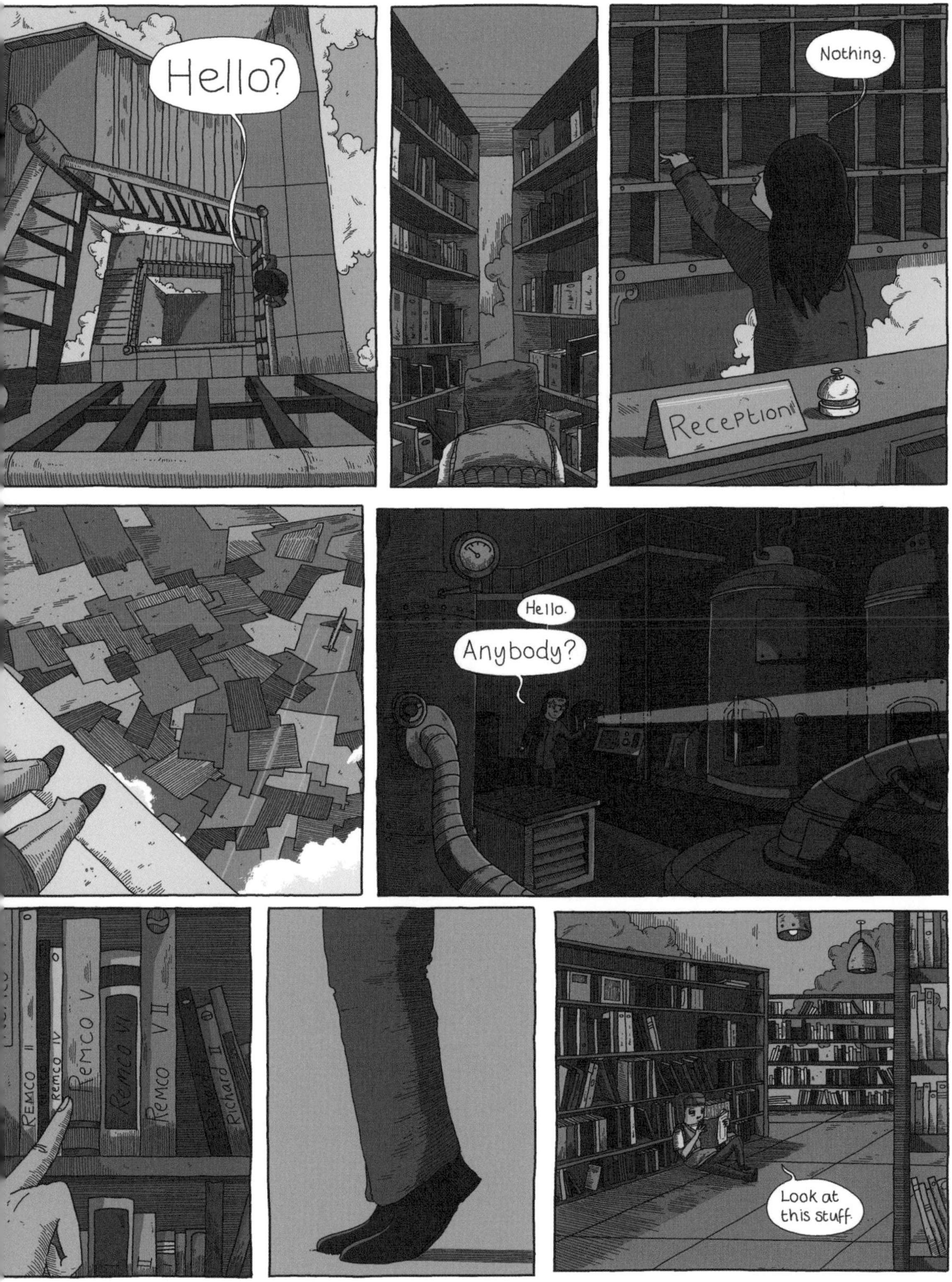
Hello?
Nothing.
Reception
Hello.
Anybody?
REMCO II
REMCO IV
REMCO V
Remco VI
Remco V II
Richard II
Look at this stuff.

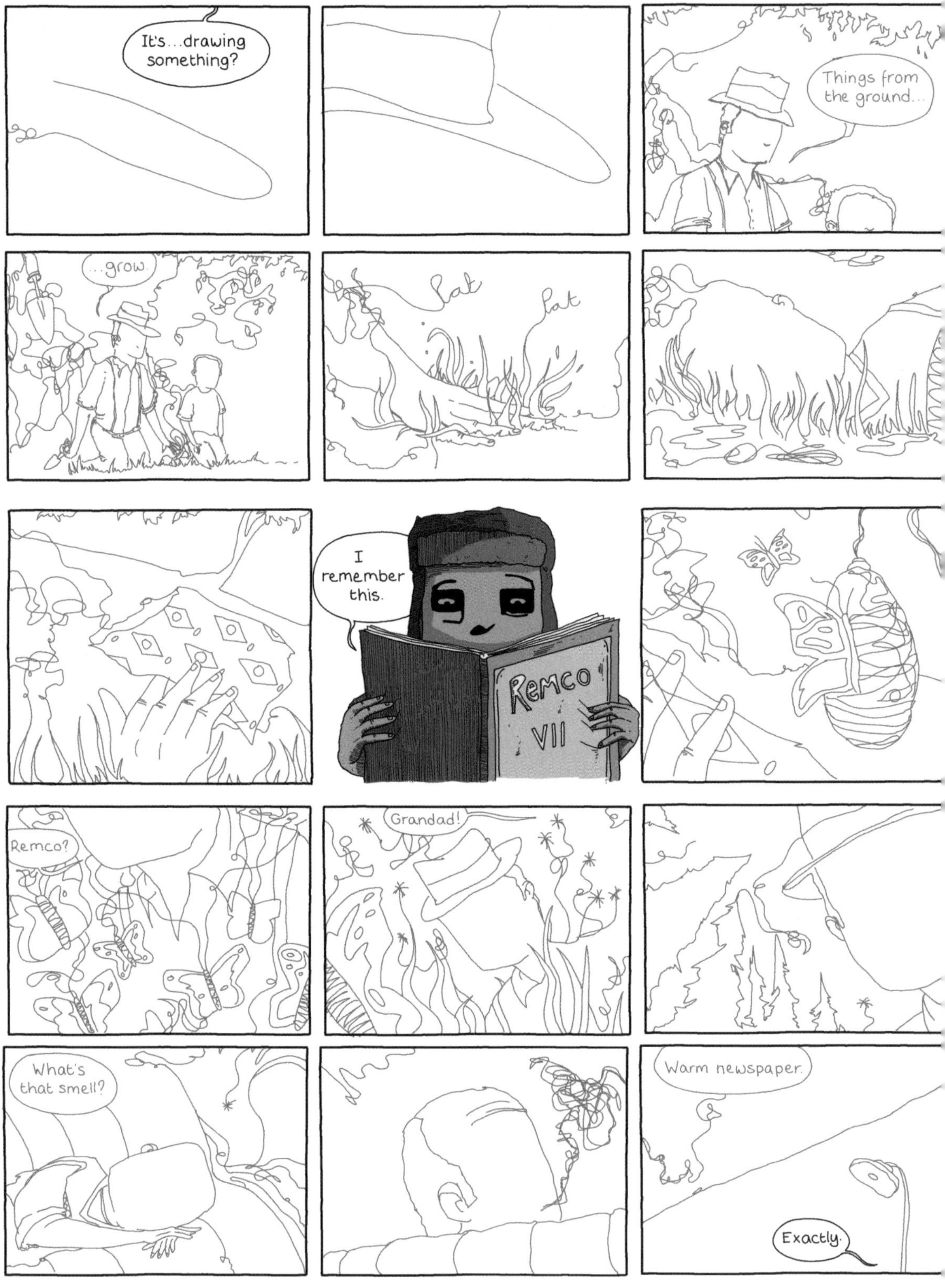
It's...drawing something?
Things from the ground...
...grow.
Pat
Pat
I remember this.
Remco VII
Remco?
Grandad!
What's that smell?
Warm newspaper.
Exactly.

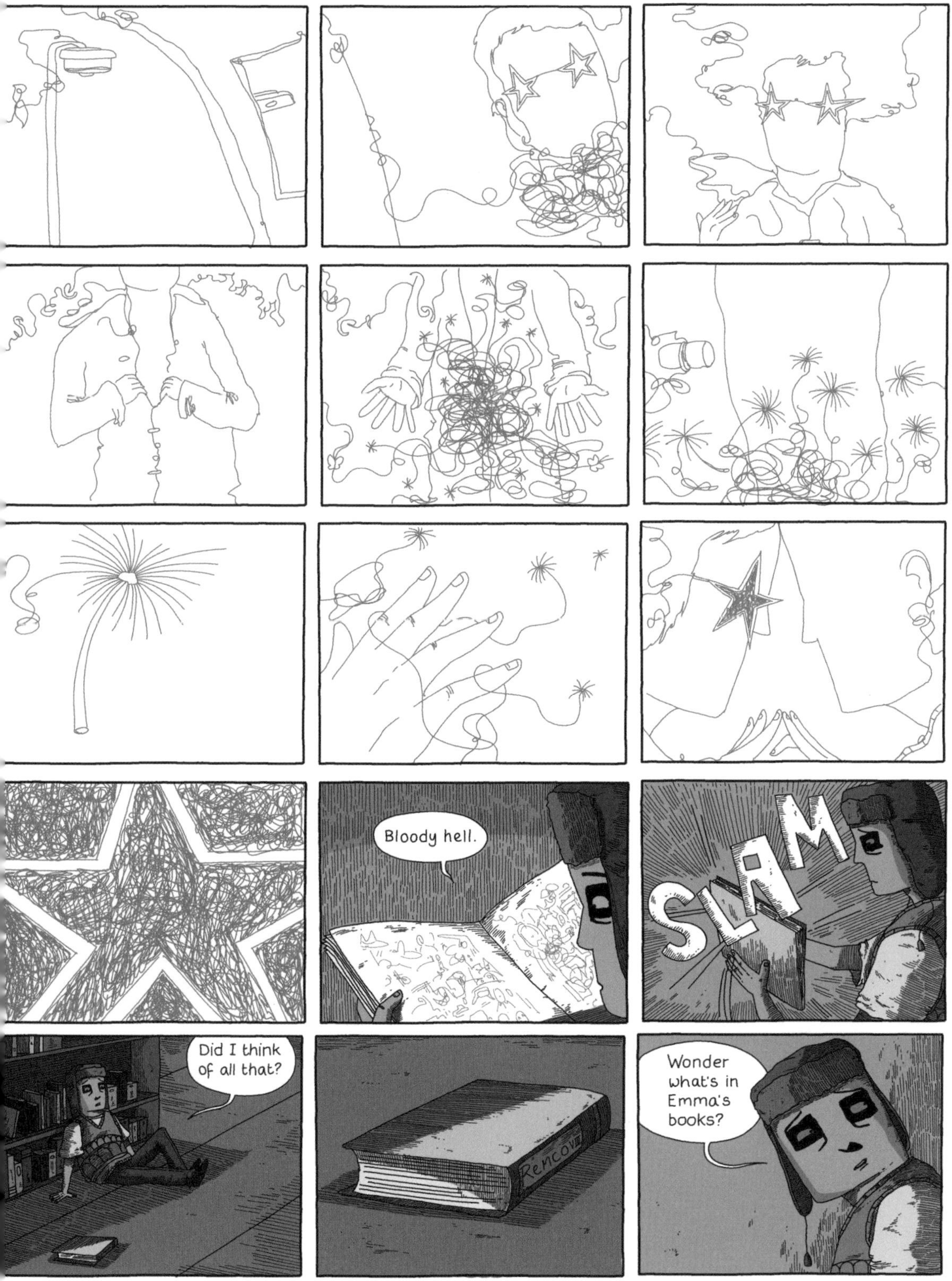
Bloody hell.
SLAM
Did I think of all that?
Rencov
Wonder what's in Emma's books?

Wow.

Emma has loads more books than me.

Huh.

They're not as much fun 'cos they don't draw in front of you.

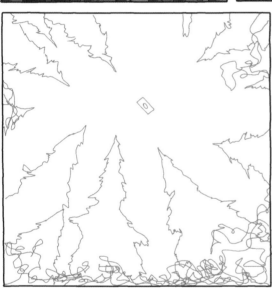

Nice. There's that thing that I drew.

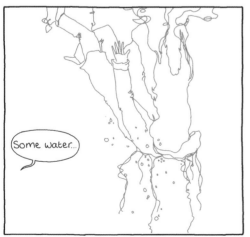

Some water...

58

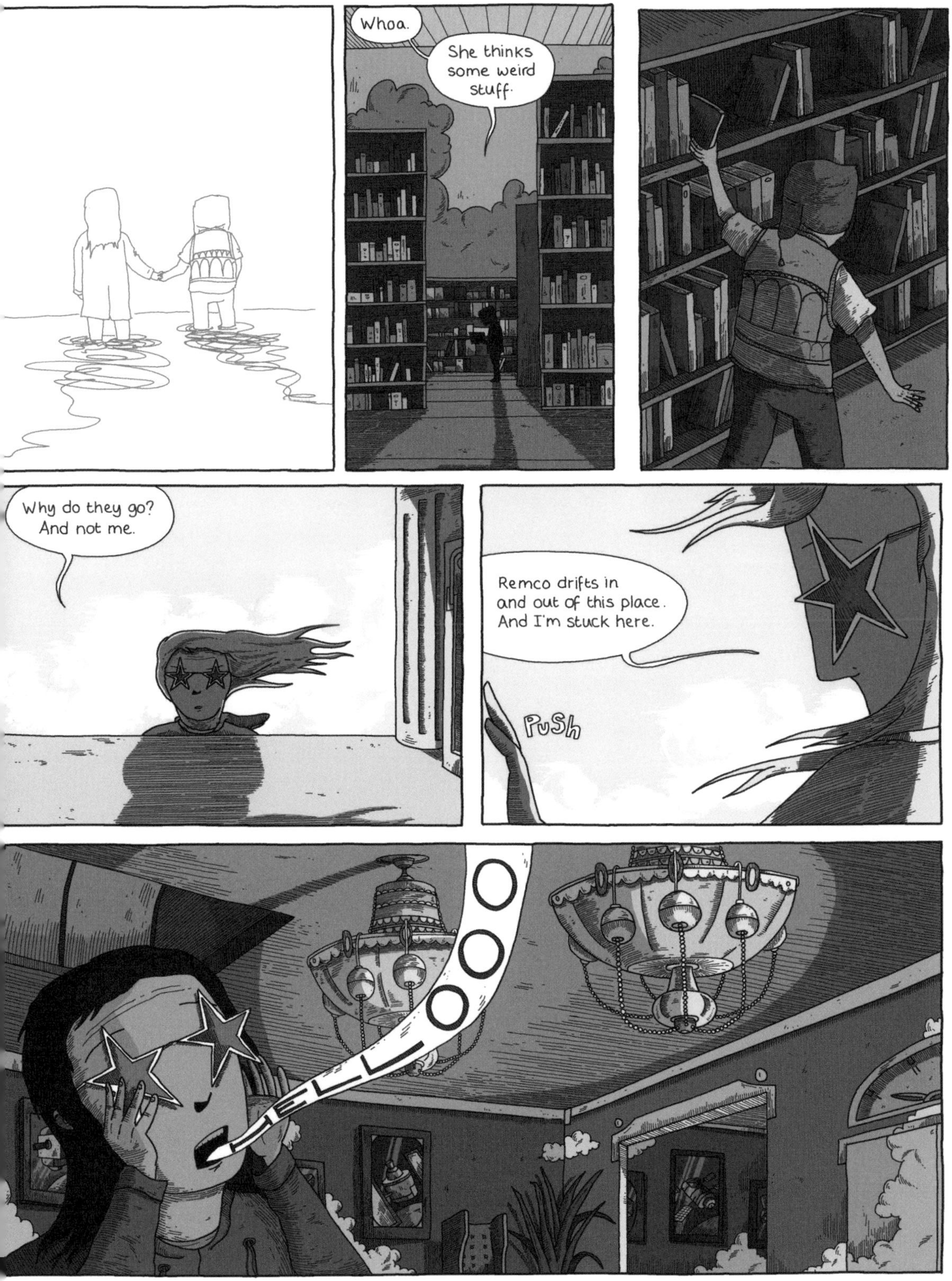
Whoa.
She thinks some weird stuff.
Why do they go? And not me.
Remco drifts in and out of this place. And I'm stuck here.
PUSH
HELLOOOO

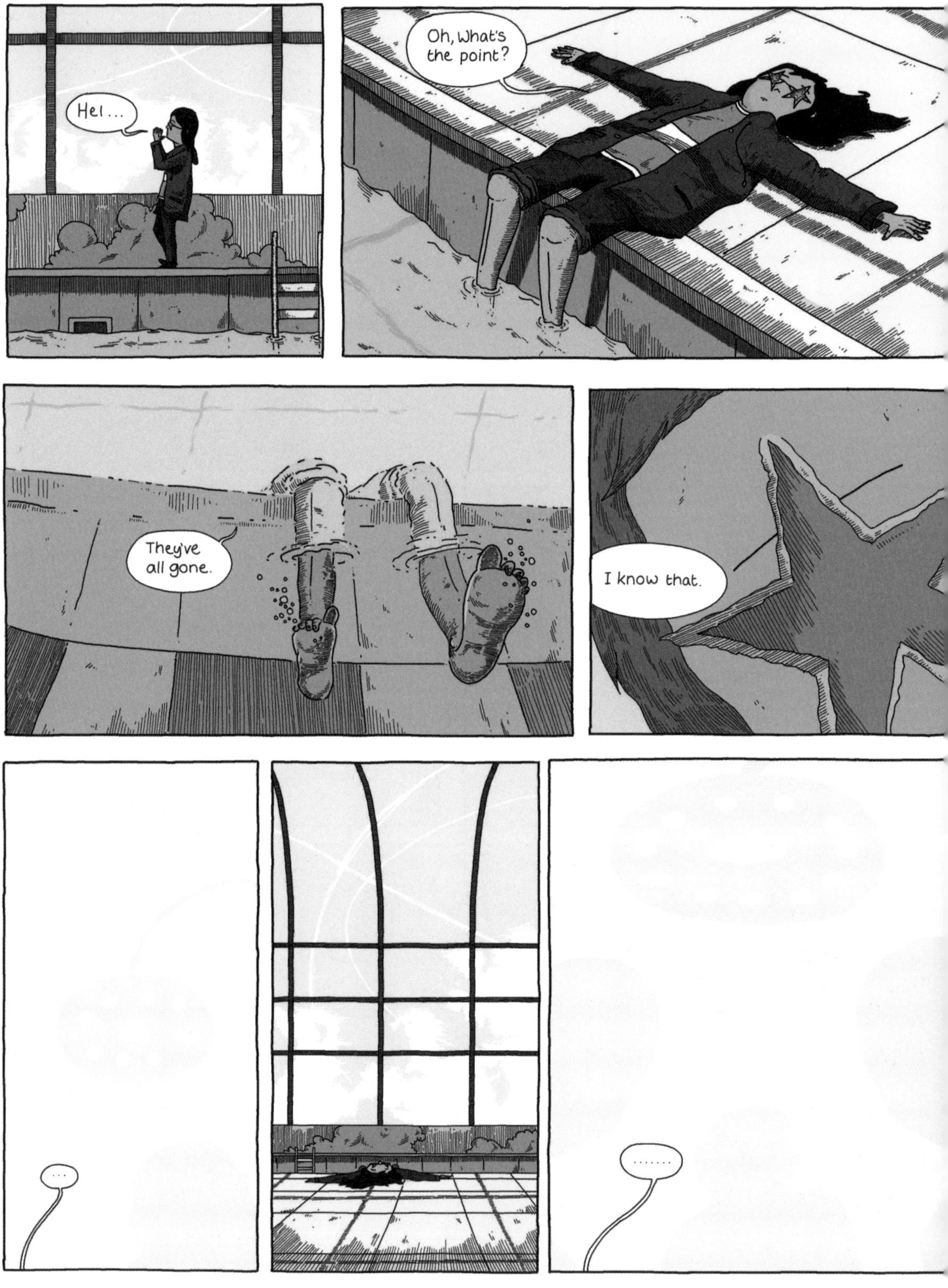
Hel...
Oh, What's the point?
They've all gone.
I know that.
...
....

Here, boy!

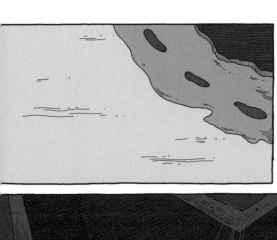

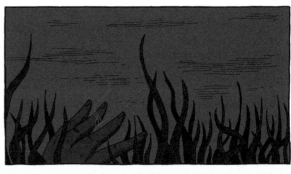

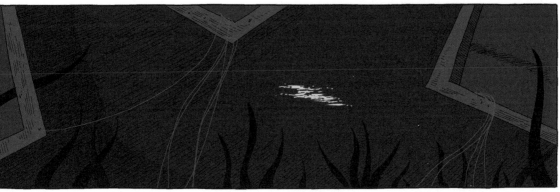

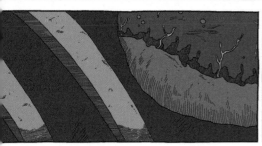

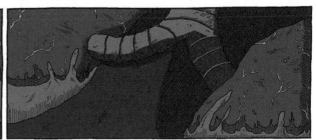

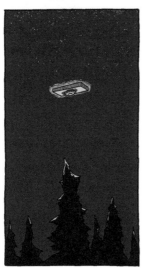

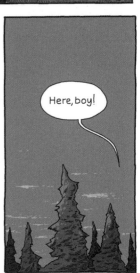

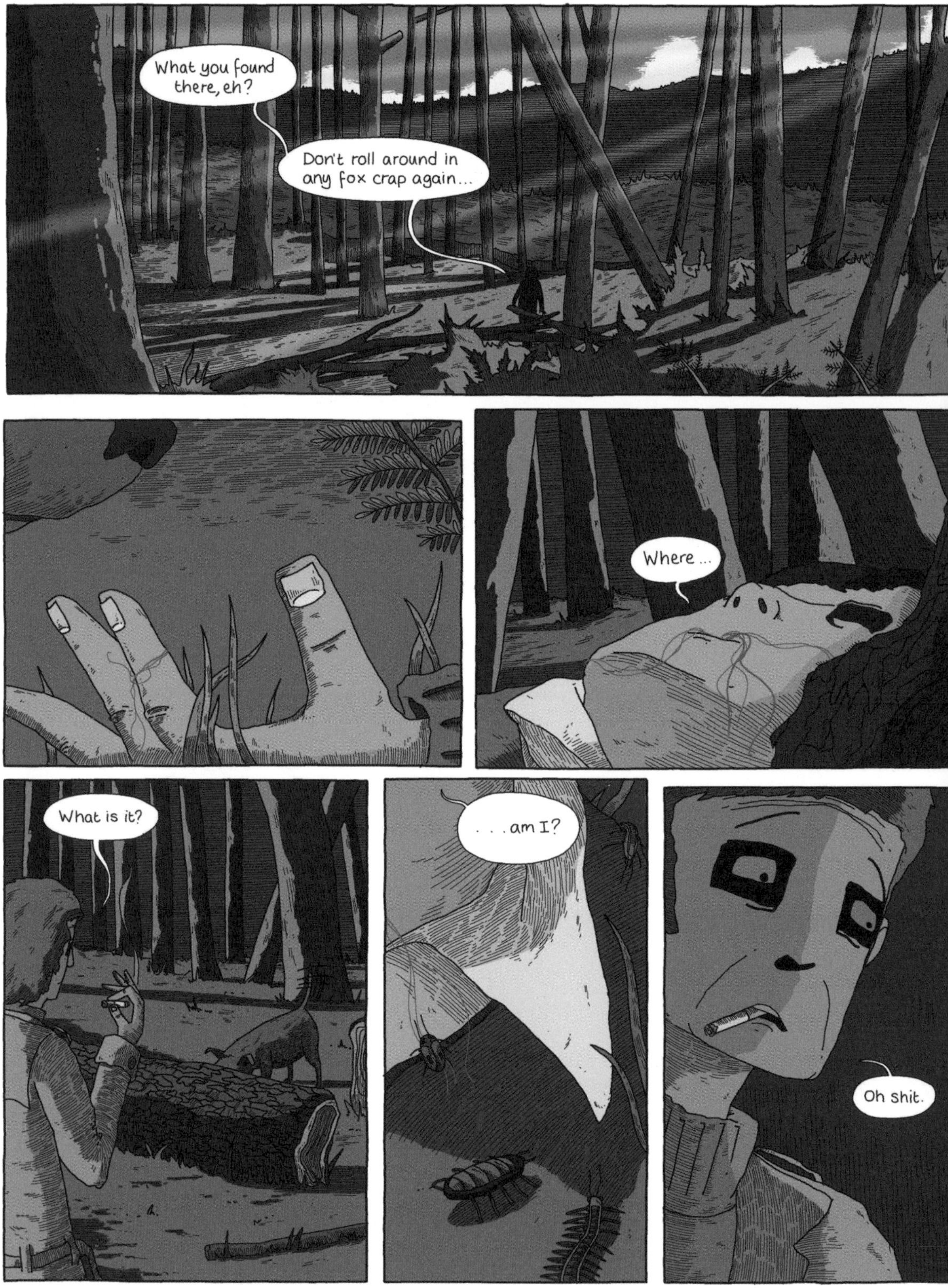
What you found there, eh?
Don't roll around in any fox crap again...
Where ...
What is it?
. . . am I?
Oh shit.

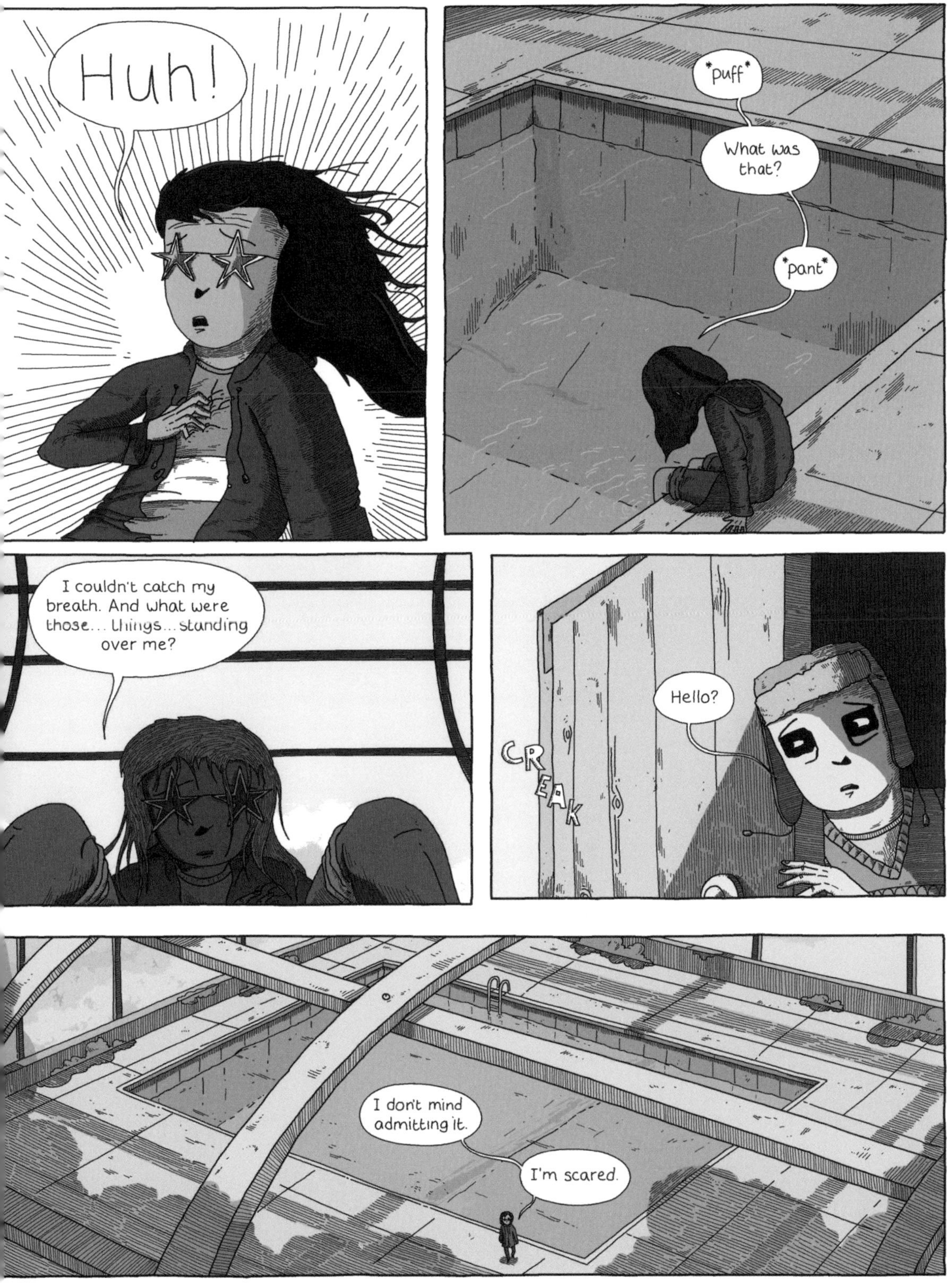

Huh!
puff
What was that?
pant
I couldn't catch my breath. And what were those... things... standing over me?
CREAK
Hello?
I don't mind admitting it.
I'm scared.

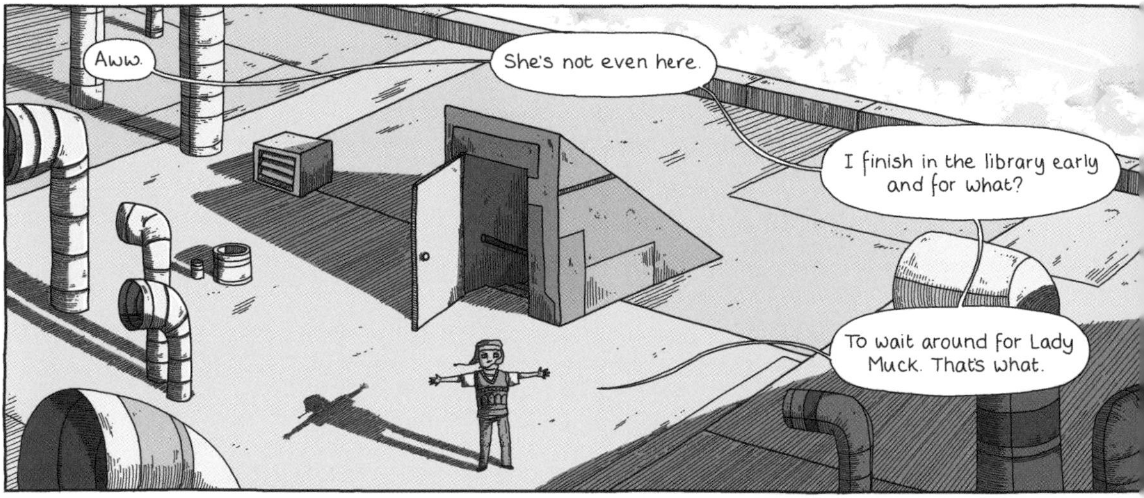
Aww.
She's not even here.
I finish in the library early and for what?
To wait around for Lady Muck. That's what.

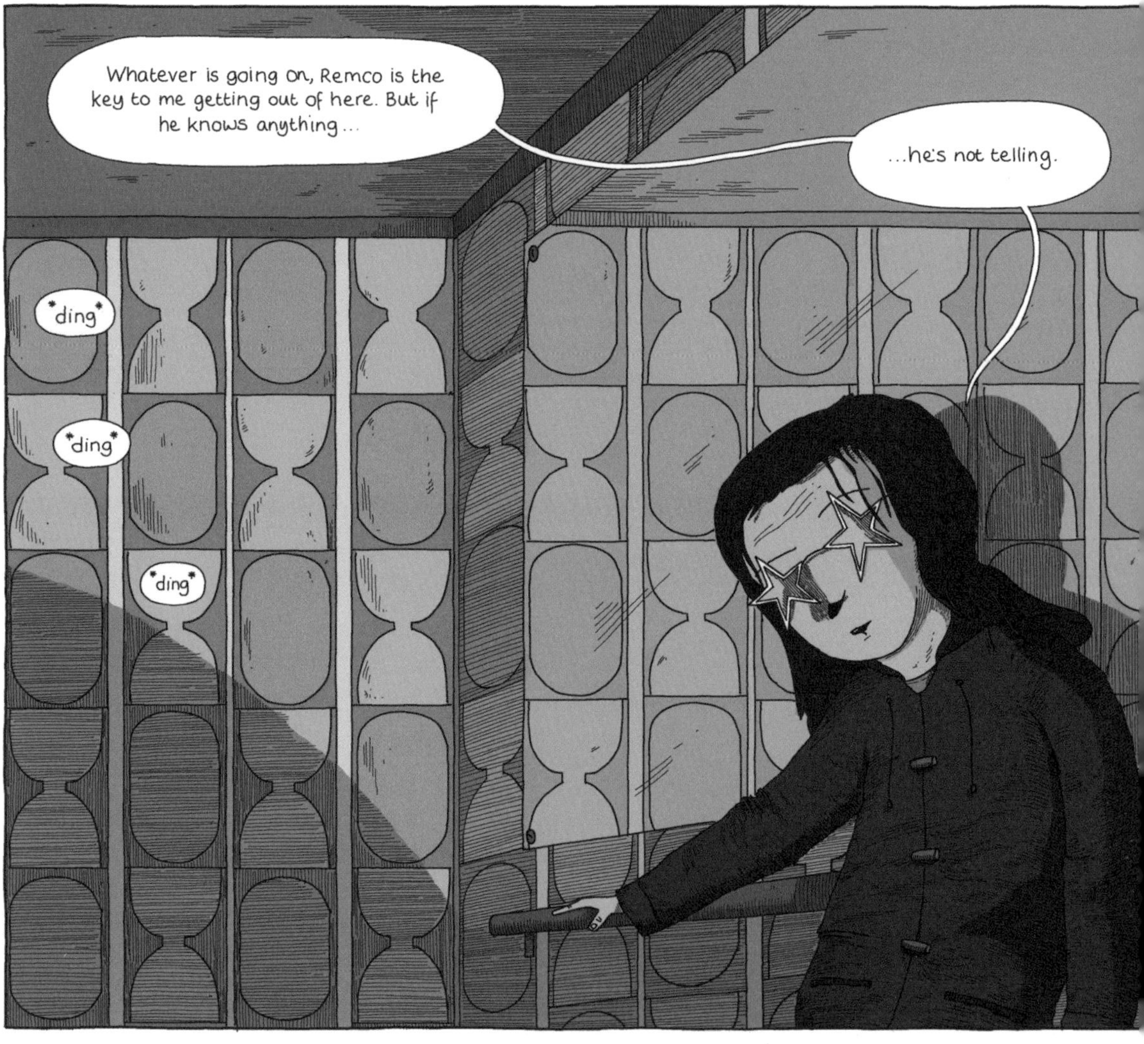
Whatever is going on, Remco is the key to me getting out of here. But if he knows anything...
...he's not telling.
ding
ding
ding

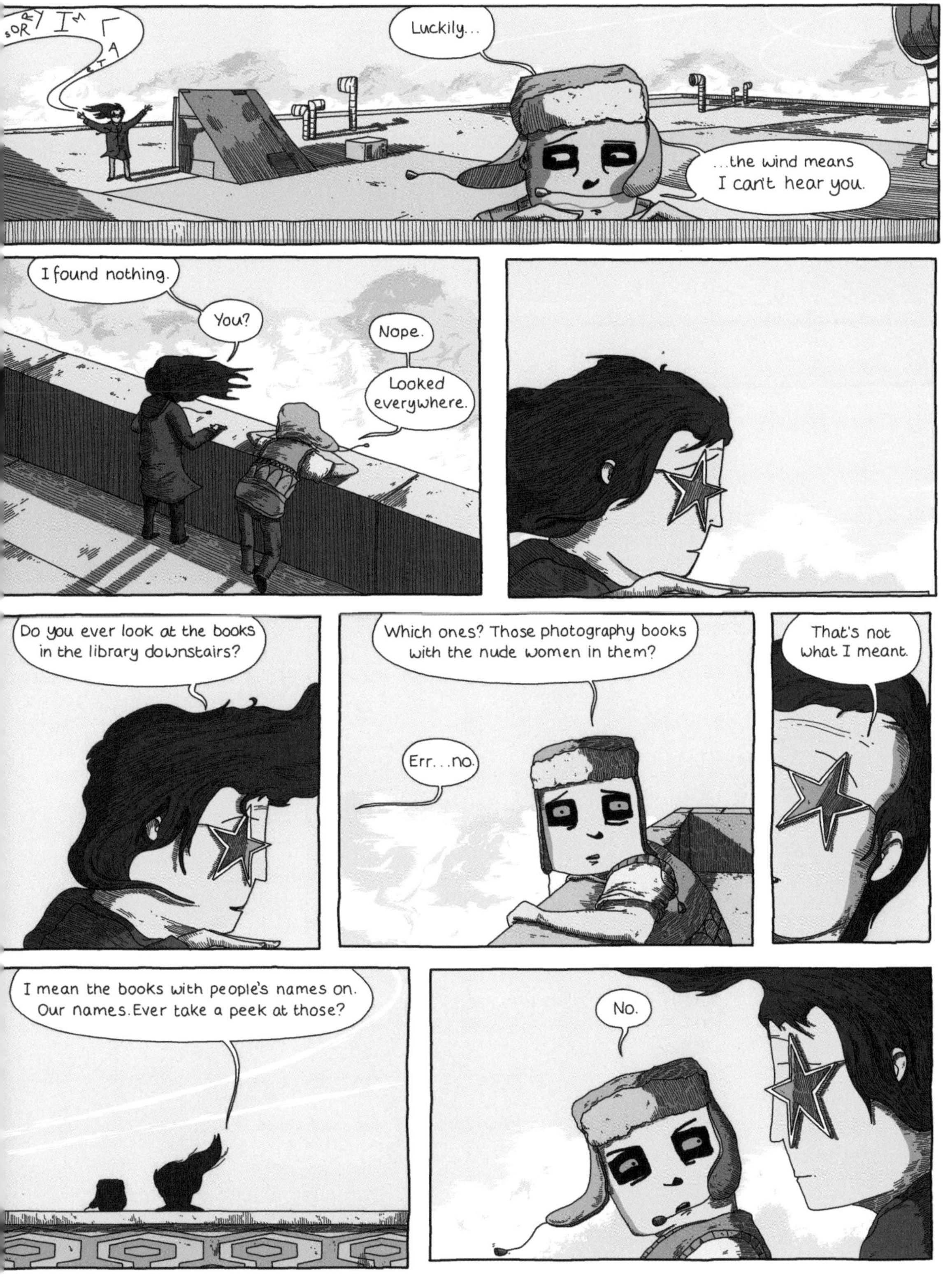
SORRY I'M LATE
Luckily...
...the wind means I can't hear you.
I found nothing.
You?
Nope.
Looked everywhere.
Do you ever look at the books in the library downstairs?
Which ones? Those photography books with the nude women in them?
Err...no.
That's not what I meant.
I mean the books with people's names on. Our names. Ever take a peek at those?
No.

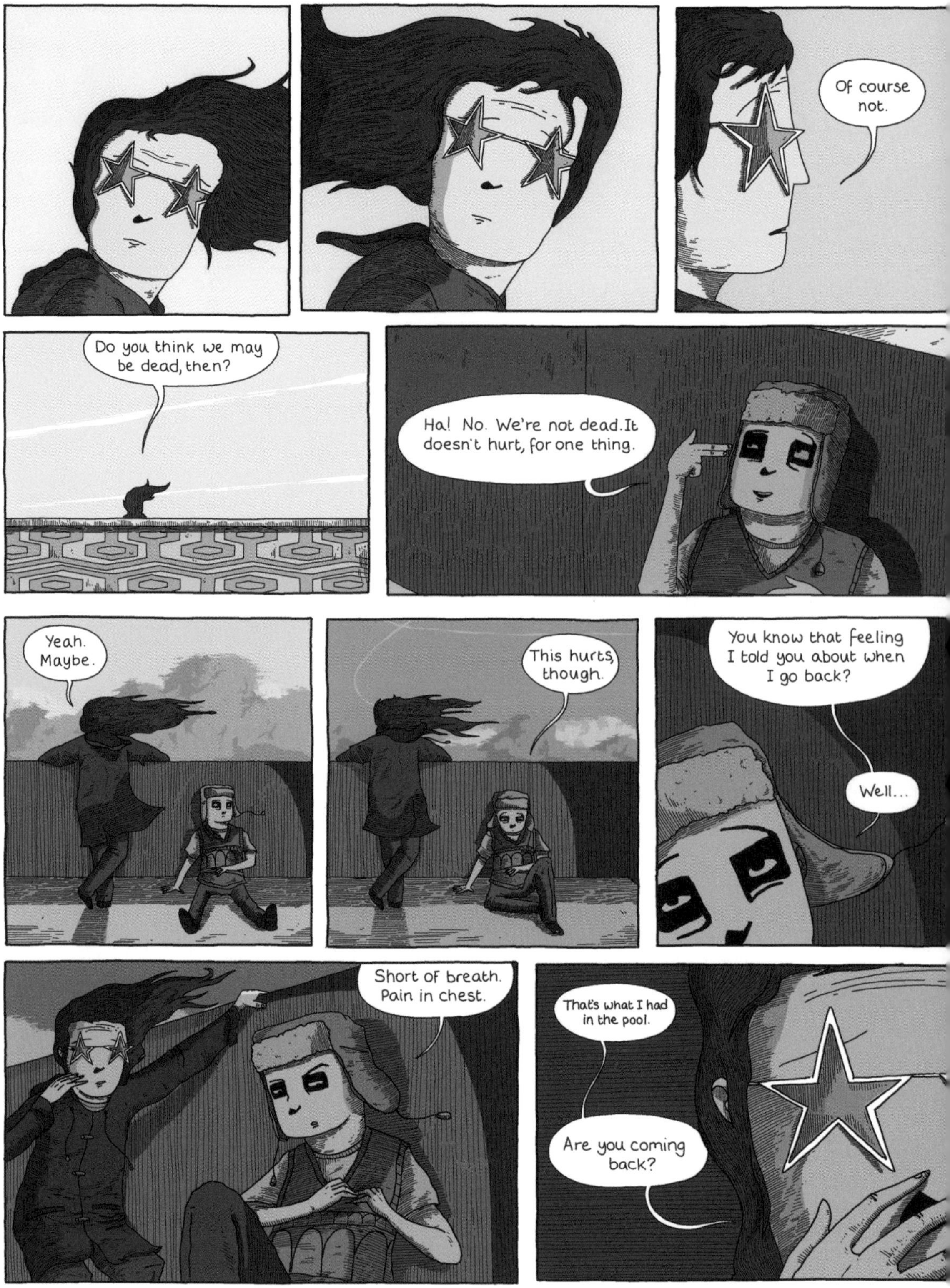
Of course not.
Do you think we may be dead, then?
Ha! No. We're not dead. It doesn't hurt, for one thing.
Yeah. Maybe.
This hurts, though.
You know that feeling I told you about when I go back?
Well...
Short of breath. Pain in chest.
That's what I had in the pool.
Are you coming back?

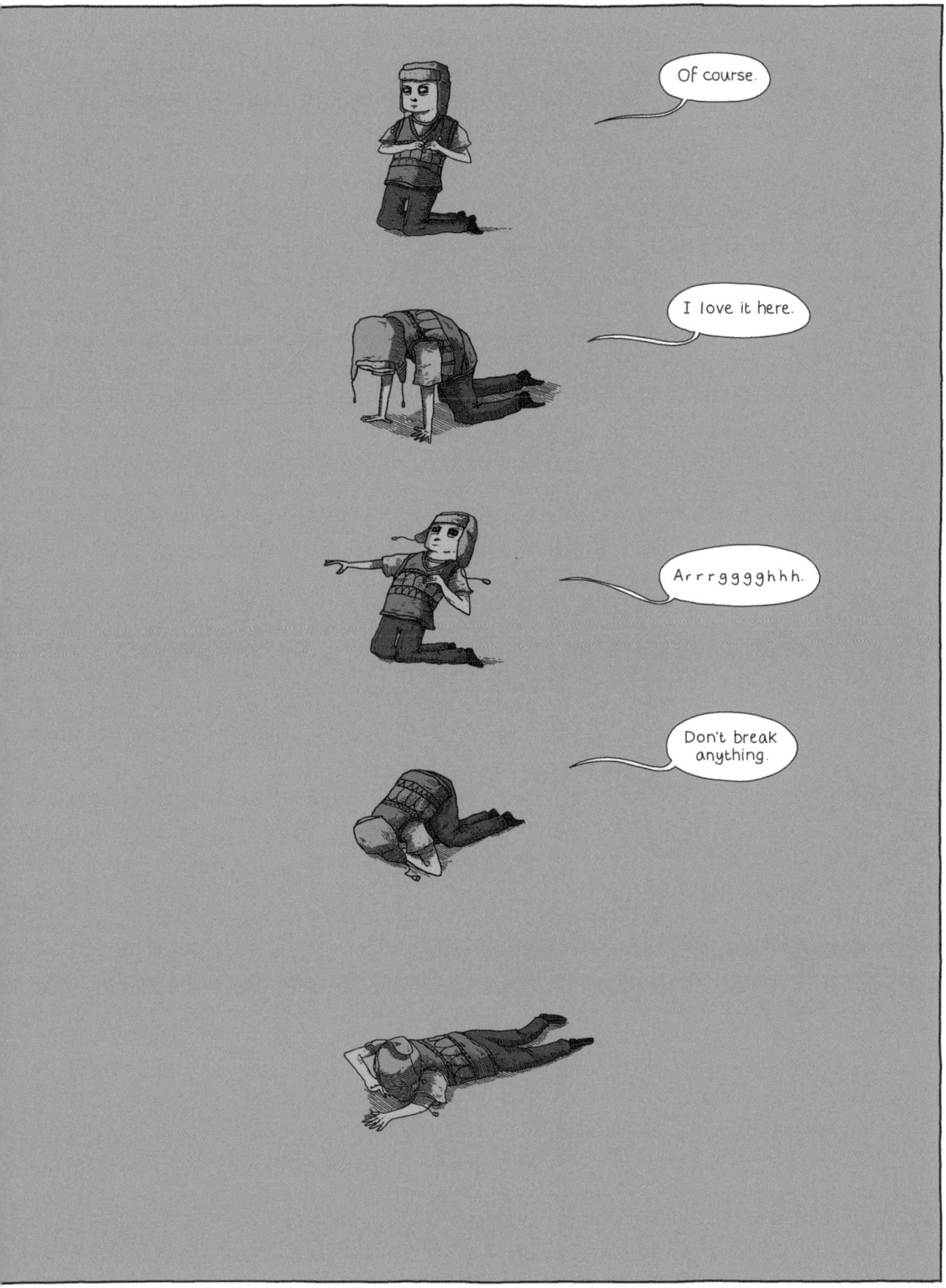
Of course.
I love it here.
Arrrggggghhh.
Don't break anything.

Hello?

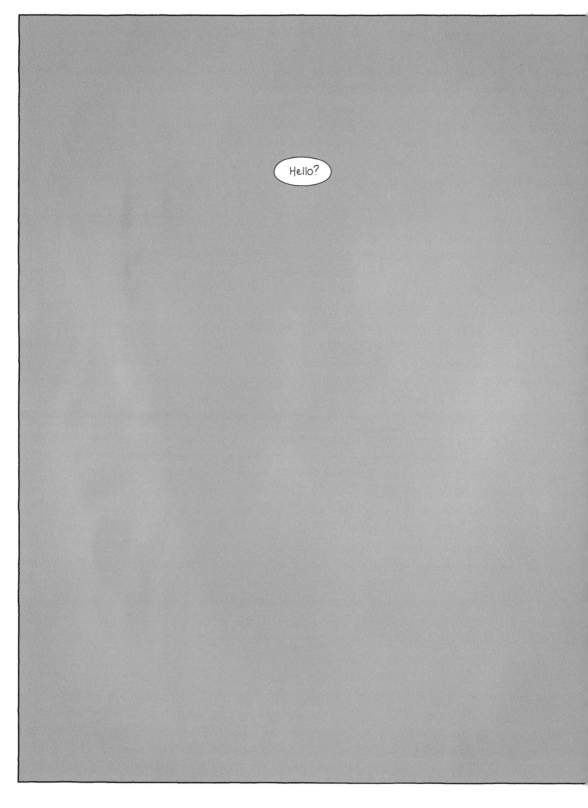

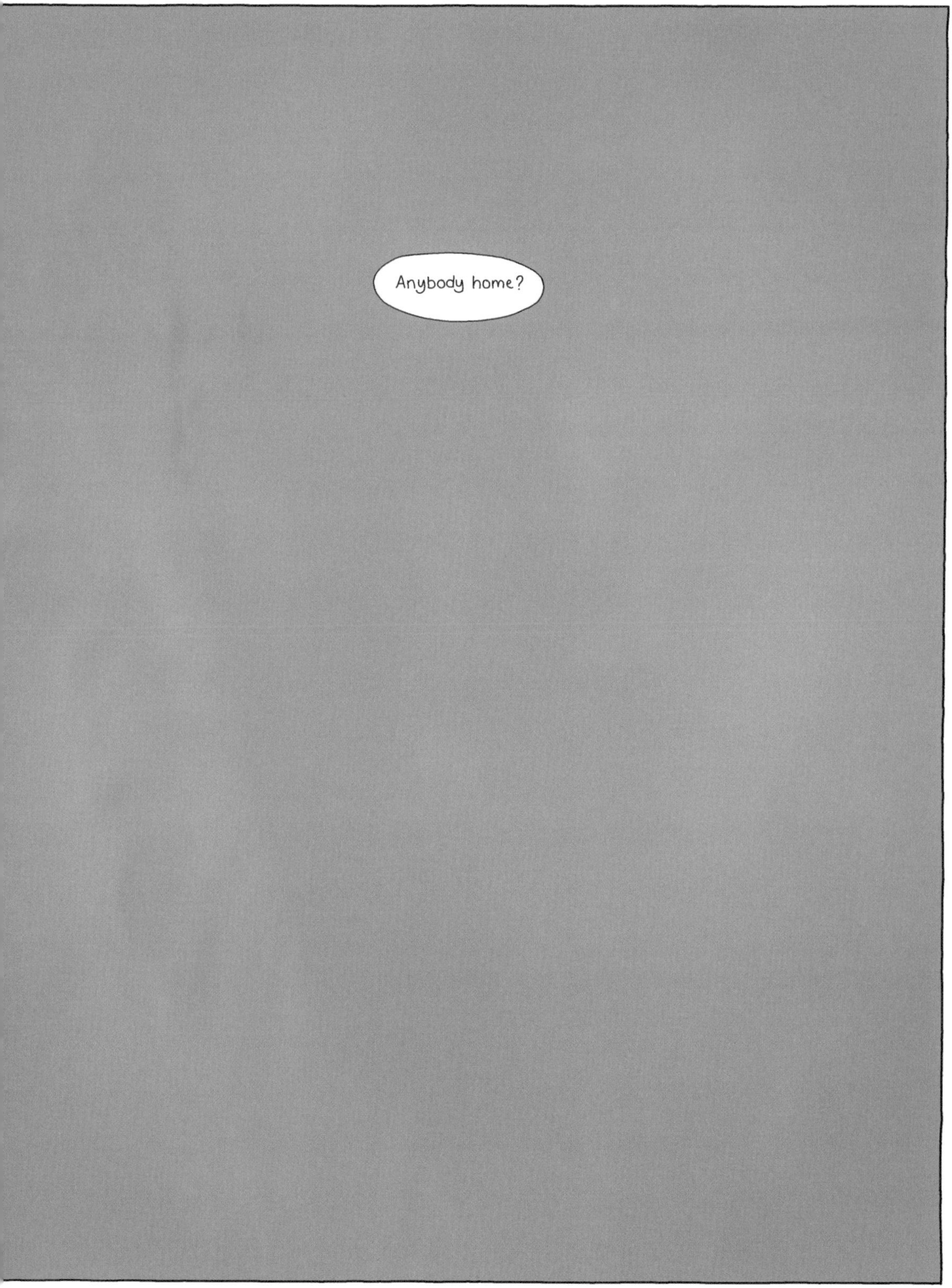
Anybody home?

Come on.
Wakey wakey. I don't want you sleeping too long.
slide

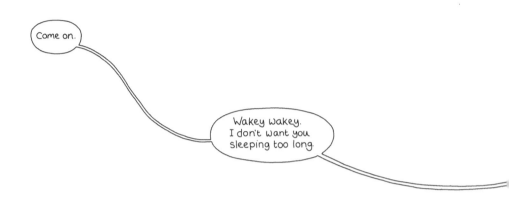

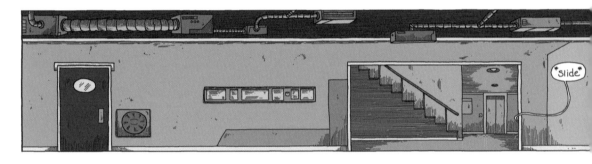

Sorry, Dad, I seem to have nodded off there.
How long was I, you know... asleep for?

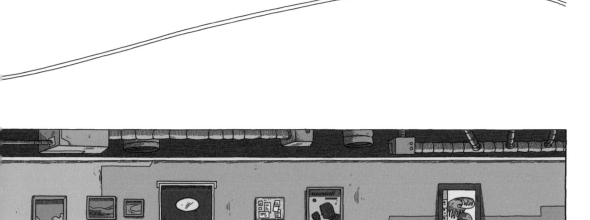

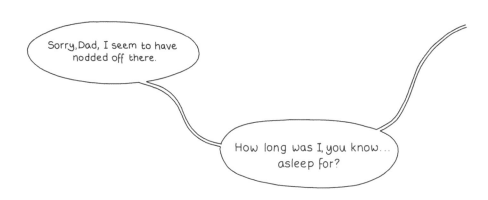

About 20 minutes.

Maybe more.

MISSING

It's odd, as it feels like hours.

Do you ever have...

No.

We don't all have your special secret powers.

Sigh.

Want to hear a real secret?

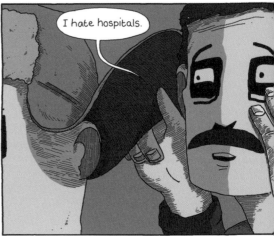

I hate hospitals.

Even when you were born here.

Rubbish, eh?

I would wait in the car park a lot of the time. Trying to look busy.

...

Where's your mum? It's nearly been an hour now.

Yeah. A long time.

I might have to go feed the meter in a bit.

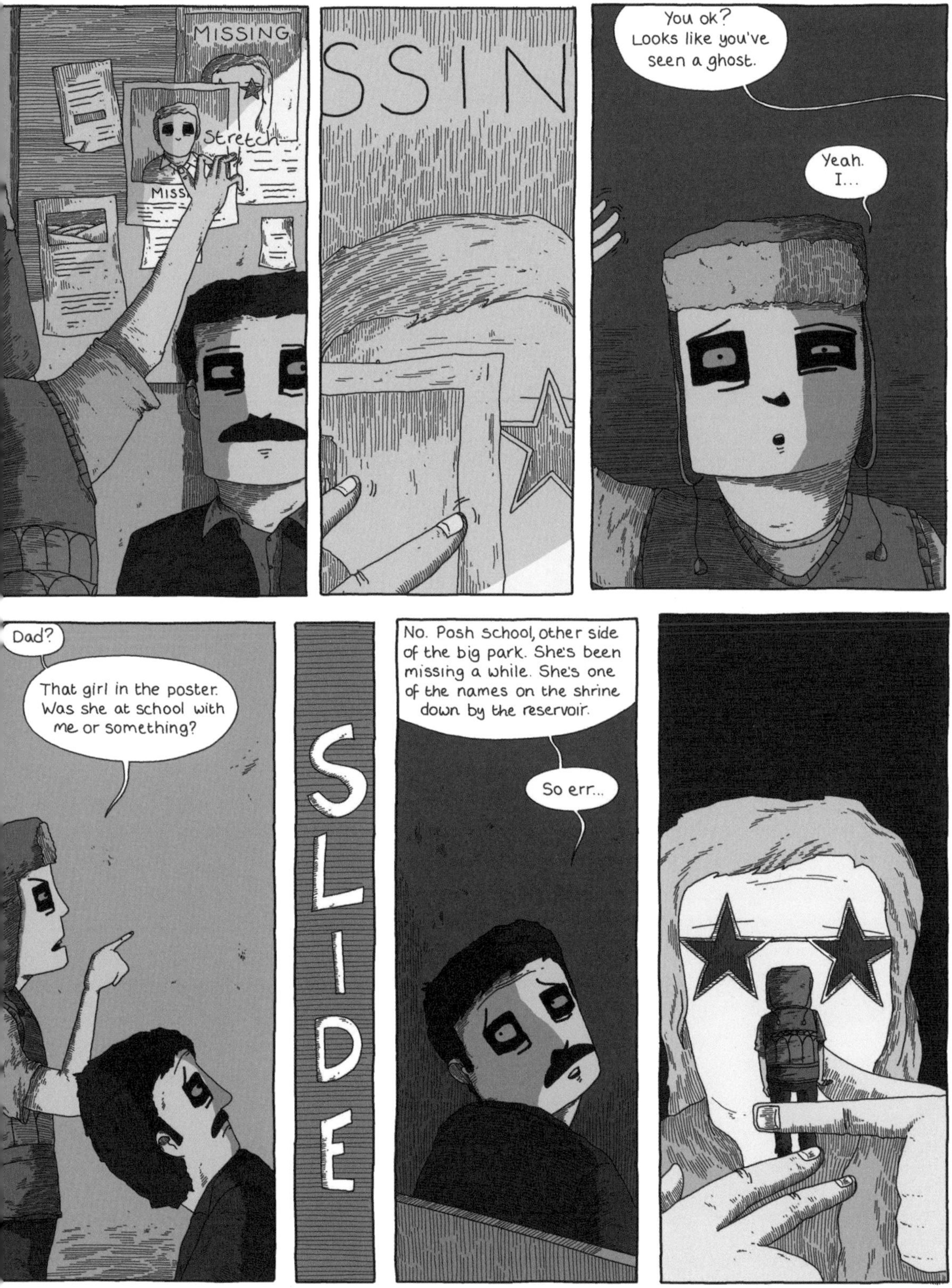
MISSING
Stretch
MISS
SSIN
You ok? Looks like you've seen a ghost.
Yeah. I...
Dad?
That girl in the poster. Was she at school with me or something?
SLIDE
No. Posh school, other side of the big park. She's been missing a while. She's one of the names on the shrine down by the reservoir.
So err...

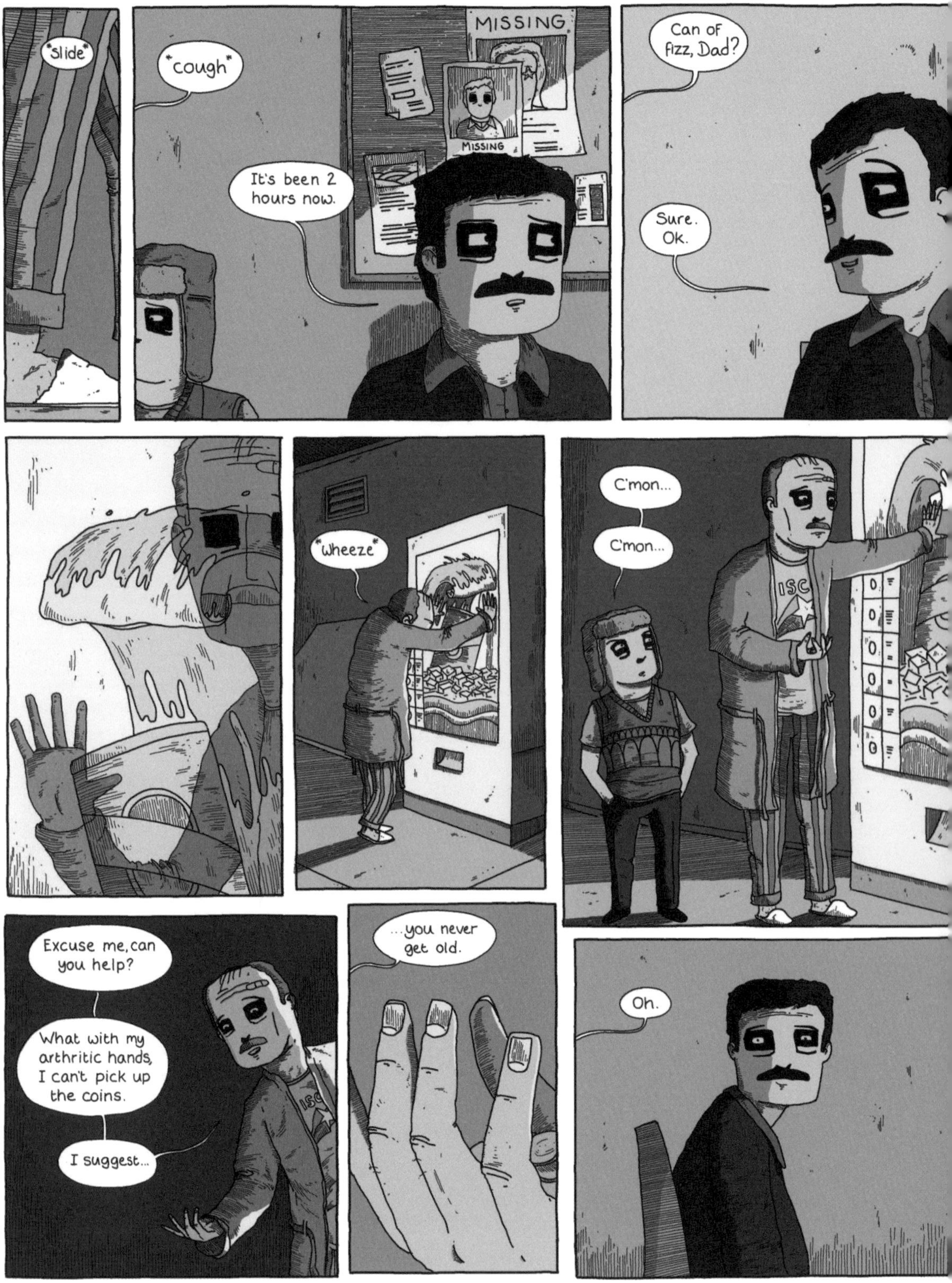
slide
cough
MISSING
MISSING
It's been 2 hours now.
Can of fizz, Dad?
Sure. Ok.
wheeze
C'mon...
C'mon...
ISC
Excuse me, can you help?
What with my arthritic hands, I can't pick up the coins.
I suggest...
...you never get old.
Oh.

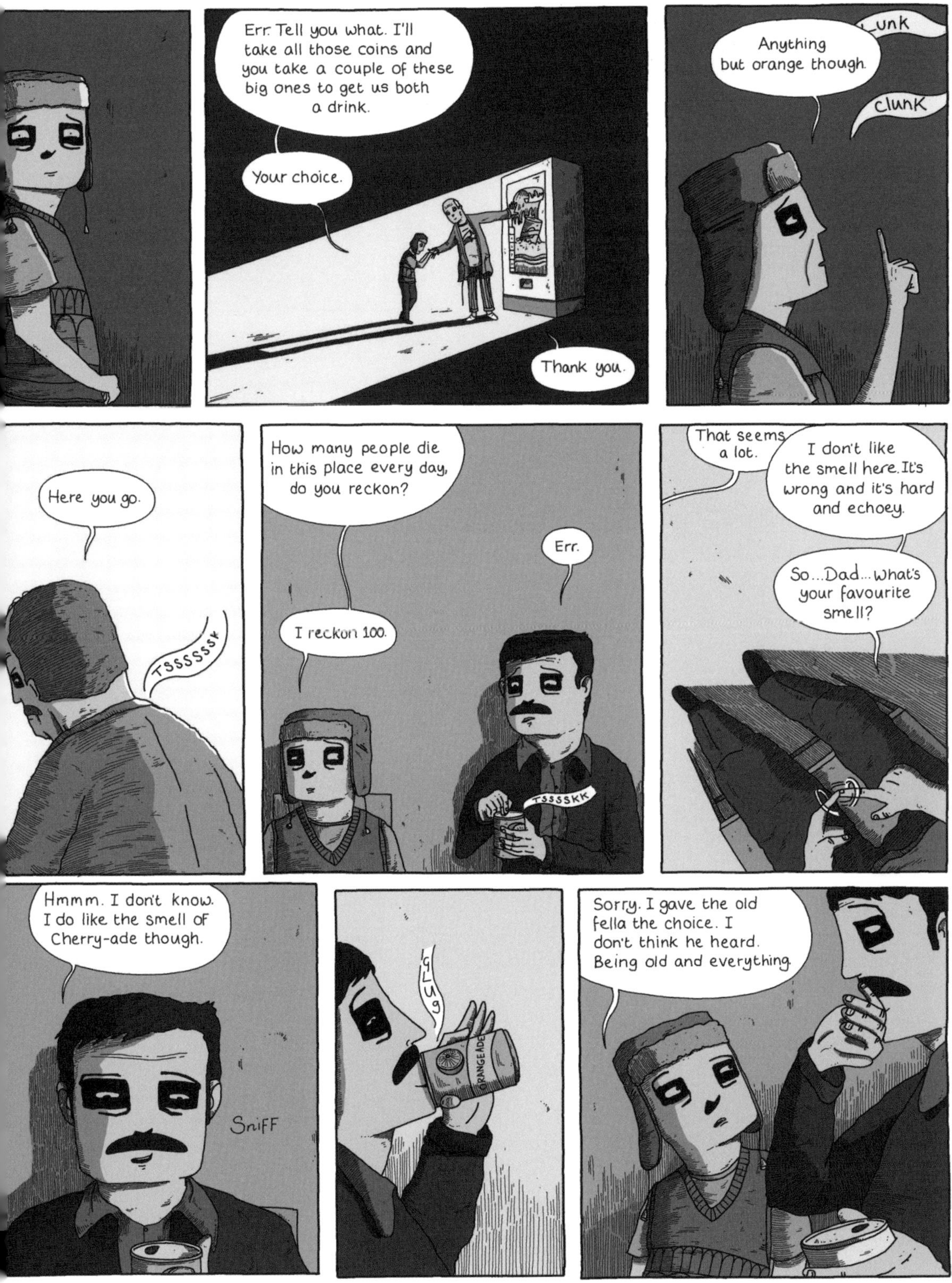
Err. Tell you what. I'll take all those coins and you take a couple of these big ones to get us both a drink.
Your choice.
Thank you.
Anything but orange though.
unk
clunK
Here you go.
TSSSSSSK
How many people die in this place every day, do you reckon?
Err.
I reckon 100.
TSSSSKK
That seems a lot.
I don't like the smell here. It's wrong and it's hard and echoey.
So...Dad...what's your favourite smell?
Hmmm. I don't know. I do like the smell of Cherry-ade though.
Sniff
GLUG
ORANGEADE
Sorry. I gave the old fella the choice. I don't think he heard. Being old and everything.

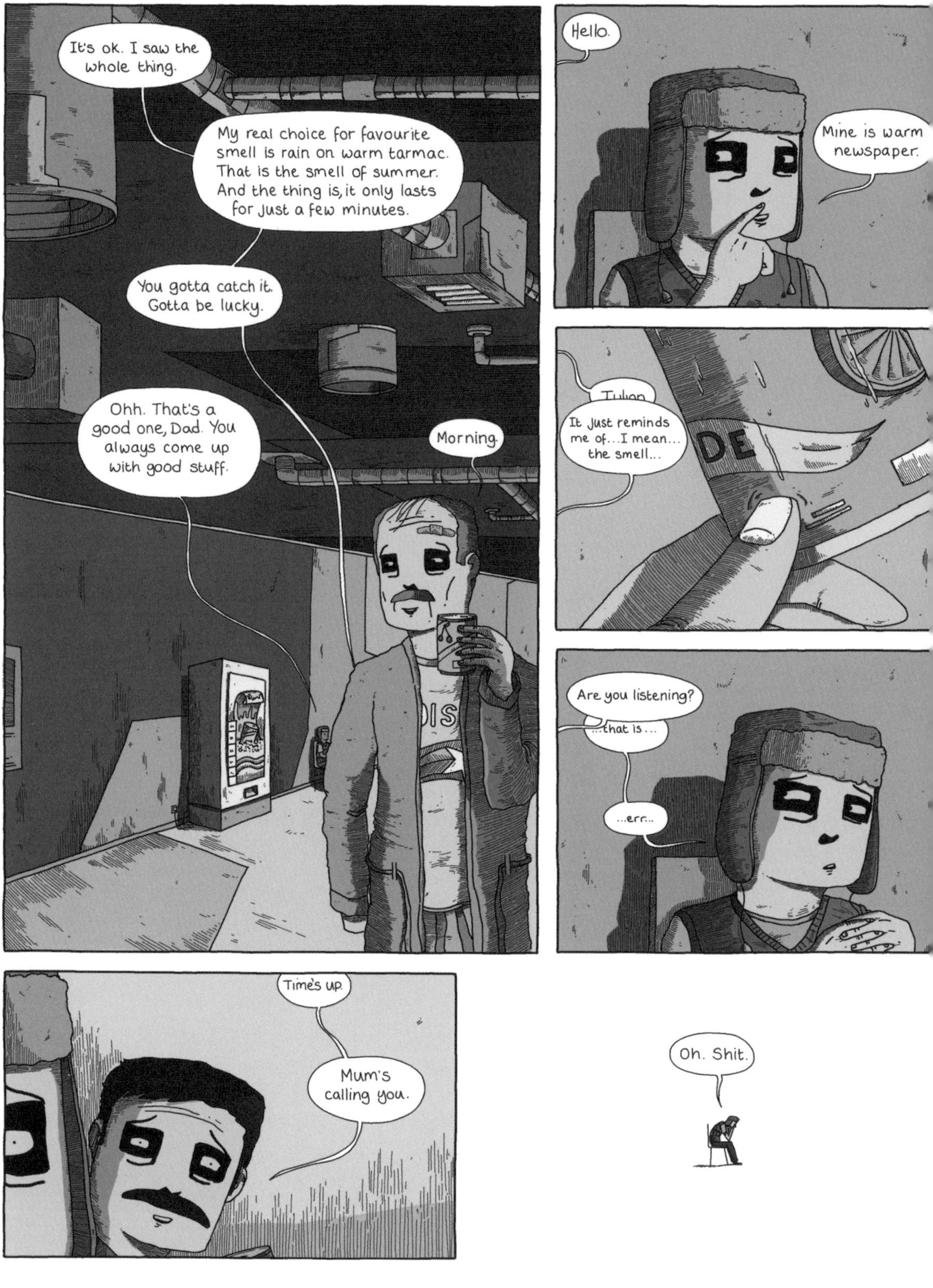
It's ok. I saw the whole thing.
My real choice for favourite smell is rain on warm tarmac. That is the smell of summer. And the thing is, it only lasts for just a few minutes.
You gotta catch it. Gotta be lucky.
Ohh. That's a good one, Dad. You always come up with good stuff.
Morning.
Hello.
Mine is warm newspaper.
It just reminds me of... I mean... the smell...
DE
Are you listening?
...that is...
...err...
Time's up.
Mum's calling you.
Oh. Shit.

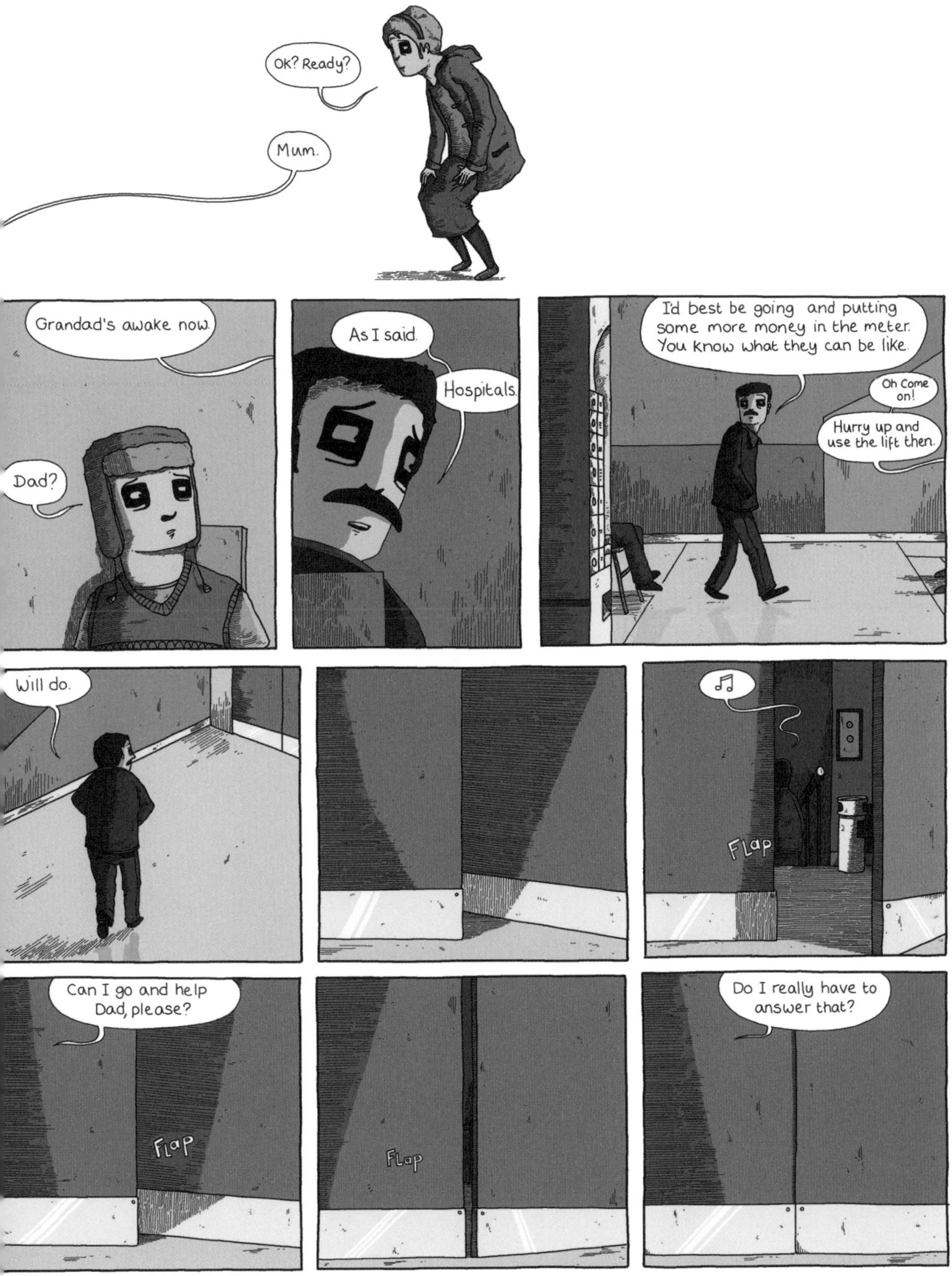
OK? Ready?
Mum.
Grandad's awake now.
Dad?
As I said.
Hospitals.
I'd best be going and putting some more money in the meter. You know what they can be like.
Oh Come on!
Hurry up and use the lift then.
Will do.
♫
FLAP
Can I go and help Dad, please?
FLAP
FLAP
Do I really have to answer that?

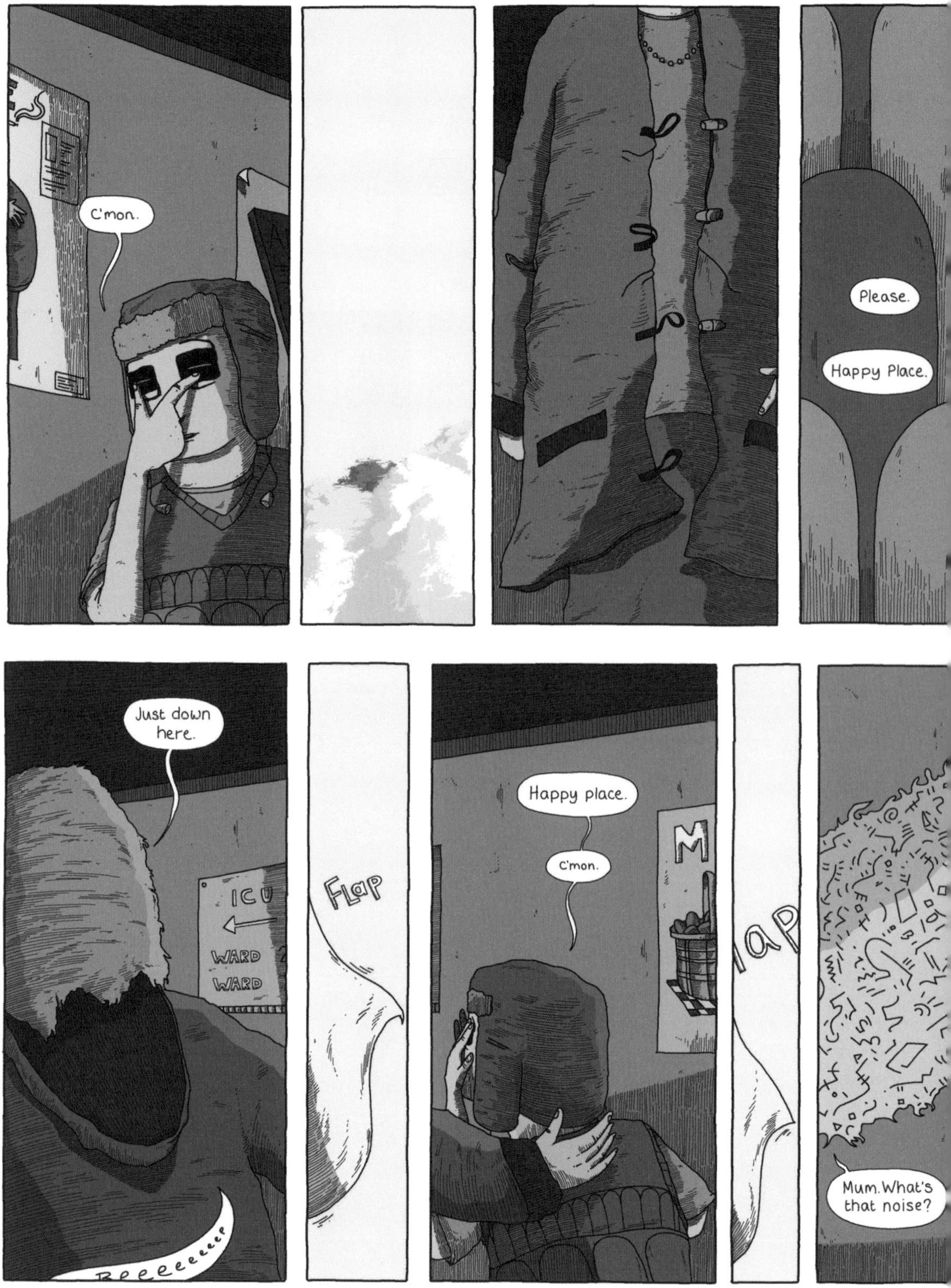
C'mon.
Please.
Happy Place.
Just down here.
ICU
WARD
WARD
Beeeeeeeeep
FLAP
Happy place.
C'mon.
lap
Mum. What's that noise?

Can we get the parents out of the ward, please?
You're going to be fine.
You Are Here

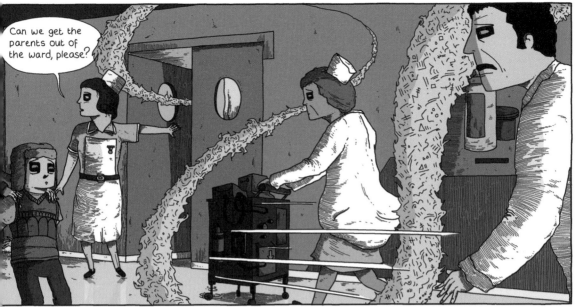

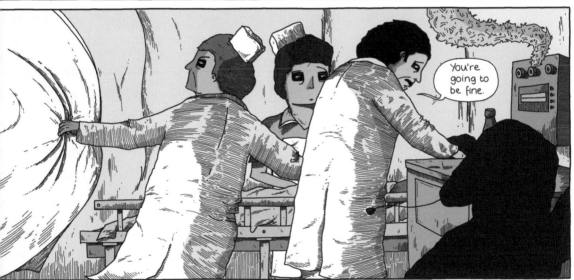

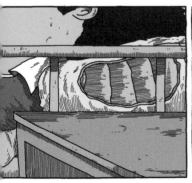

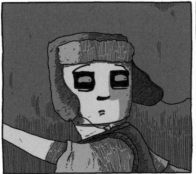

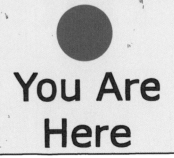

I C U
Ward

Are
re

Now, listen. I'm sure that boy back there will be fine.

Honestly.

Ok.

Good boy.

Ok, say hello to Grandad. I'll just be outside.

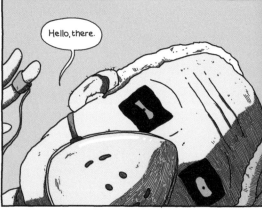

Hello, there.

YOu

H

Hi.

It's good to see you. Come closer. I know I'm old, but there's no need to be afraid.

Ha.

cough

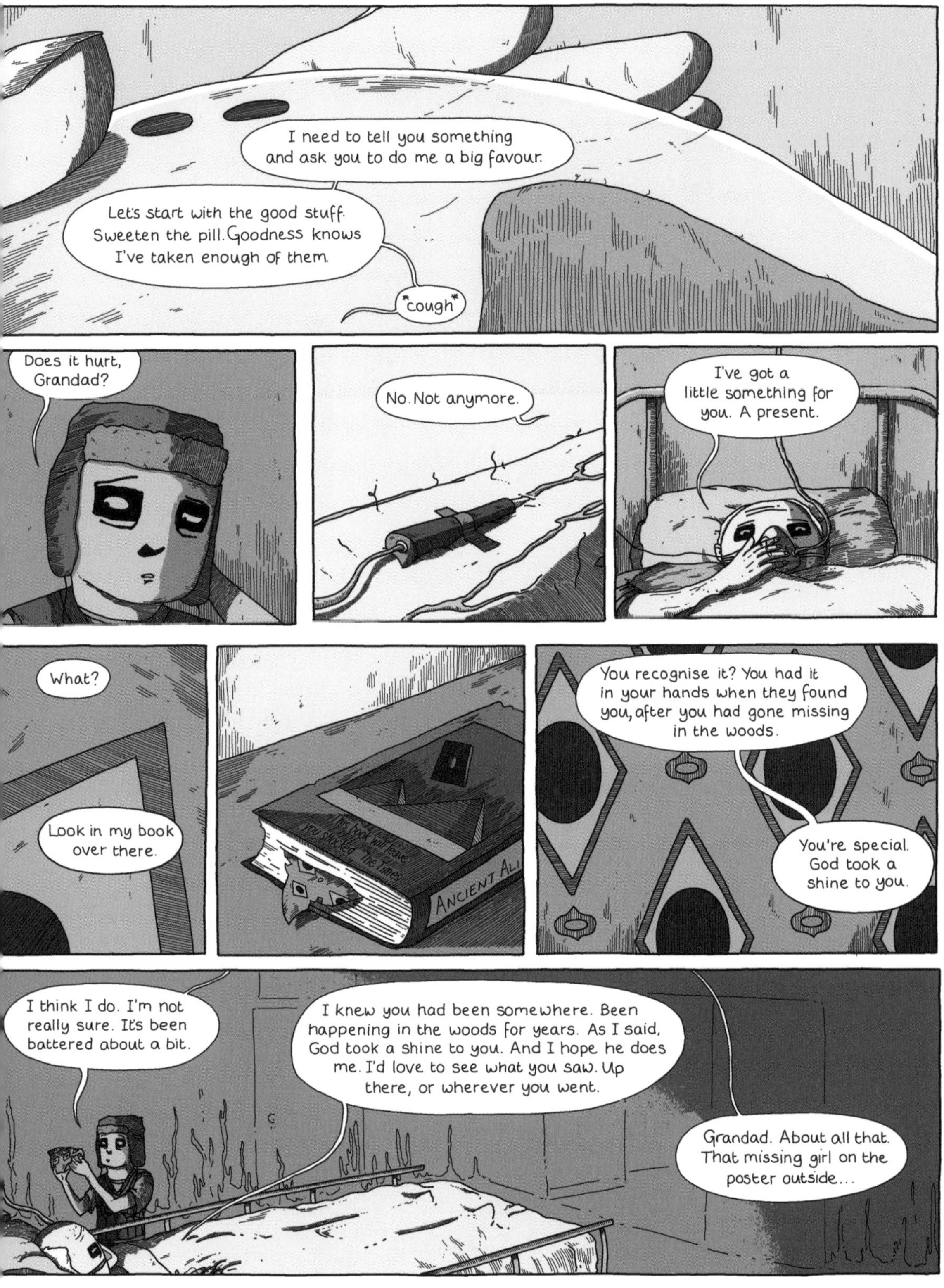
I need to tell you something and ask you to do me a big favour.
Let's start with the good stuff. Sweeten the pill. Goodness knows I've taken enough of them.
cough
Does it hurt, Grandad?
No. Not anymore.
I've got a little something for you. A present.
What?
Look in my book over there.
This book will leave you shocked - The Times
ANCIENT ALI
You recognise it? You had it in your hands when they found you, after you had gone missing in the woods.
You're special. God took a shine to you.
I think I do. I'm not really sure. It's been battered about a bit.
I knew you had been somewhere. Been happening in the woods for years. As I said, God took a shine to you. And I hope he does me. I'd love to see what you saw. Up there, or wherever you went.
Grandad. About all that. That missing girl on the poster outside...

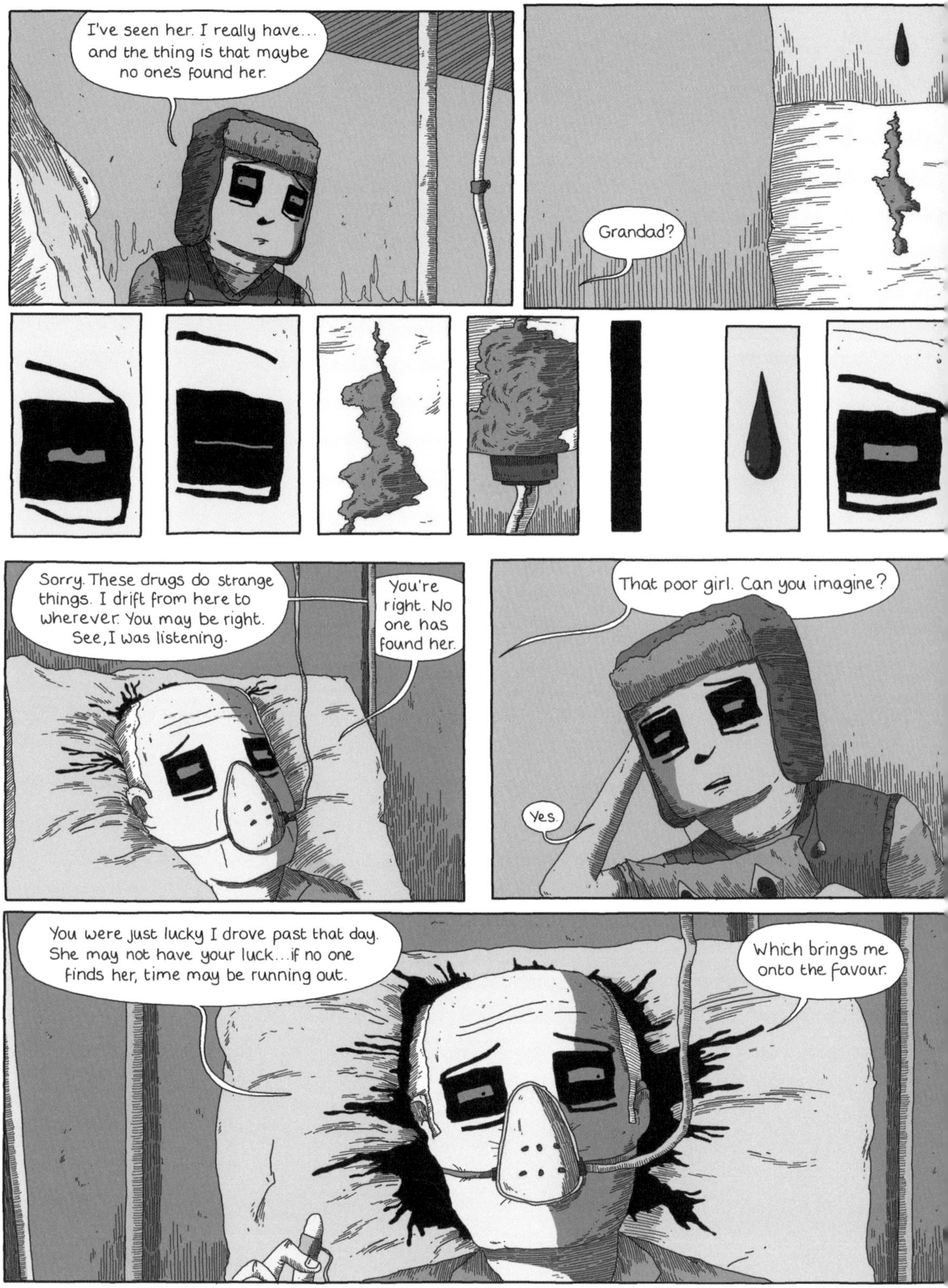
I've seen her. I really have... and the thing is that maybe no one's found her.
Grandad?
Sorry. These drugs do strange things. I drift from here to wherever. You may be right. See, I was listening.
You're right. No one has found her.
That poor girl. Can you imagine?
Yes.
You were just lucky I drove past that day. She may not have your luck...if no one finds her, time may be running out.
Which brings me onto the favour.

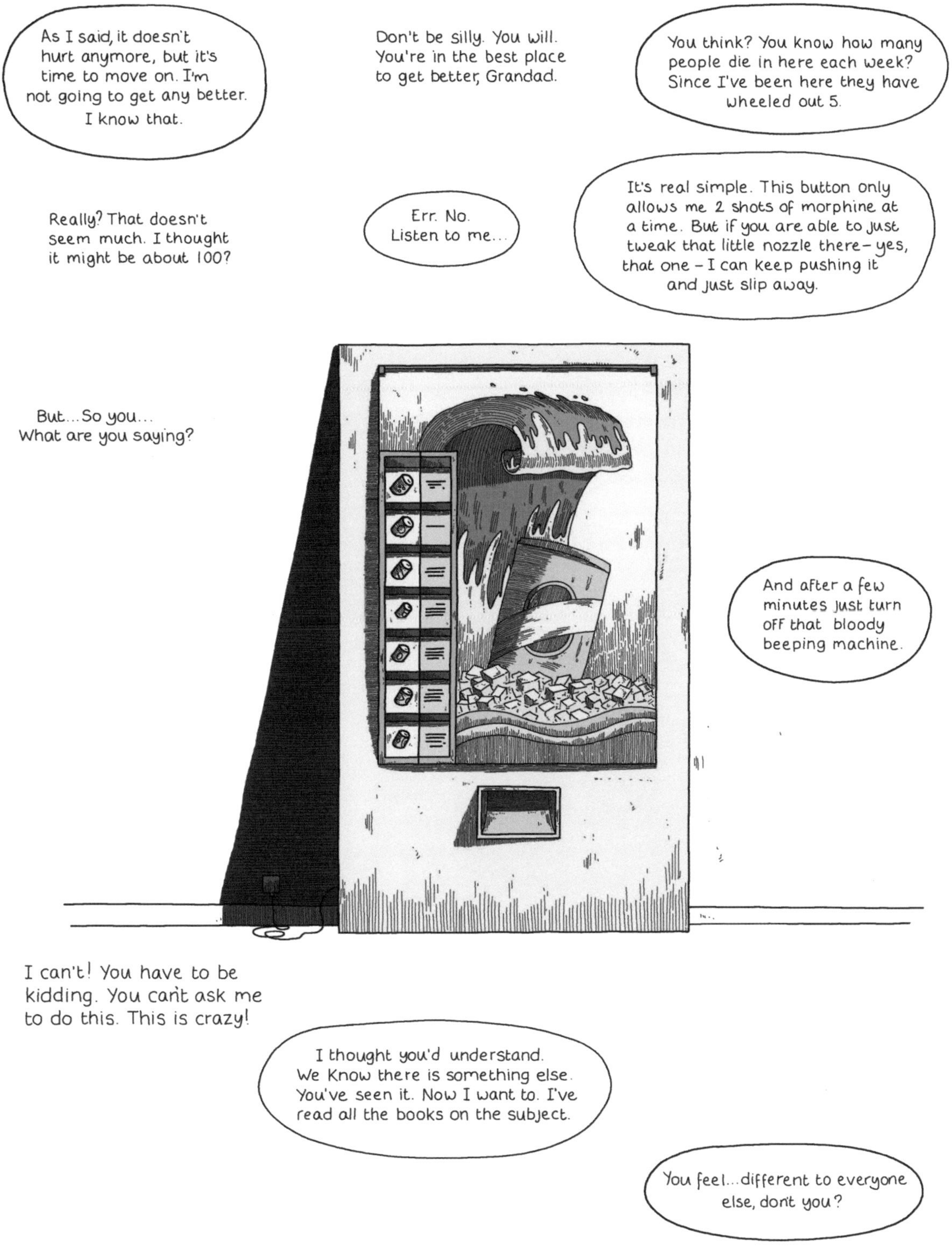
As I said, it doesn't hurt anymore, but it's time to move on. I'm not going to get any better. I know that.
Don't be silly. You will. You're in the best place to get better, Grandad.
You think? You know how many people die in here each week? Since I've been here they have wheeled out 5.
Really? That doesn't seem much. I thought it might be about 100?
Err. No. Listen to me...
It's real simple. This button only allows me 2 shots of morphine at a time. But if you are able to just tweak that little nozzle there - yes, that one - I can keep pushing it and just slip away.
But... So you... What are you saying?
And after a few minutes just turn off that bloody beeping machine.
I can't! You have to be kidding. You can't ask me to do this. This is crazy!
I thought you'd understand. We Know there is something else. You've seen it. Now I want to. I've read all the books on the subject.
You feel... different to everyone else, don't you?

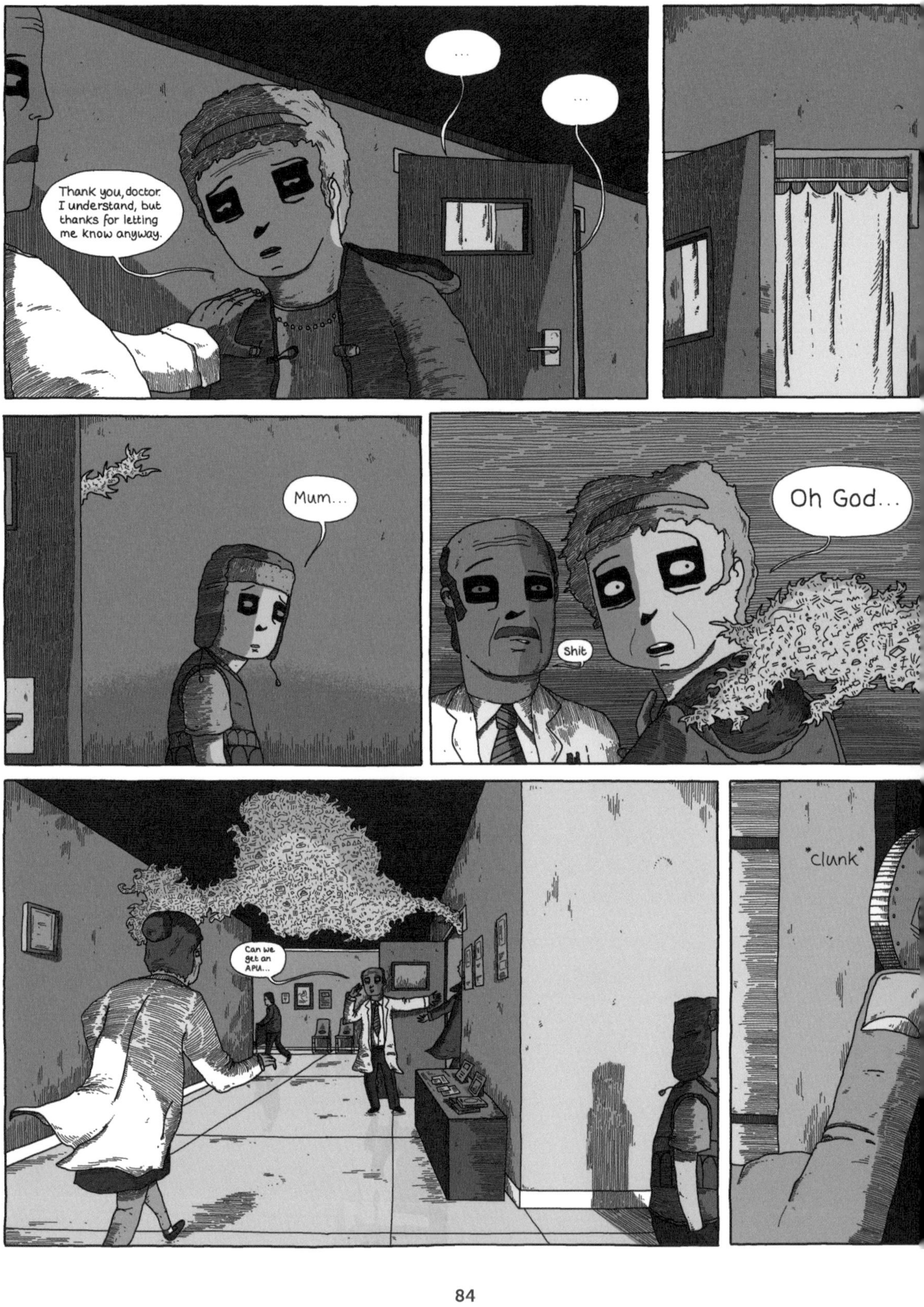
...
...
Thank you, doctor. I understand, but thanks for letting me know anyway.
Mum...
Oh God...
Shit
Can we get an APU...
clunk

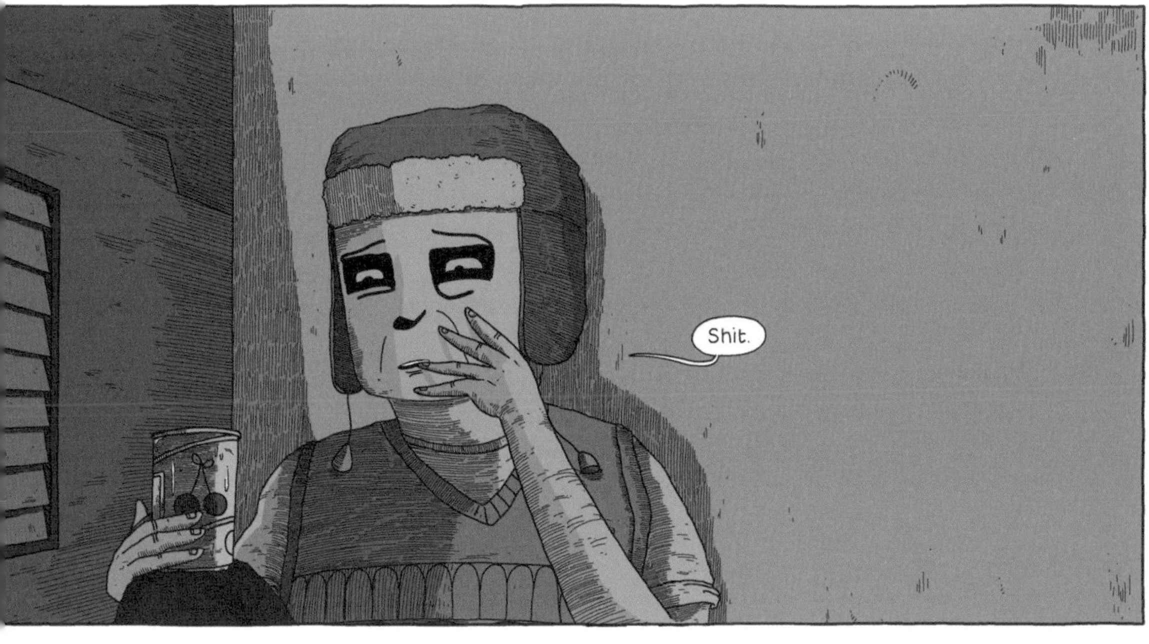
Shit.

5th May

1981

He's been looking at my book! Little sod.

Dirty fingers all over it. Especially this bit...

EMMA

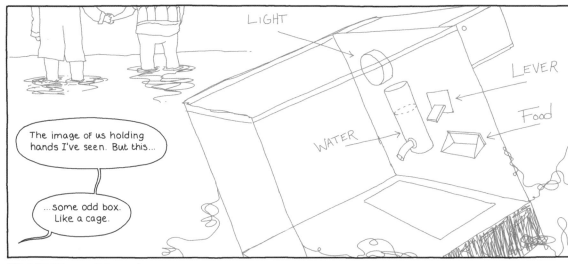

LIGHT

LEVER

Food

WATER

The image of us holding hands I've seen. But this...

...some odd box. Like a cage.

Hey!

Oh, this isn't good.

ding

ding

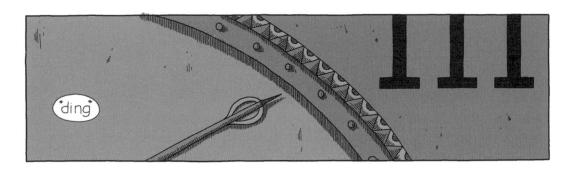

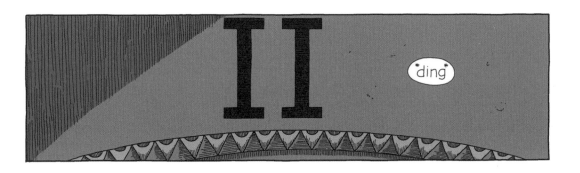

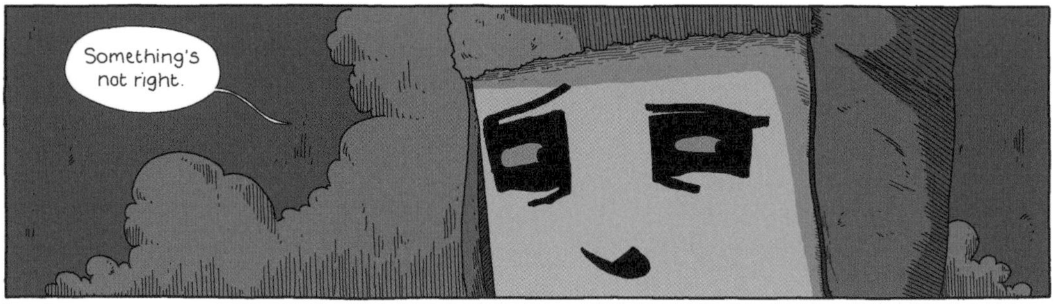
Something's not right.

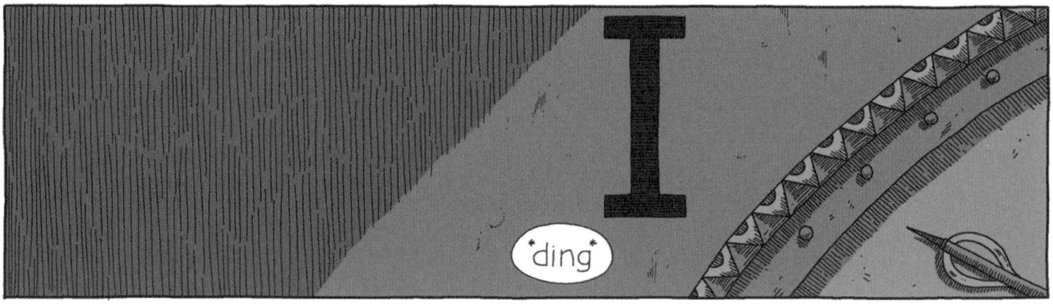
ding

click
Maybe the paintings have changed?

ding
G

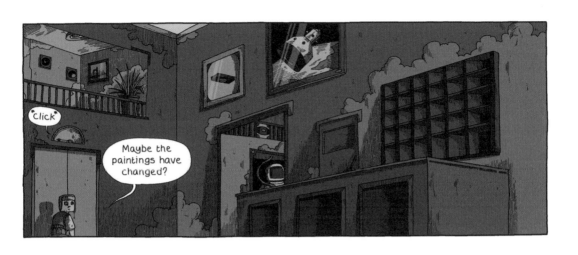

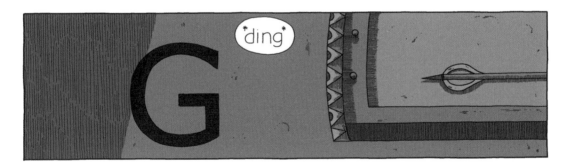

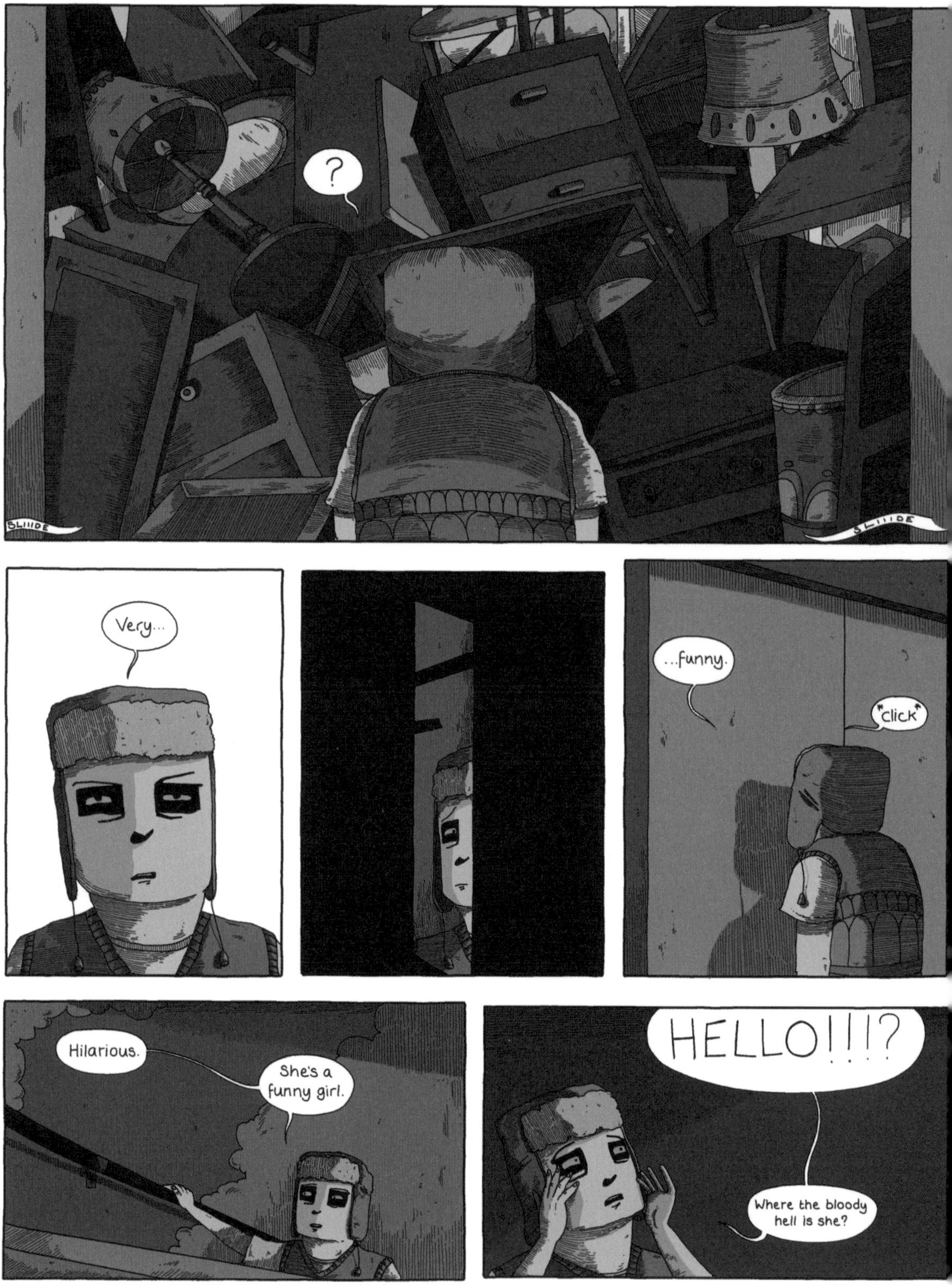
?
SLIIIDE
SLIIIDE
Very...
...funny.
click
Hilarious.
She's a funny girl.
HELLO!!!?
Where the bloody hell is she?

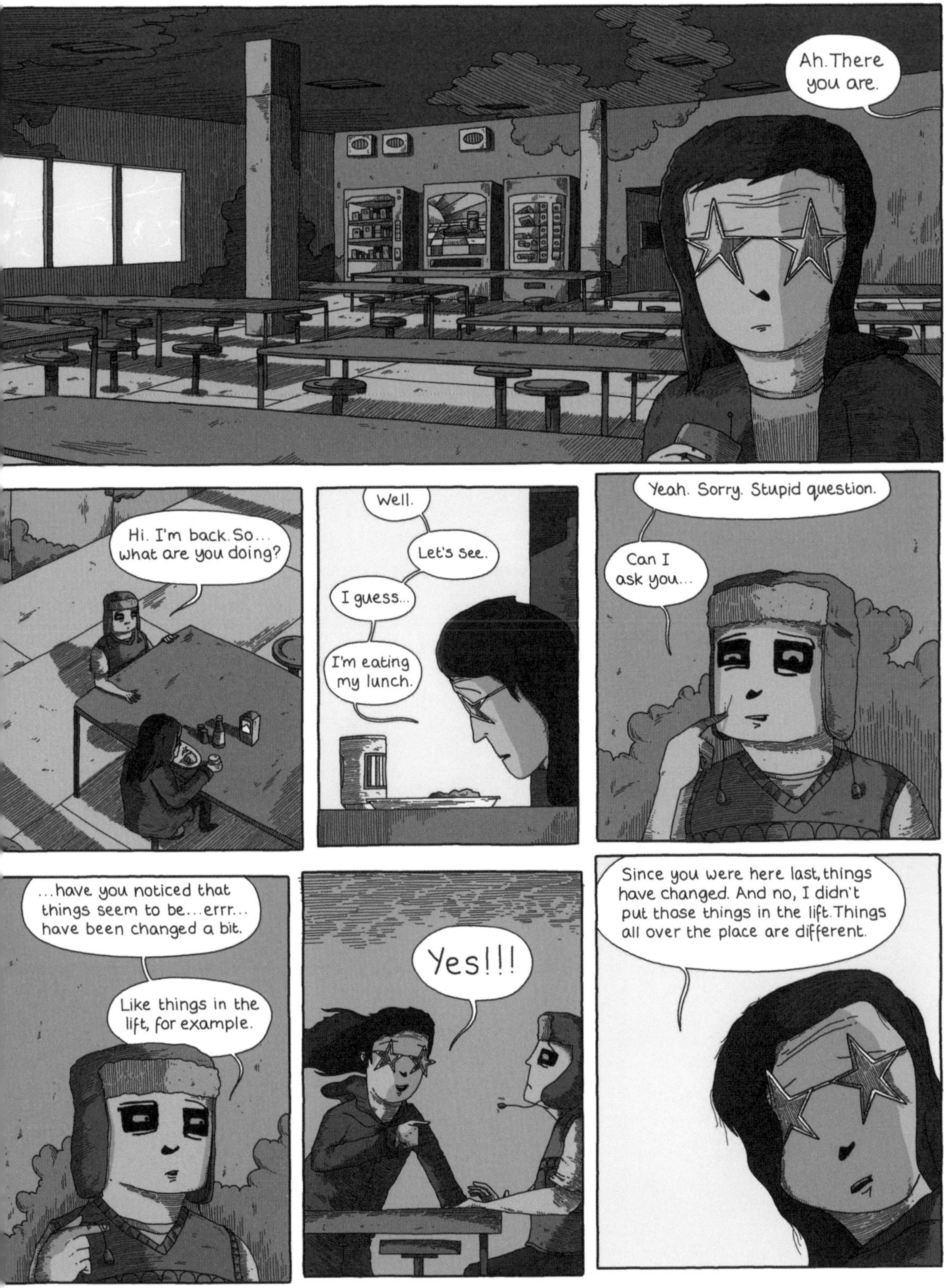
Ah. There you are.
Hi. I'm back. So... what are you doing?
Well.
Let's see.
I guess...
I'm eating my lunch.
Yeah. Sorry. Stupid question.
Can I ask you...
...have you noticed that things seem to be... errr... have been changed a bit.
Like things in the lift, for example.
Yes!!!
Since you were here last, things have changed. And no, I didn't put those things in the lift. Things all over the place are different.

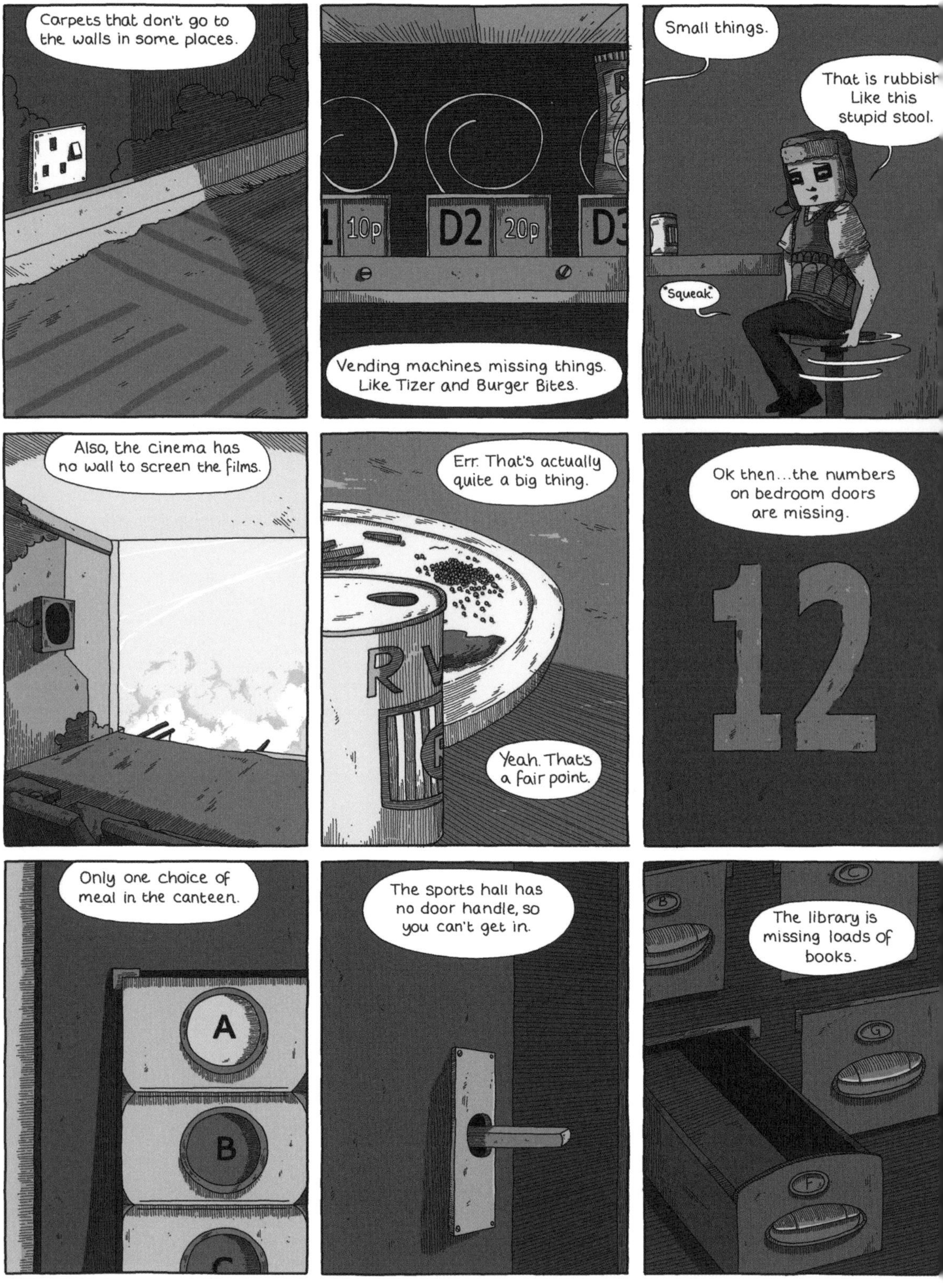
Carpets that don't go to the walls in some places.
10p
D2
20p
Vending machines missing things. Like Tizer and Burger Bites.
Small things.
That is rubbish Like this stupid stool.
Squeak
Also, the cinema has no wall to screen the films.
Err. That's actually quite a big thing.
Yeah. That's a fair point.
Ok then...the numbers on bedroom doors are missing.
12
Only one choice of meal in the canteen.
A
B
The sports hall has no door handle, so you can't get in.
The library is missing loads of books.

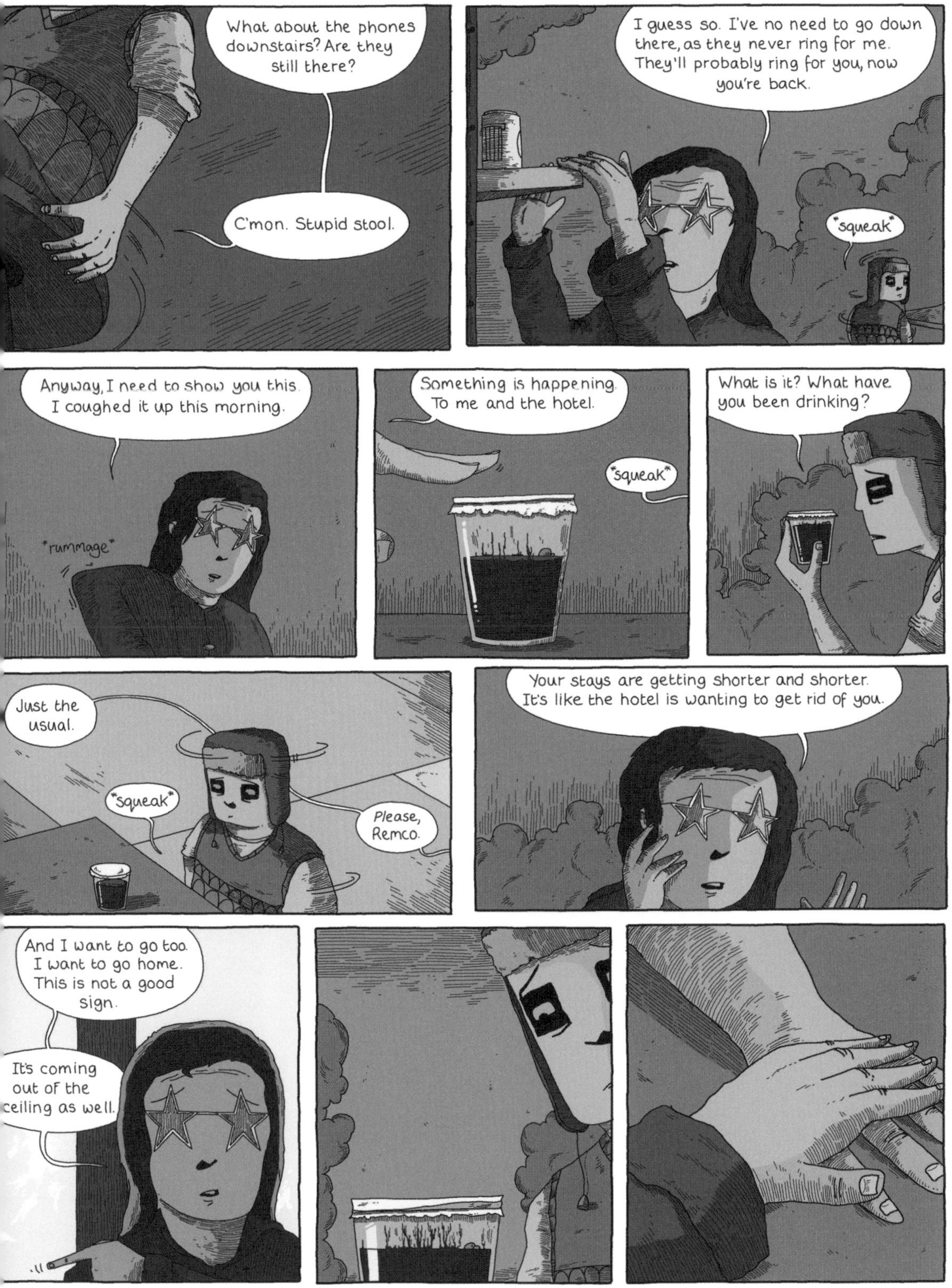
What about the phones downstairs? Are they still there?
C'mon. Stupid stool.
I guess so. I've no need to go down there, as they never ring for me. They'll probably ring for you, now you're back.
squeak
Anyway, I need to show you this. I coughed it up this morning.
rummage
Something is happening. To me and the hotel.
squeak
What is it? What have you been drinking?
Just the usual.
squeak
Please, Remco.
Your stays are getting shorter and shorter. It's like the hotel is wanting to get rid of you.
And I want to go too. I want to go home. This is not a good sign.
It's coming out of the ceiling as well.

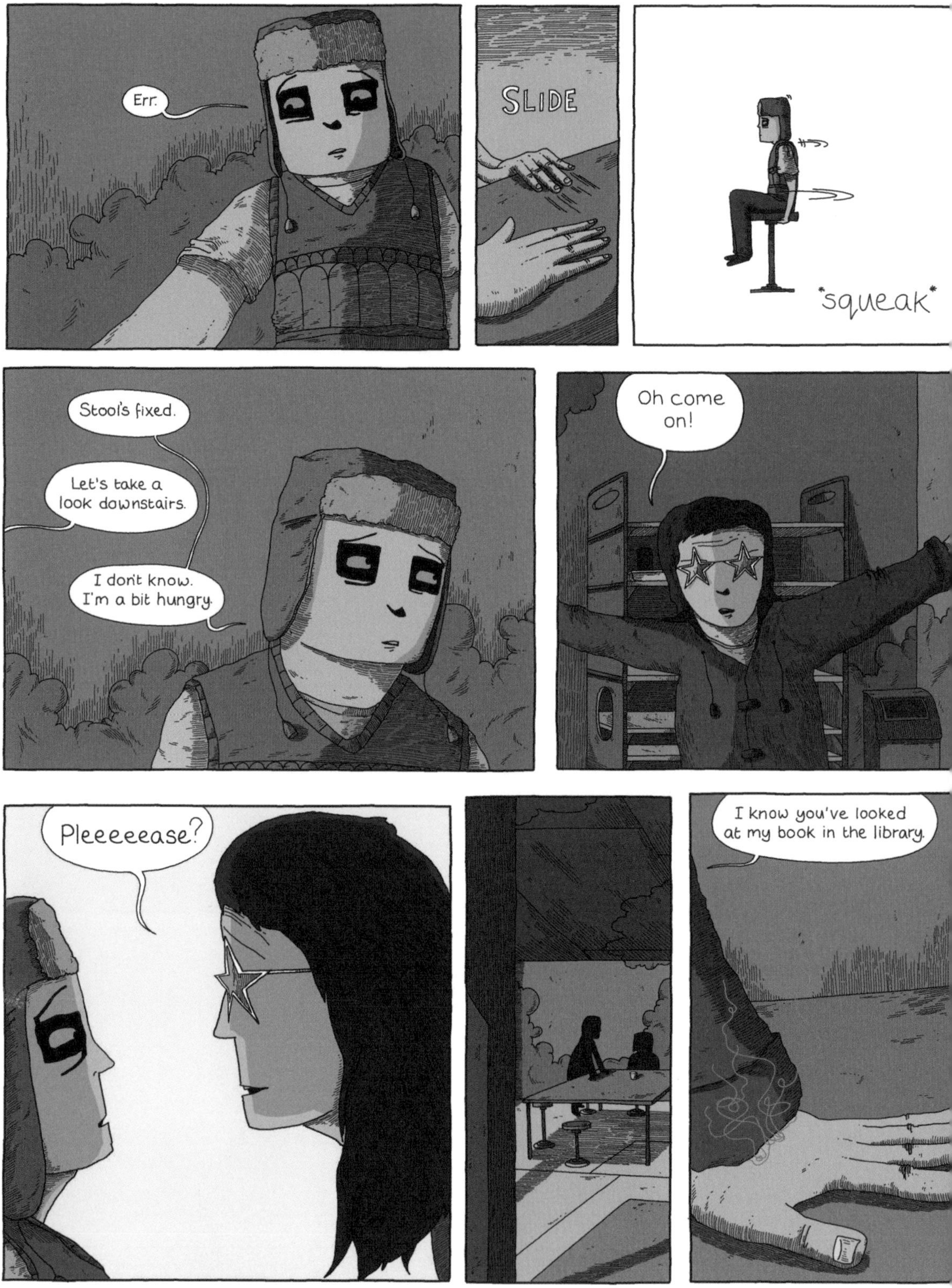

Err.
SLIDE
squeak
Stool's fixed.
Let's take a look downstairs.
I don't know. I'm a bit hungry.
Oh come on!
Pleeeeease?
I know you've looked at my book in the library.

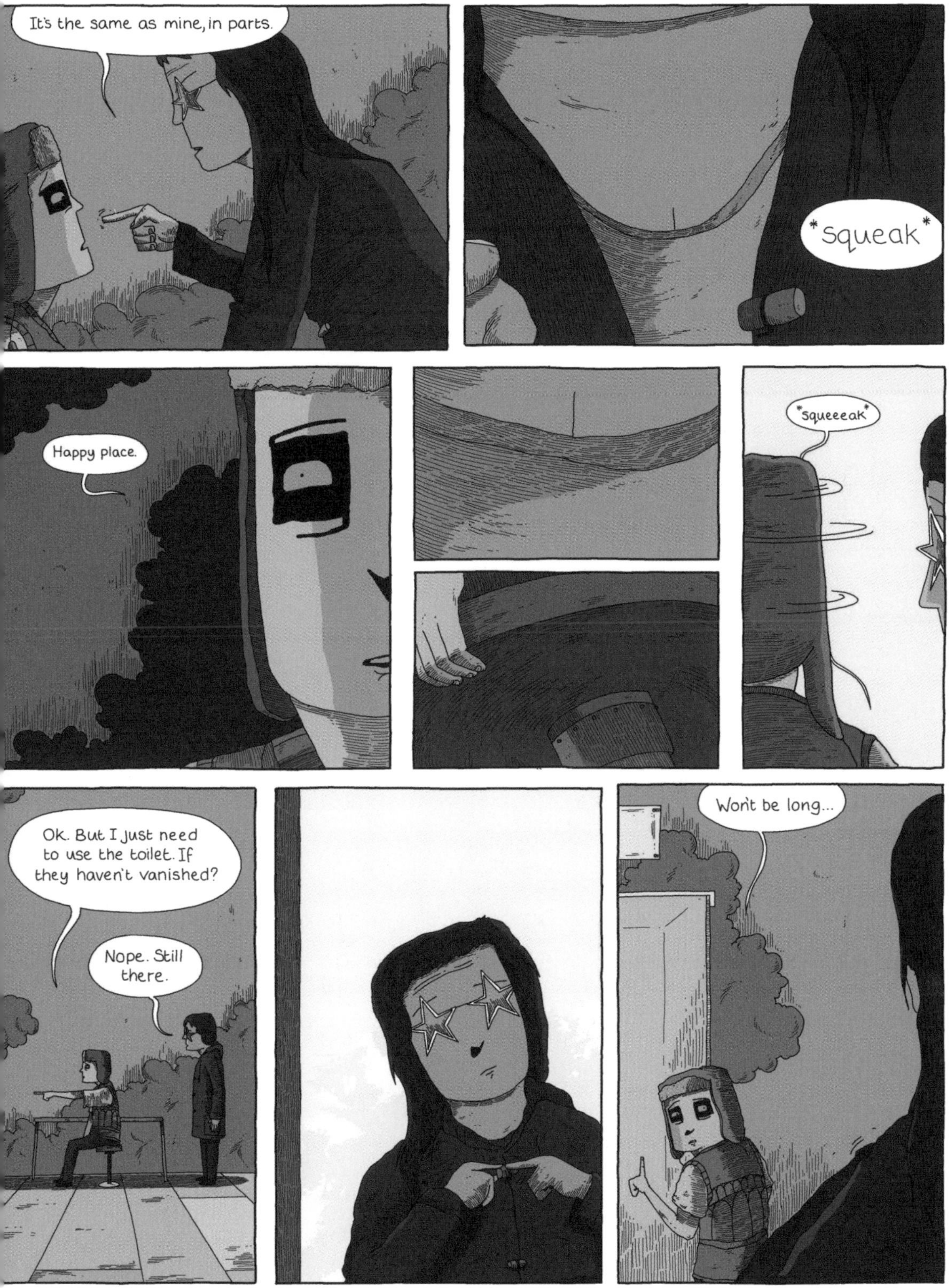
It's the same as mine, in parts.
squeak
Happy place.
squeeeak
Ok. But I just need to use the toilet. If they haven't vanished?
Nope. Still there.
Won't be long...

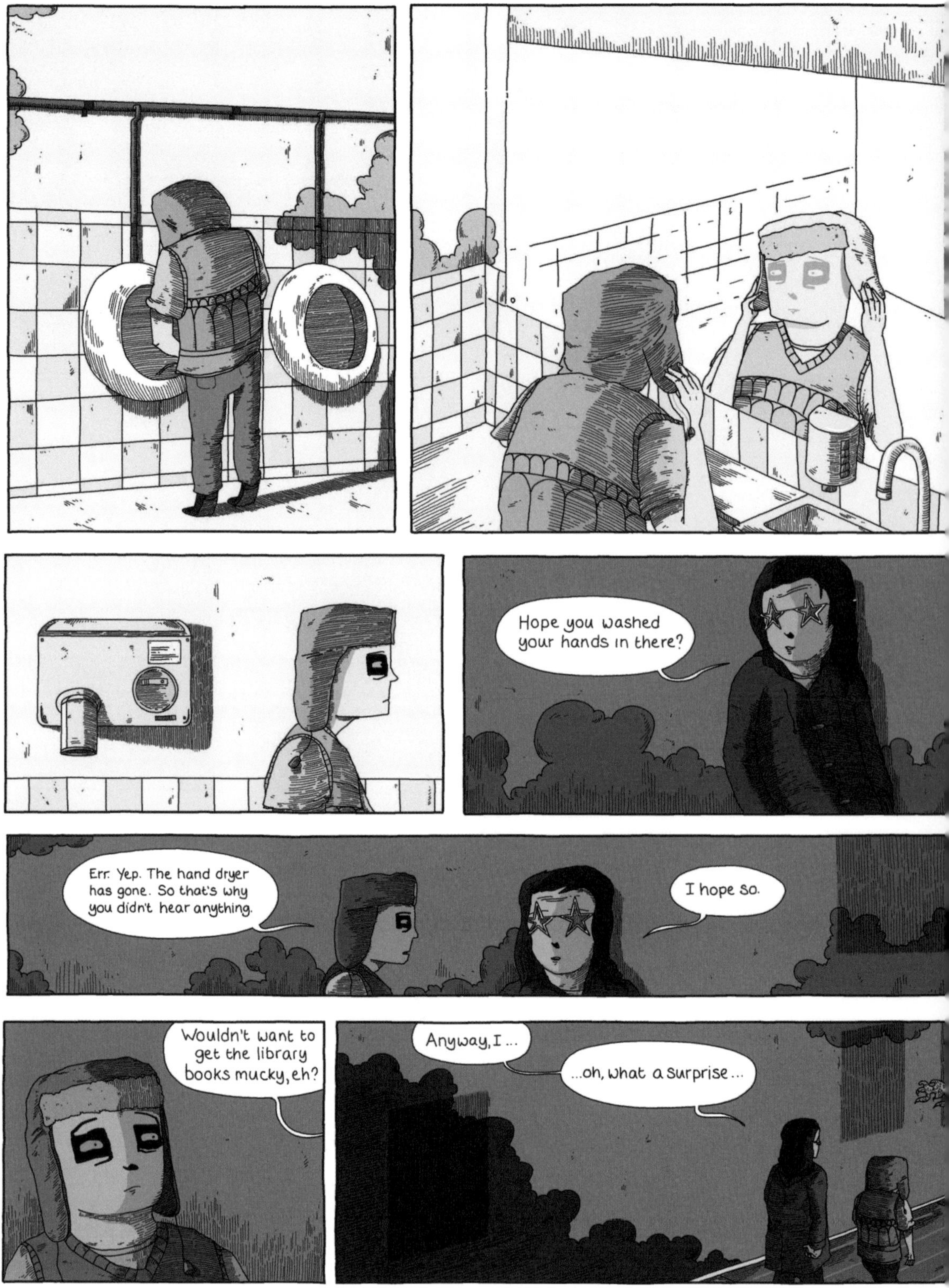
Hope you washed your hands in there?
Err. Yep. The hand dryer has gone. So that's why you didn't hear anything.
I hope so.
Wouldn't want to get the library books mucky, eh?
Anyway, I...
...oh, what a surprise...

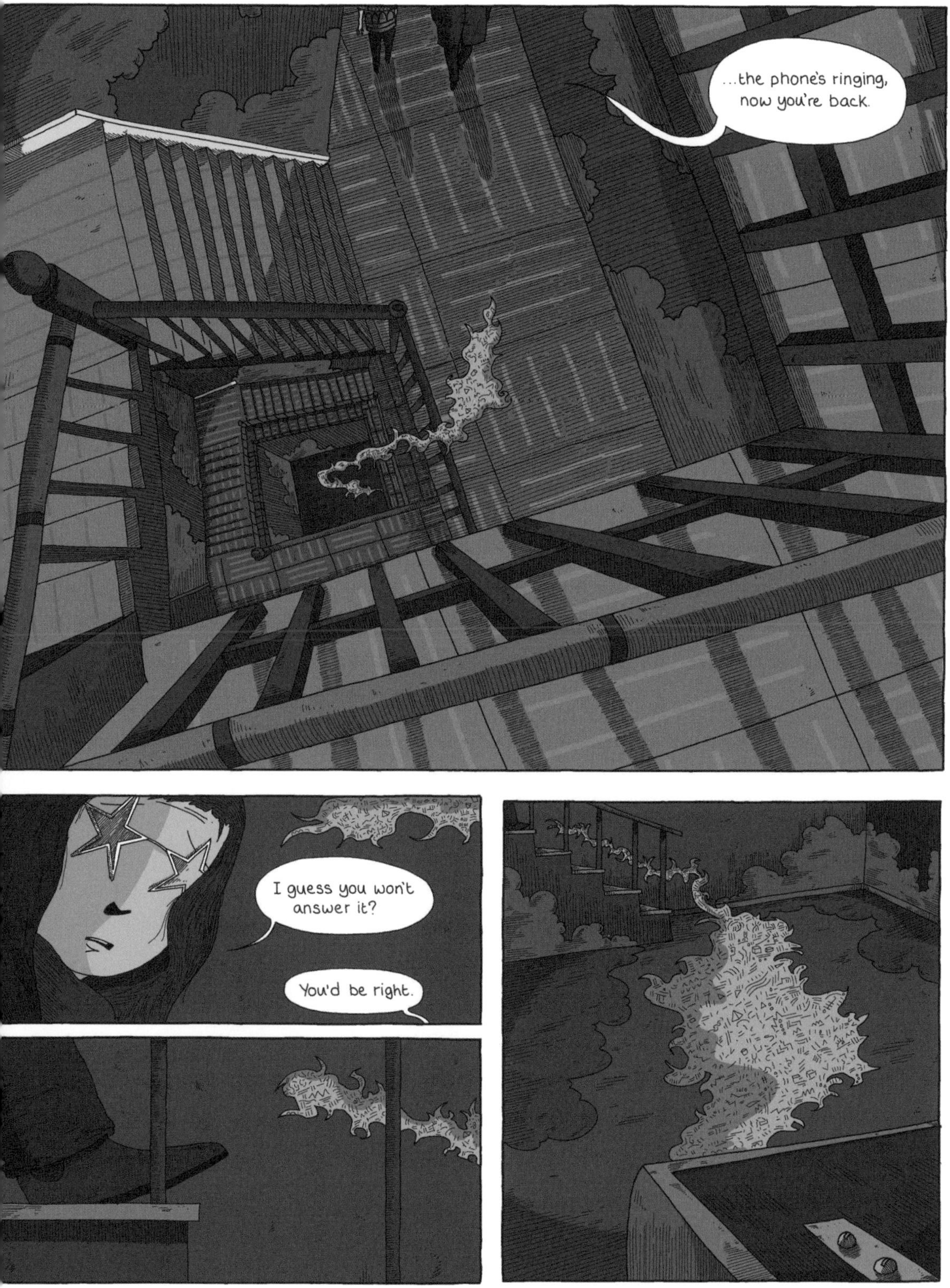
...the phone's ringing, now you're back.
I guess you won't answer it?
You'd be right.

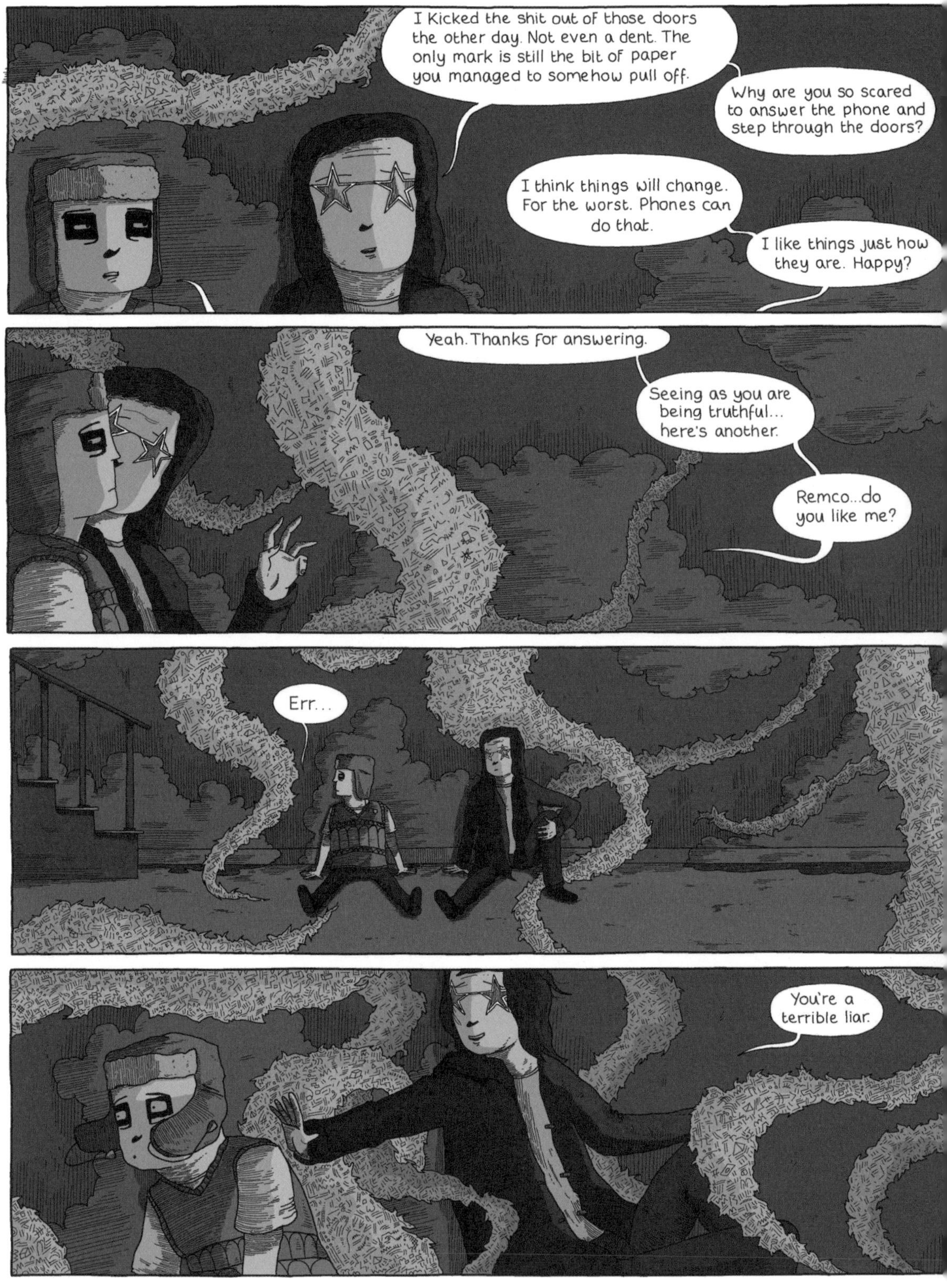
I Kicked the shit out of those doors the other day. Not even a dent. The only mark is still the bit of paper you managed to somehow pull off.
Why are you so scared to answer the phone and step through the doors?
I think things will change. For the worst. Phones can do that.
I like things just how they are. Happy?
Yeah. Thanks for answering.
Seeing as you are being truthful... here's another.
Remco...do you like me?
Err...
You're a terrible liar.

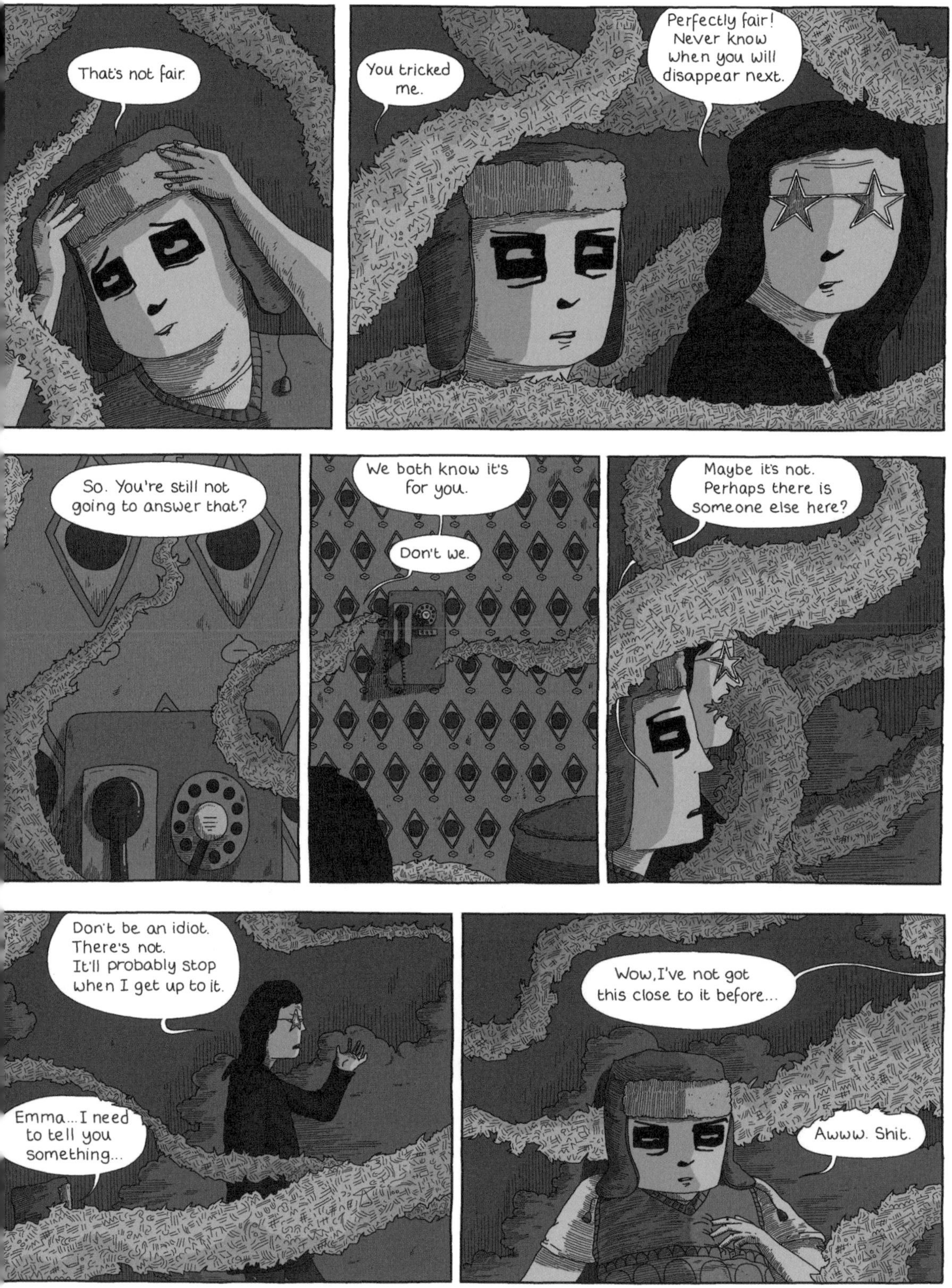
That's not fair.
You tricked me.
Perfectly fair! Never know when you will disappear next.
So. You're still not going to answer that?
We both know it's for you.
Don't we.
Maybe it's not. Perhaps there is someone else here?
Don't be an idiot. There's not. It'll probably stop when I get up to it.
Emma... I need to tell you something...
Wow, I've not got this close to it before...
Awww. Shit.

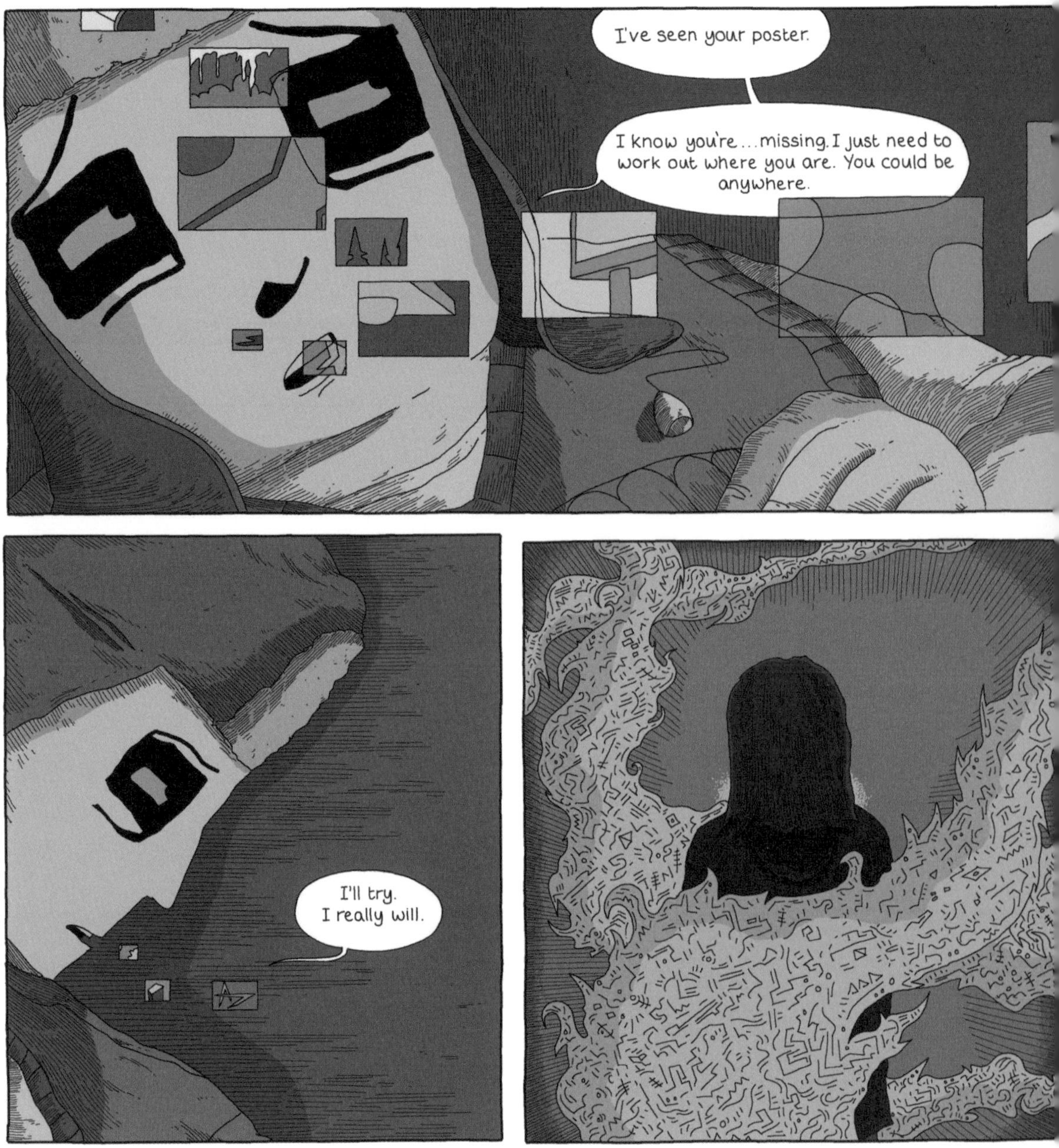
I've seen your poster.
I know you're ... missing. I just need to work out where you are. You could be anywhere.
I'll try. I really will.

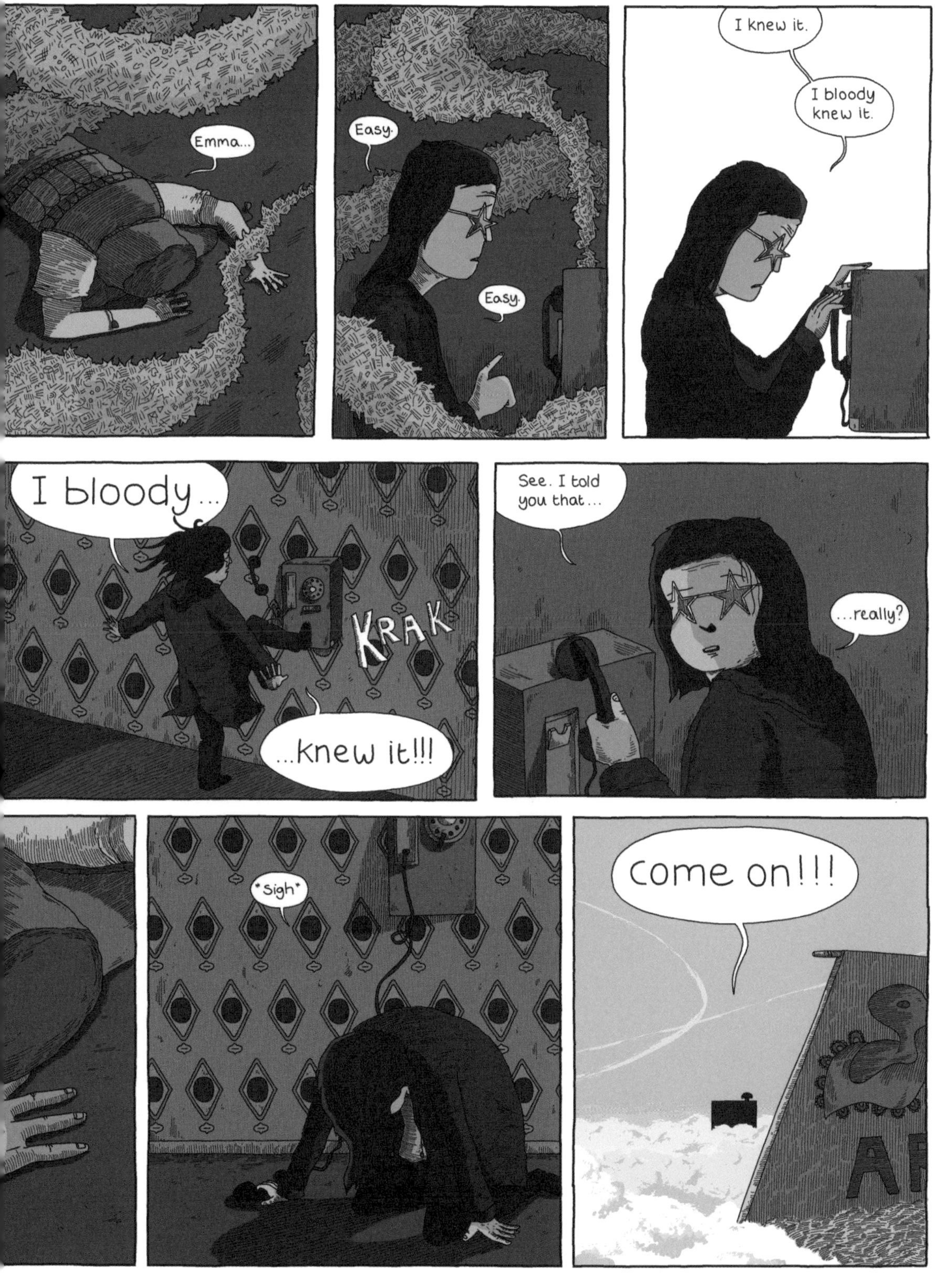
Emma...
Easy.
Easy.
I knew it.
I bloody knew it.
I bloody...
KRAK
...knew it!!!
See. I told you that...
...really?
Sigh
Come on!!!

6th May

1981

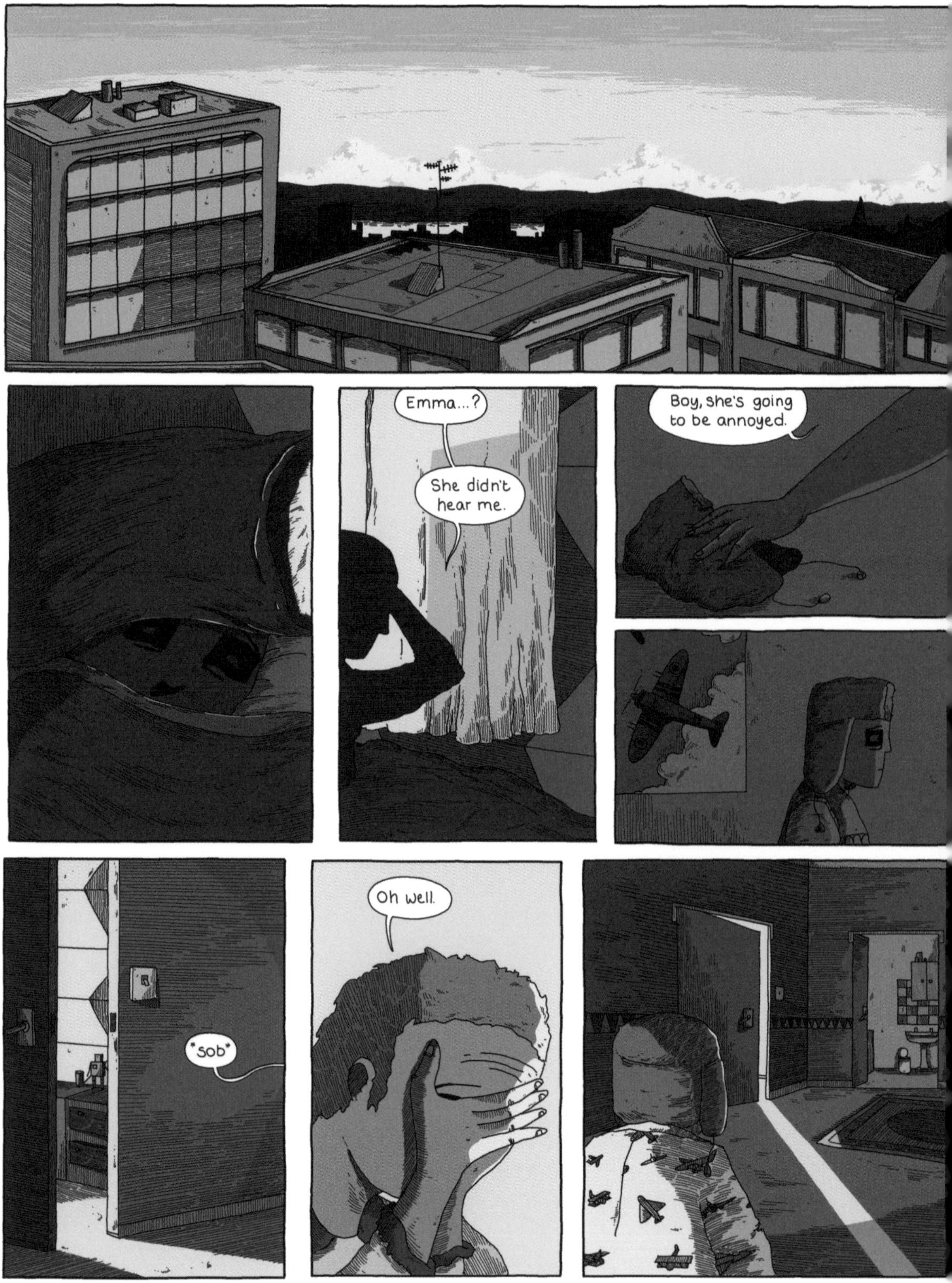
Emma...?
She didn't hear me.
Boy, she's going to be annoyed.
sob
Oh well.

I'll phone in to work and say you are taking a day off.

Thank you.

You should go for a walk. Should be a nice day. Think the fresh air will do you good. Clear your head a bit.

I know.

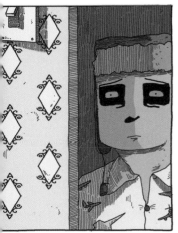

I'm not sure about anything at the moment.

I feel like a helpless child.

And my Dad can't help me.

My Dad...

Oh God.

I think Dad understood what goes on in his mind.

I mean he found him on that bus shelter. We were miles away...

...I wasn't there.

You can't blame yourself for that.

Why not? I let him cycle around the woods. Kids have gone missing for years.

And lots of kids have played in the woods and nothing bad has happened.

He's safer playing in the woods than he is out on the streets.

That's not the point, is it.

Oh, I don't know.

Nor do I.

Dad?

Hi, there.

sob

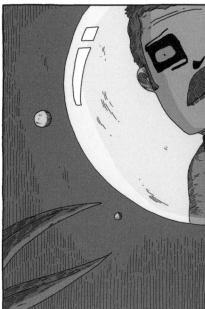

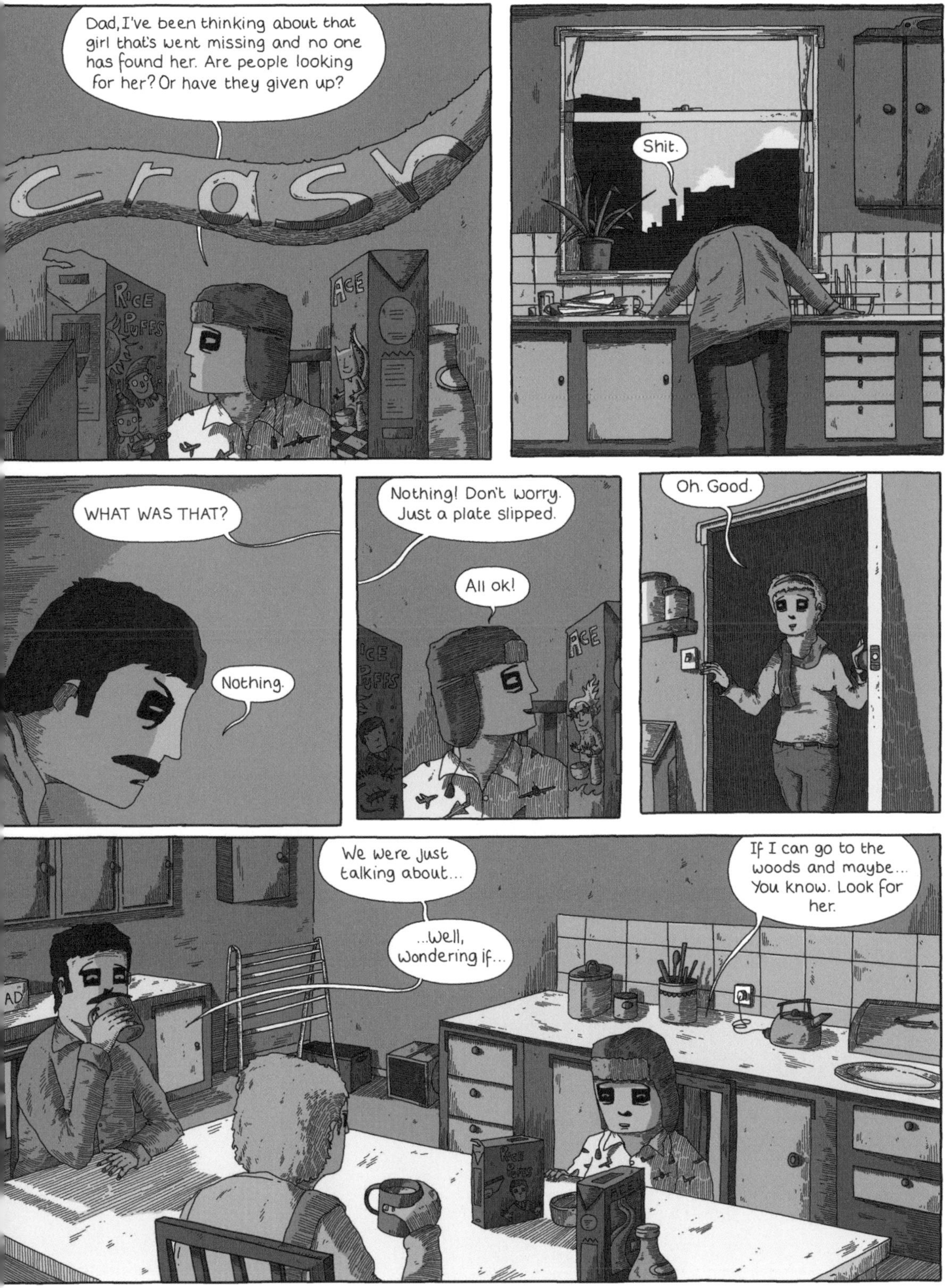
Dad, I've been thinking about that girl that's went missing and no one has found her. Are people looking for her? Or have they given up?
crash
RICE PUFFS
ACE
Shit.
WHAT WAS THAT?
Nothing.
Nothing! Don't worry. Just a plate slipped.
All ok!
Oh. Good.
We were just talking about...
...Well, wondering if...
If I can go to the woods and maybe... You know. Look for her.

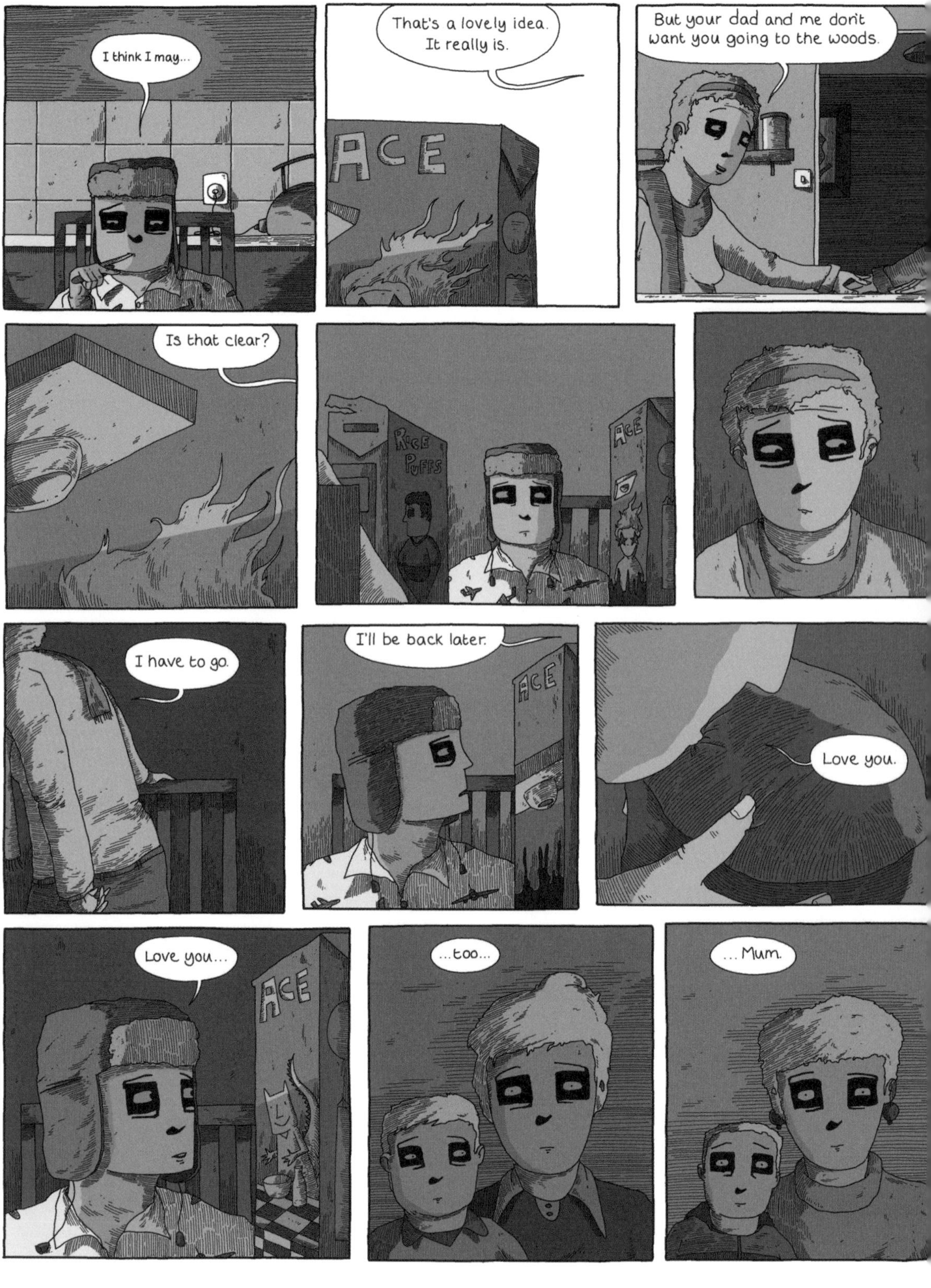
I think I may...
That's a lovely idea. It really is.
ACE
But your dad and me don't want you going to the woods.
Is that clear?
RICE PUFFS
ACE
I have to go.
I'll be back later.
ACE
Love you.
Love you...
ACE
...too...
...Mum.

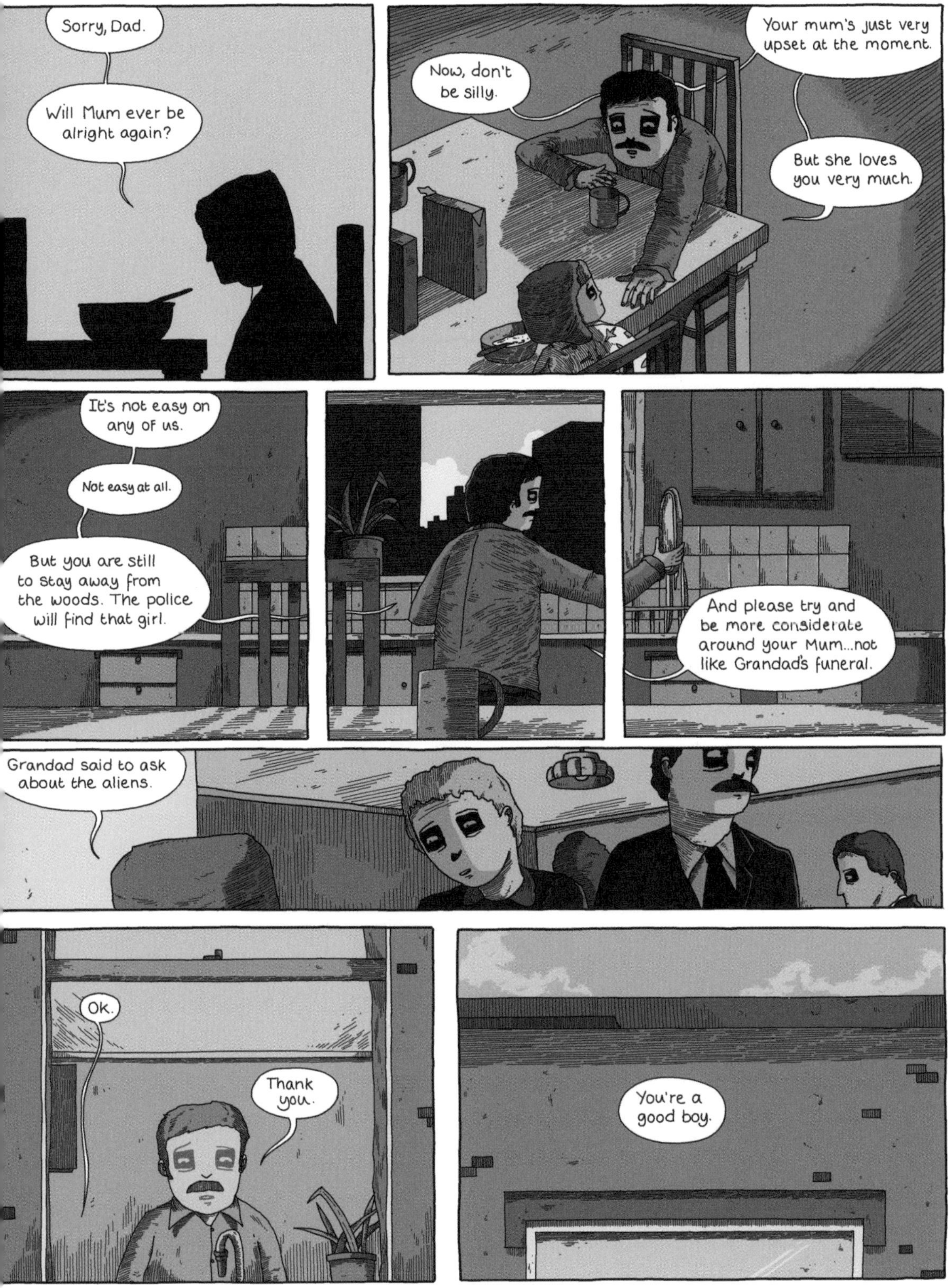

Sorry, Dad.
Will Mum ever be alright again?
Now, don't be silly.
Your mum's just very upset at the moment.
But she loves you very much.
It's not easy on any of us.
Not easy at all.
But you are still to stay away from the woods. The police will find that girl.
And please try and be more considerate around your Mum...not like Grandad's funeral.
Grandad said to ask about the aliens.
Ok.
Thank you.
You're a good boy.

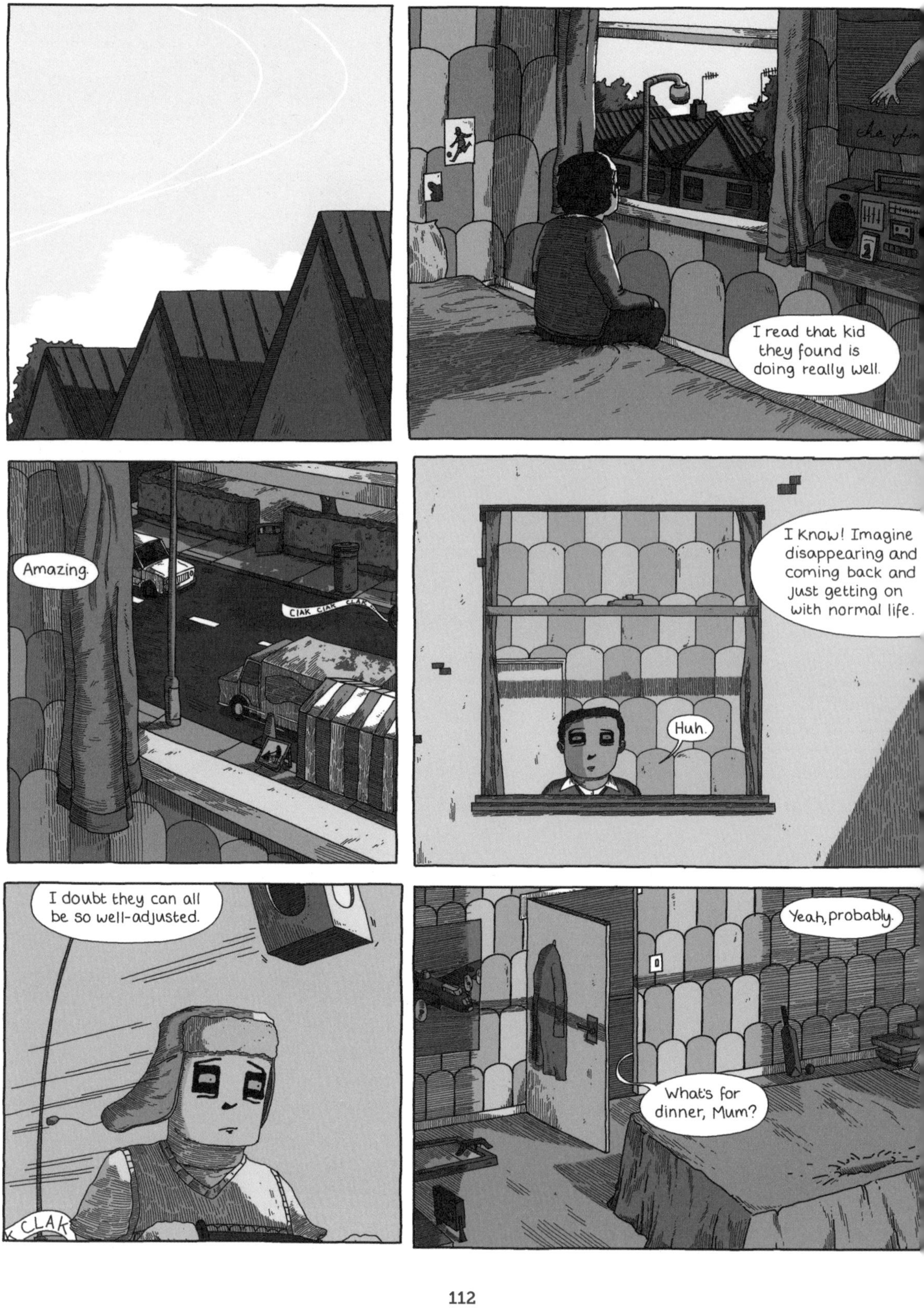
I read that kid they found is doing really well.
Amazing.
CIAK CIAK CLAK
I know! Imagine disappearing and coming back and just getting on with normal life.
Huh.
I doubt they can all be so well-adjusted.
CLAK
Yeah, probably.
What's for dinner, Mum?

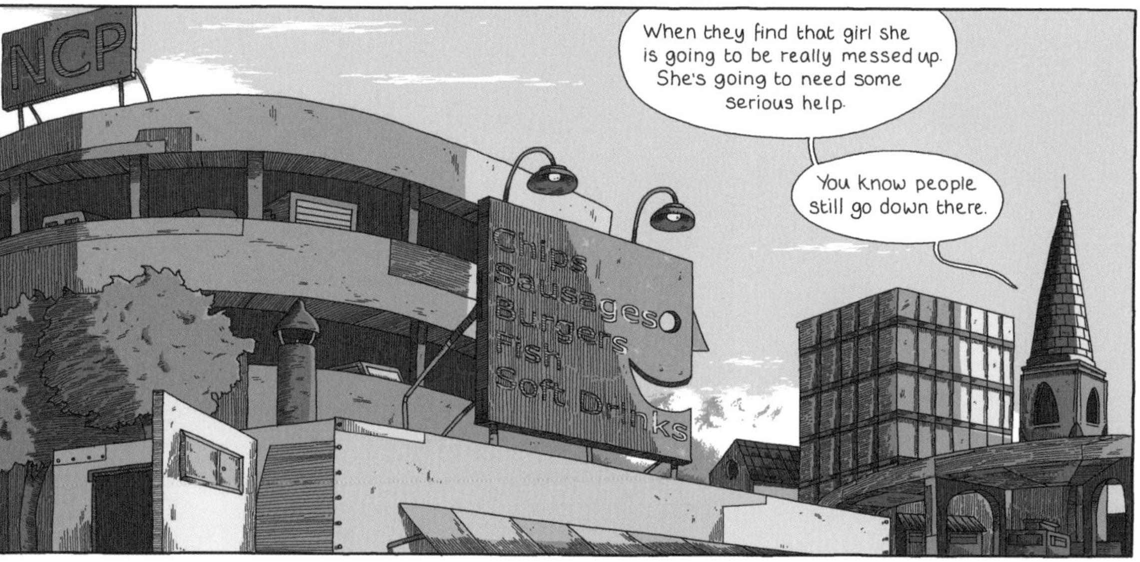
NCP
Chips
Sausages
Burgers
Fish
Soft Drinks
When they find that girl she is going to be really messed up. She's going to need some serious help.
You know people still go down there.

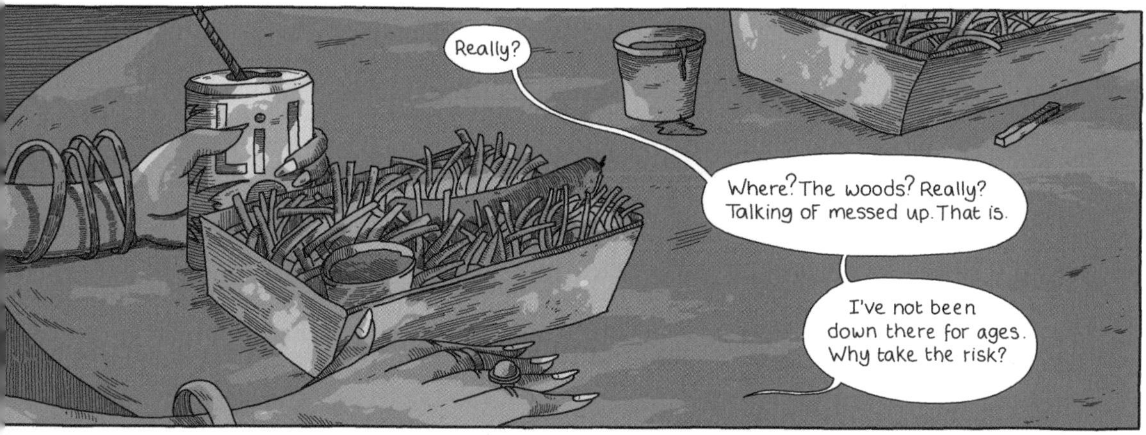
Really?
Where? The woods? Really? Talking of messed up. That is.
I've not been down there for ages. Why take the risk?

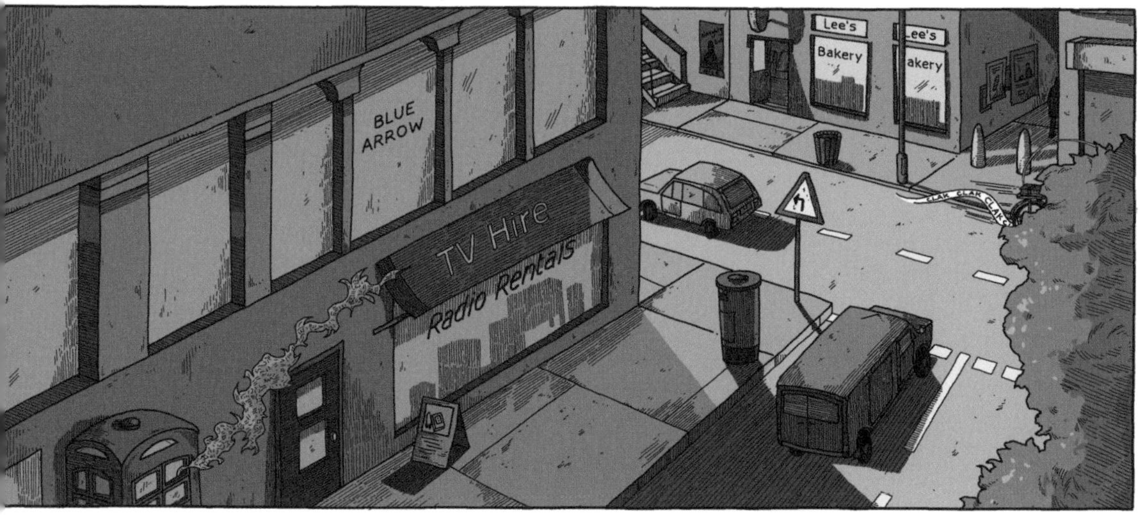
BLUE ARROW
TV Hire
Radio Rentals
Lee's
Bakery

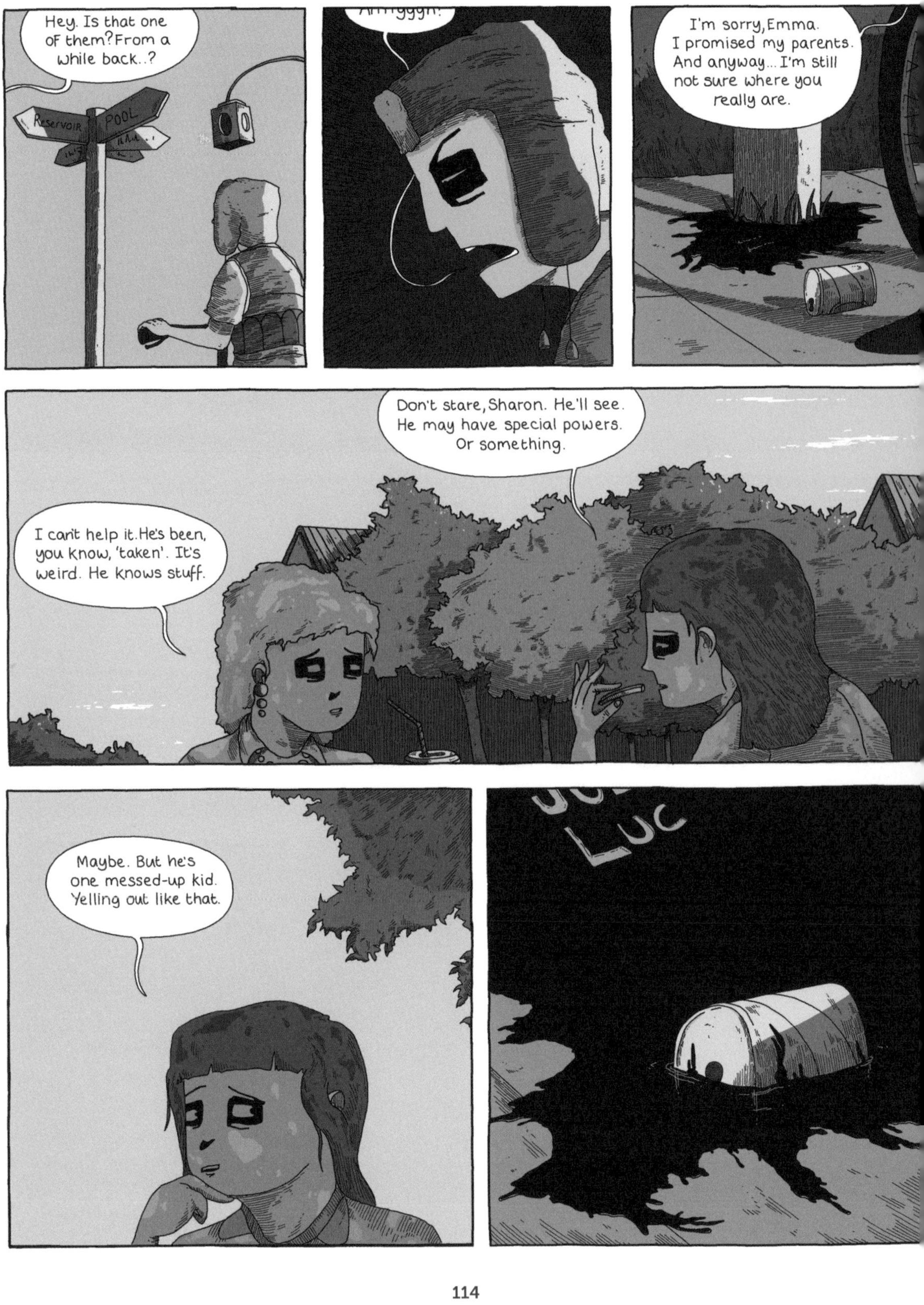
Hey. Is that one of them? From a while back..?
Reservoir
POOL
I'm sorry, Emma. I promised my parents. And anyway... I'm still not sure where you really are.
Don't stare, Sharon. He'll see. He may have special powers. Or something.
I can't help it. He's been, you know, 'taken'. It's weird. He knows stuff.
Maybe. But he's one messed-up kid. Yelling out like that.

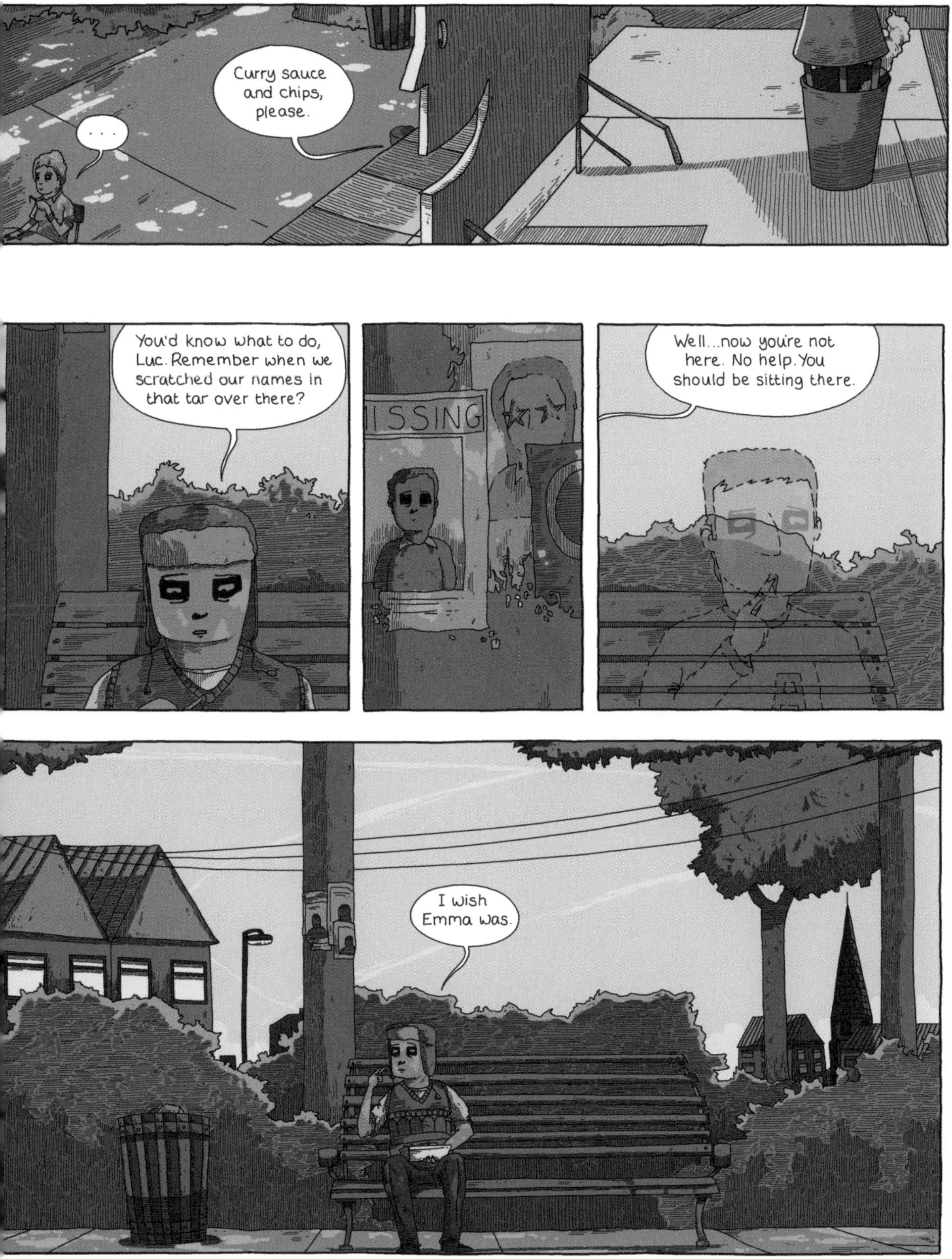
Curry sauce and chips, please.
. . .
You'd know what to do, Luc. Remember when we scratched our names in that tar over there?
ISSING
Well...now you're not here. No help. You should be sitting there.
I wish Emma was.

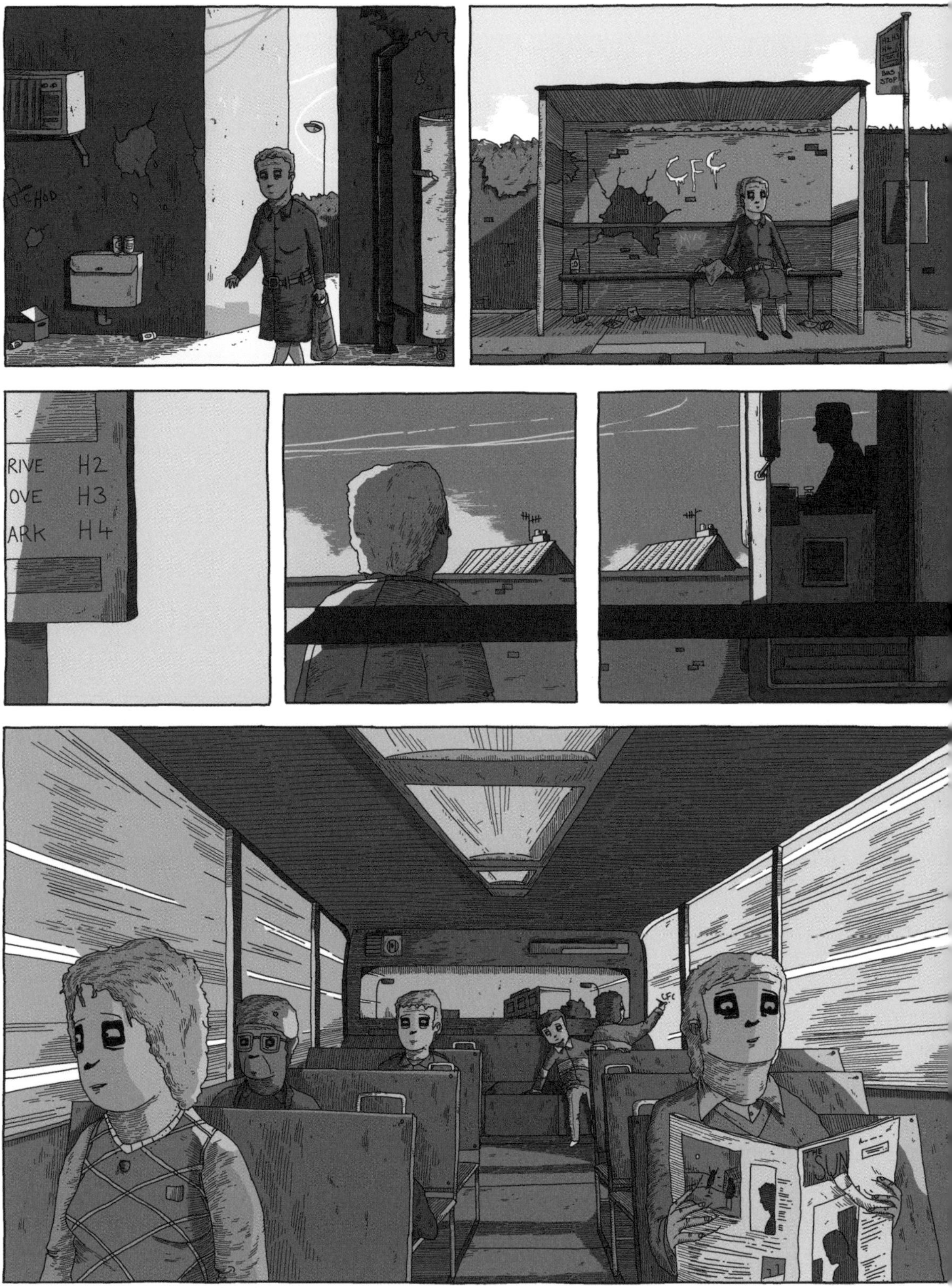
CHOD
CFC
BUS STOP
RIVE H2
OVE H3
ARK H4
THE SUN

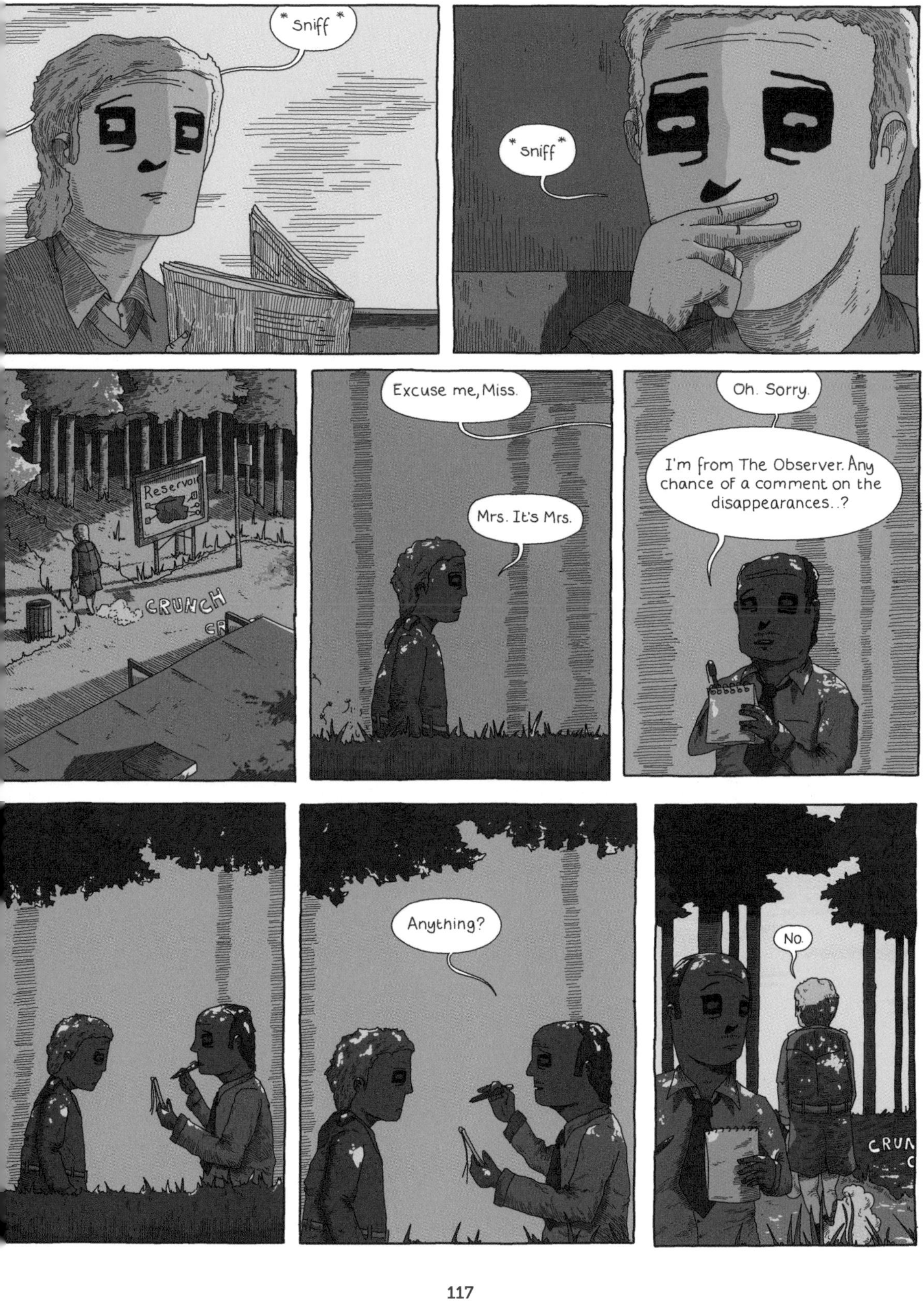
sniff
sniff
Reservoir
CRUNCH
CR
Excuse me, Miss.
Mrs. It's Mrs.
Oh. Sorry.
I'm from The Observer. Any chance of a comment on the disappearances..?
Anything?
No.
CRUN
C

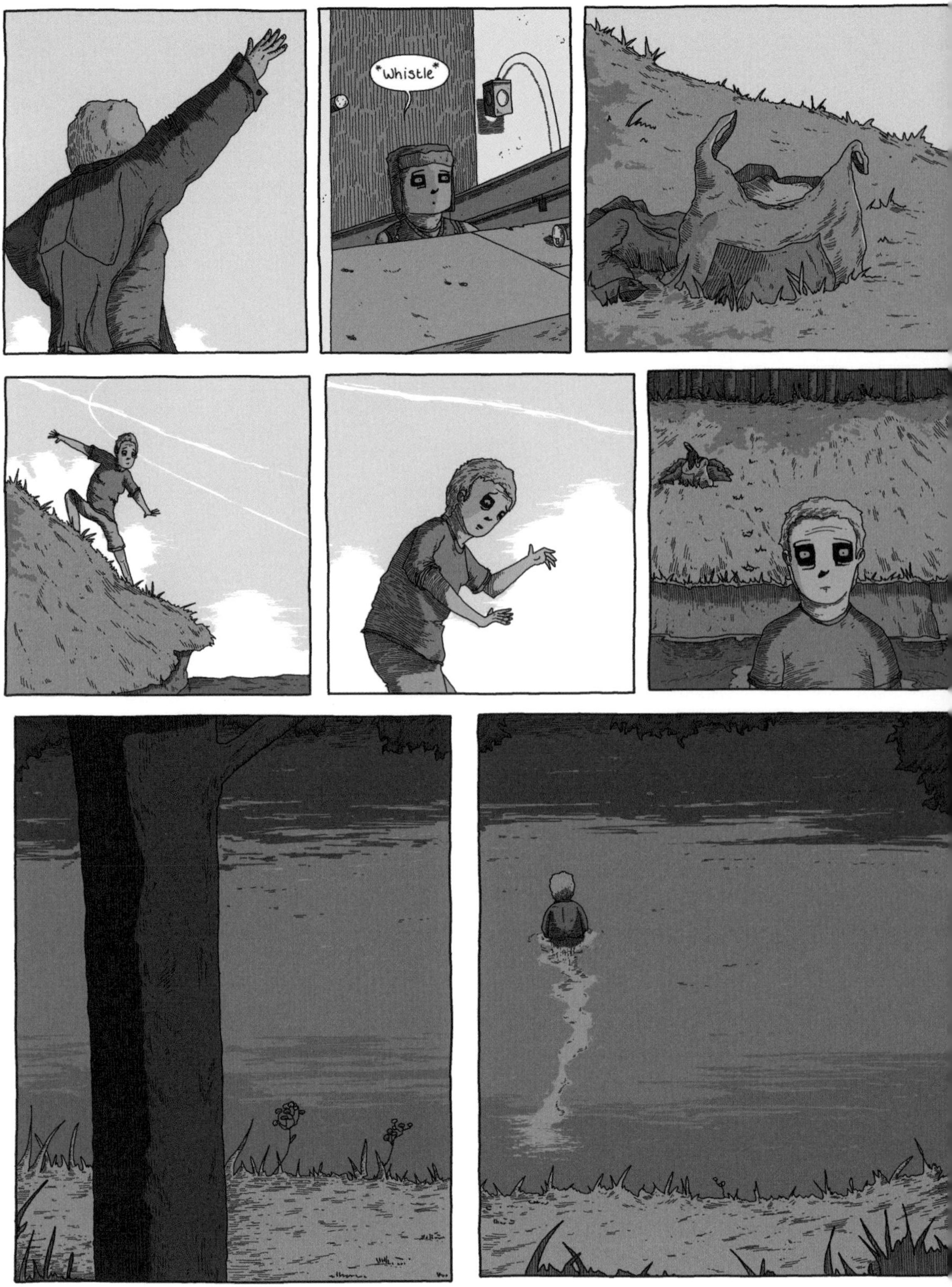
Whistle

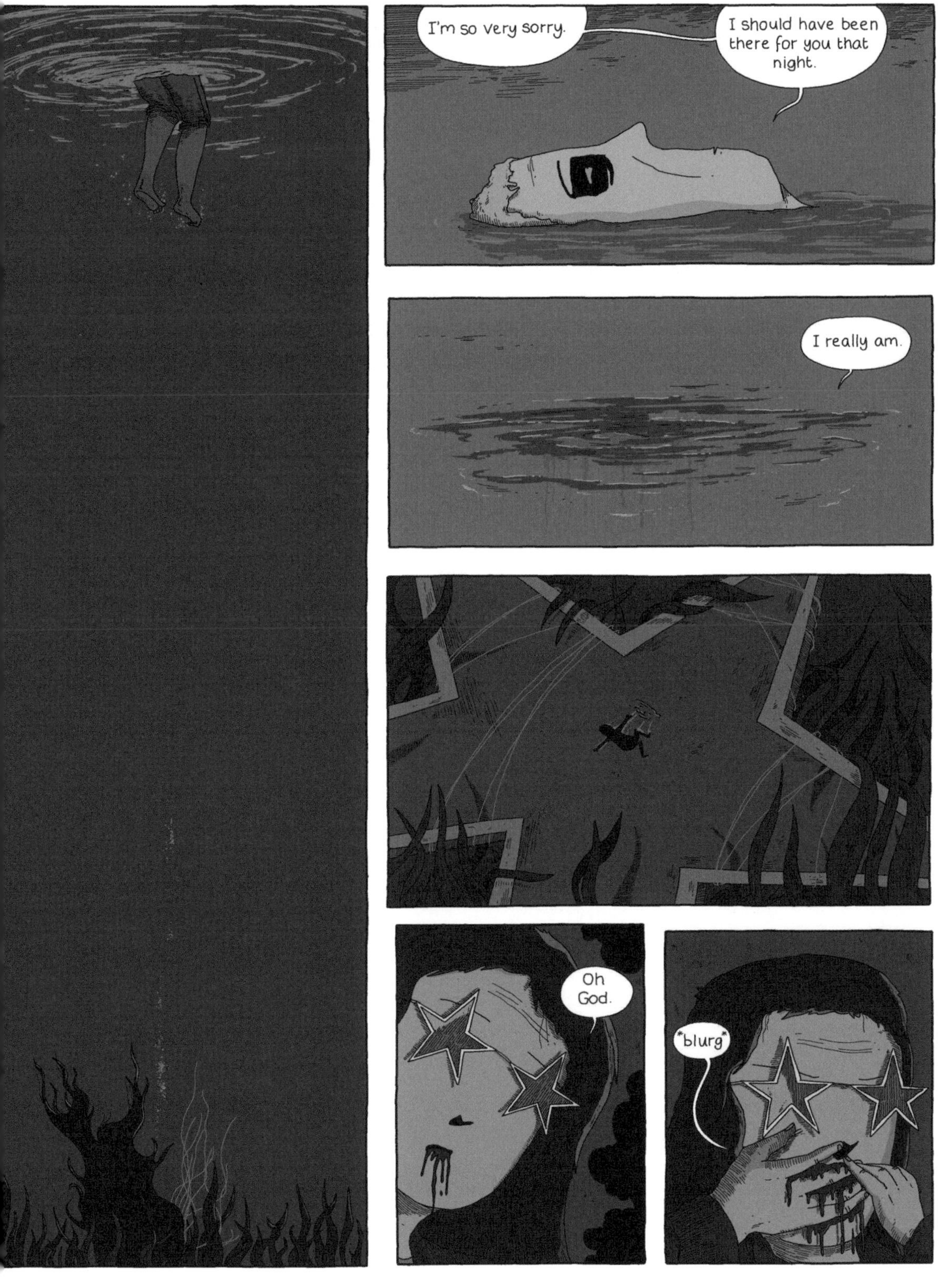
I'm so very sorry.
I should have been there for you that night.
I really am.
Oh God.
blurg

KLAP
blurrgh
Is this it?
Hey! Space Boy!
Daniel. Grant.

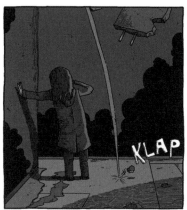

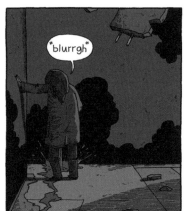

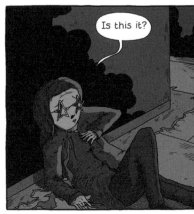

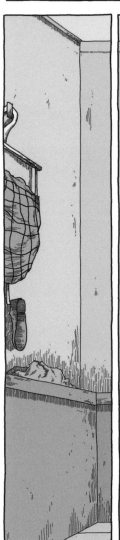

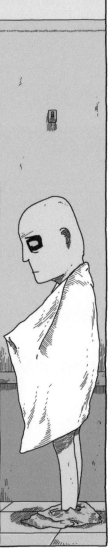

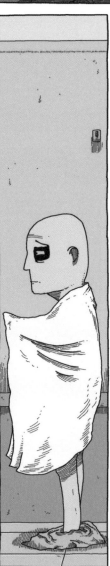

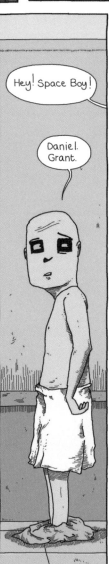

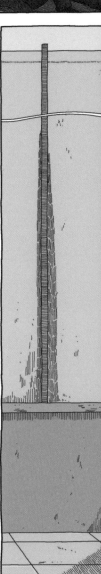

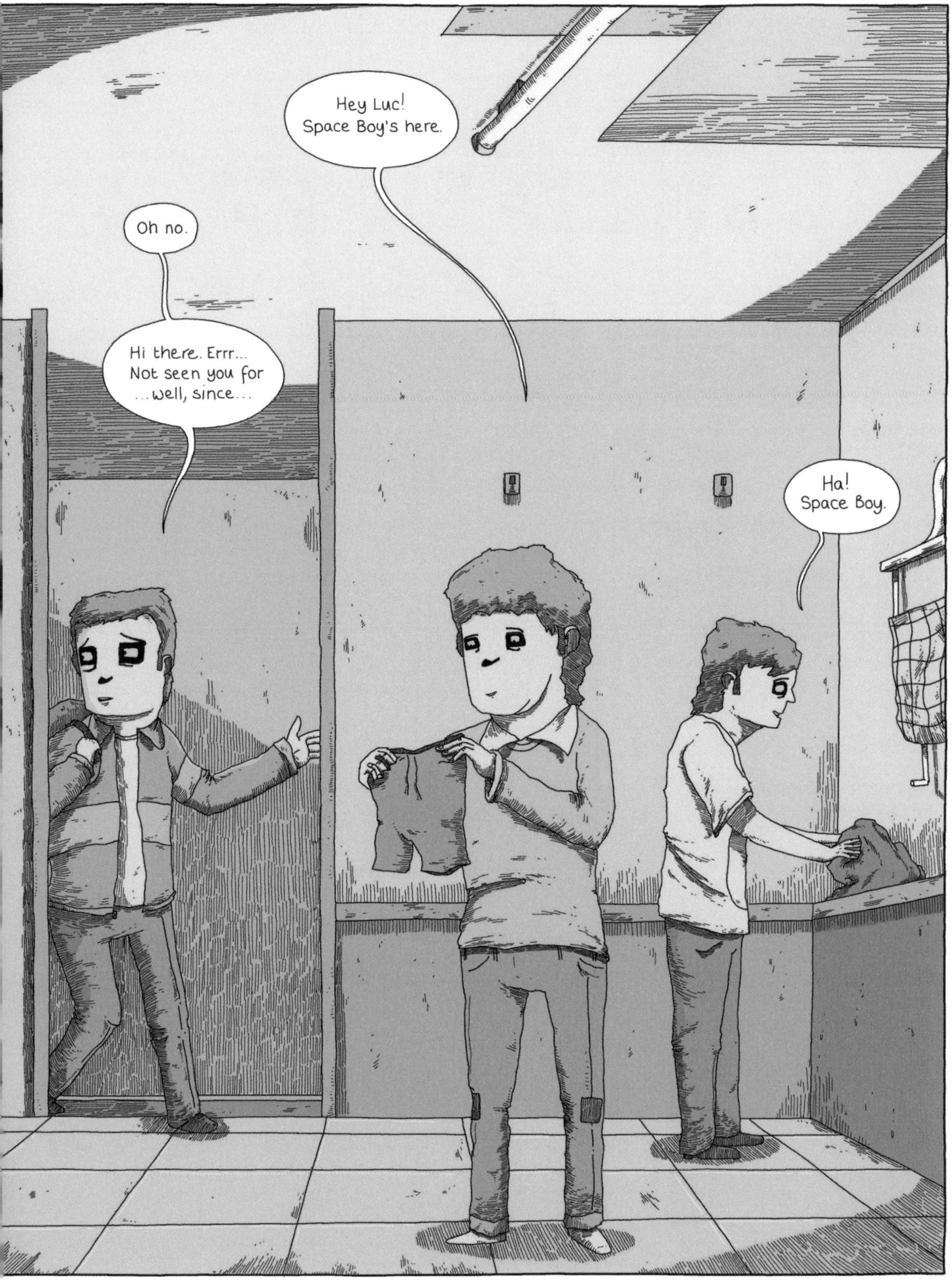
Oh no.
Hi there. Errr... Not seen you for ...well, since...
Hey Luc! Space Boy's here.
Ha! Space Boy.

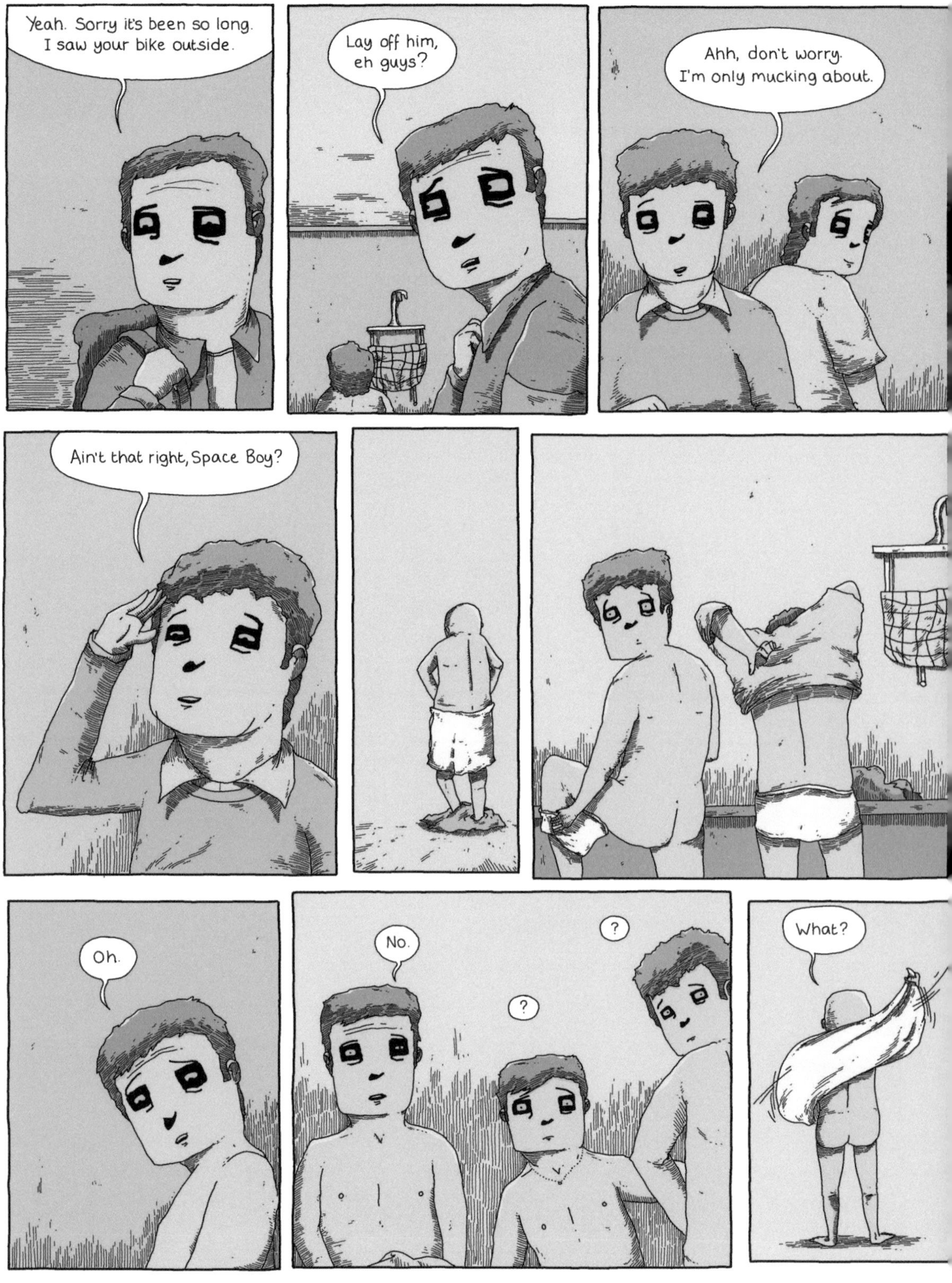
Yeah. Sorry it's been so long. I saw your bike outside.
Lay off him, eh guys?
Ahh, don't worry. I'm only mucking about.
Ain't that right, Space Boy?
Oh.
No.
?
?
What?

Oh my God.

He's as bald as a coot below as he is on his head!

Shit.

Perhaps he is an alien after all?

Beam me up, baldy.

Ha. What is it? Something prosper..?

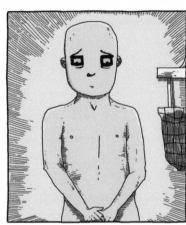

I remember now. Be old and prosper!

Is that it?

Leave him alone, boys.

It's probably good you aren't coming to the beach with all of us tomorrow.

Someone might mistake you for an eel.

And harpoon you.

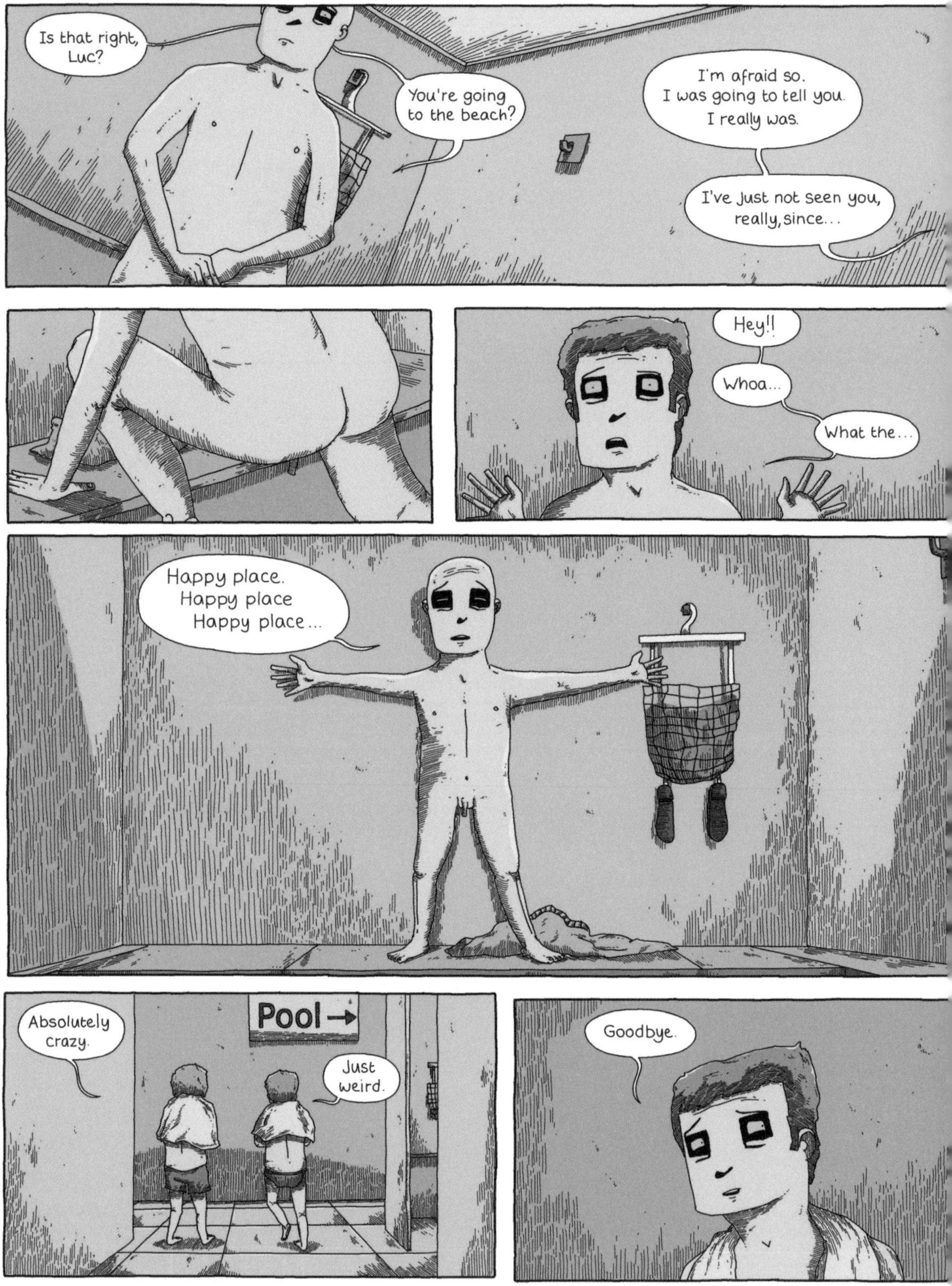
Is that right, Luc?
You're going to the beach?
I'm afraid so. I was going to tell you. I really was.
I've just not seen you, really, since...
Hey!!
Whoa...
What the...
Happy place. Happy place Happy place...
Pool →
Absolutely crazy.
Just weird.
Goodbye.

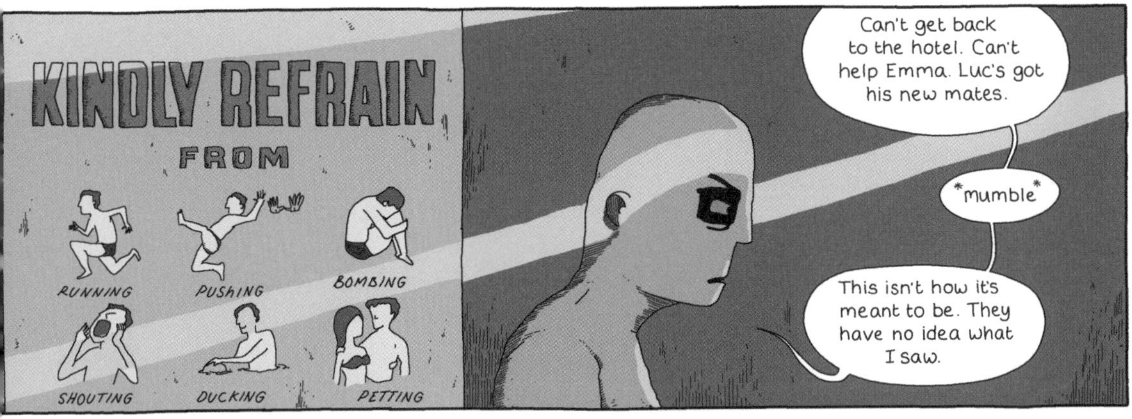
KINDLY REFRAIN
FROM
RUNNING
PUSHING
BOMBING
SHOUTING
DUCKING
PETTING
Can't get back to the hotel. Can't help Emma. Luc's got his new mates.
mumble
This isn't how it's meant to be. They have no idea what I saw.

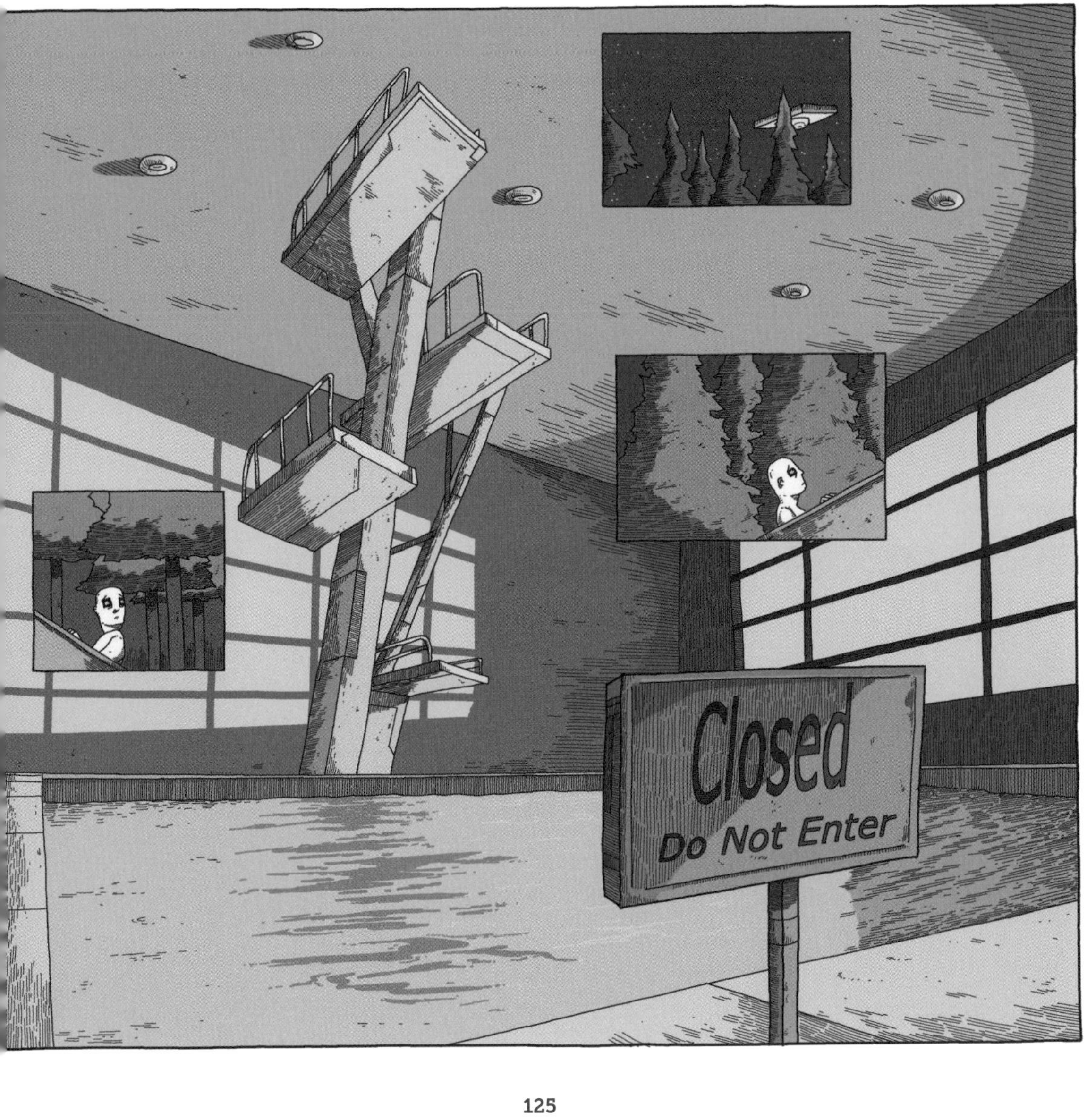
Closed
Do Not Enter

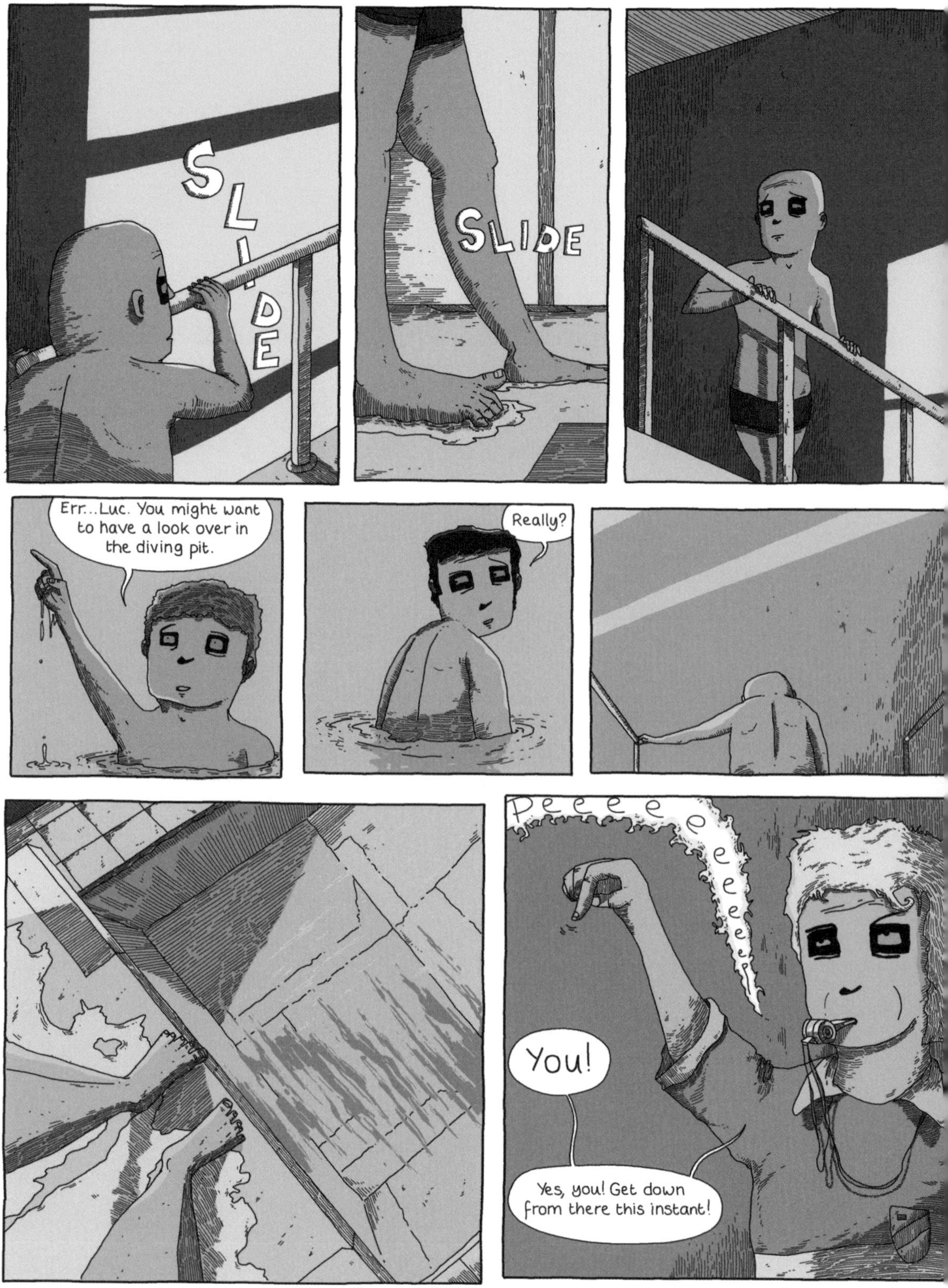
SLIDE
SLIDE
Err...Luc. You might want to have a look over in the diving pit.
Really?
Peeeeeeeeeeep
You!
Yes, you! Get down from there this instant!

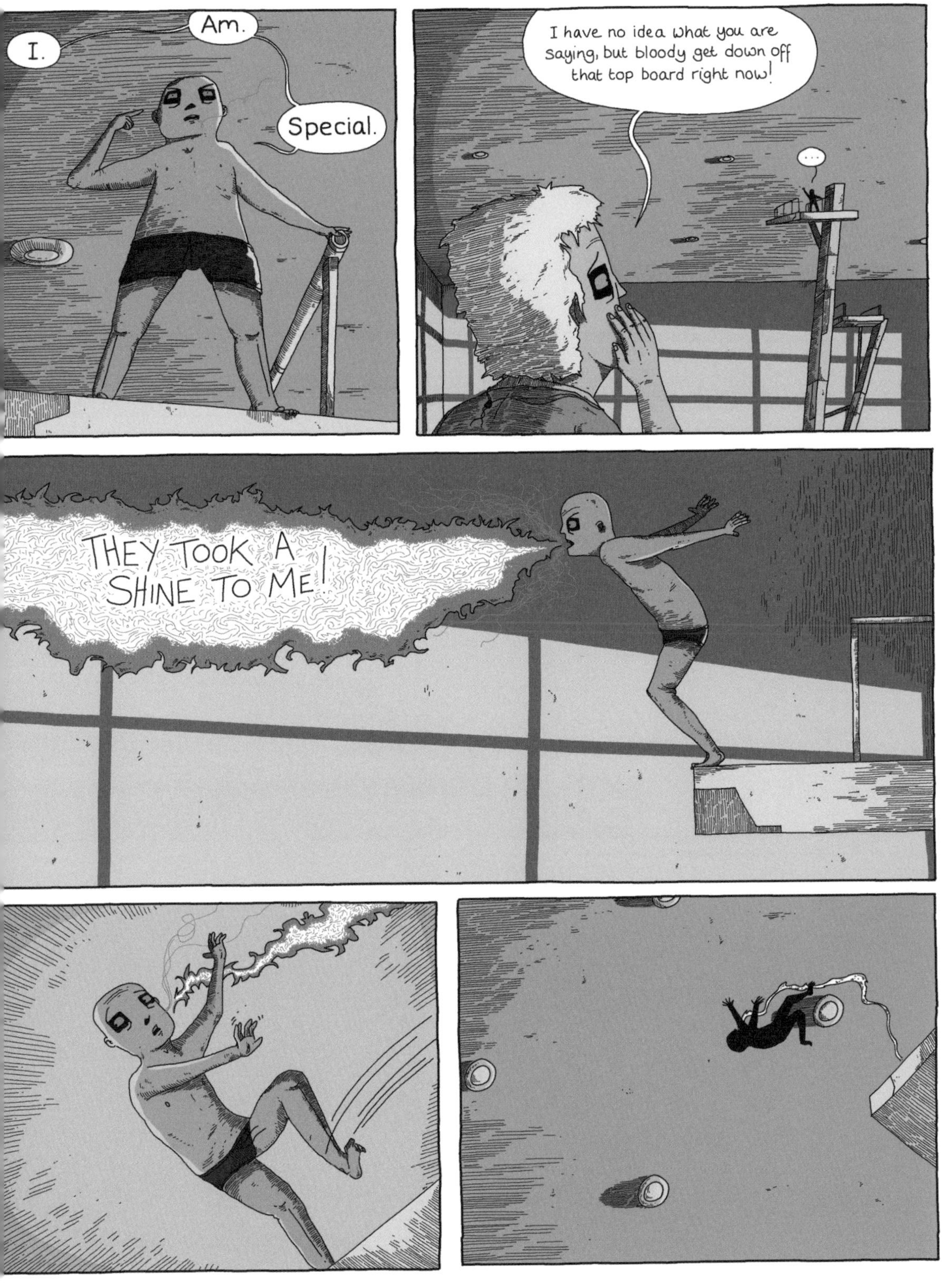
I.
Am.
Special.
I have no idea what you are saying, but bloody get down off that top board right now!
...
THEY TOOK A SHINE TO ME!

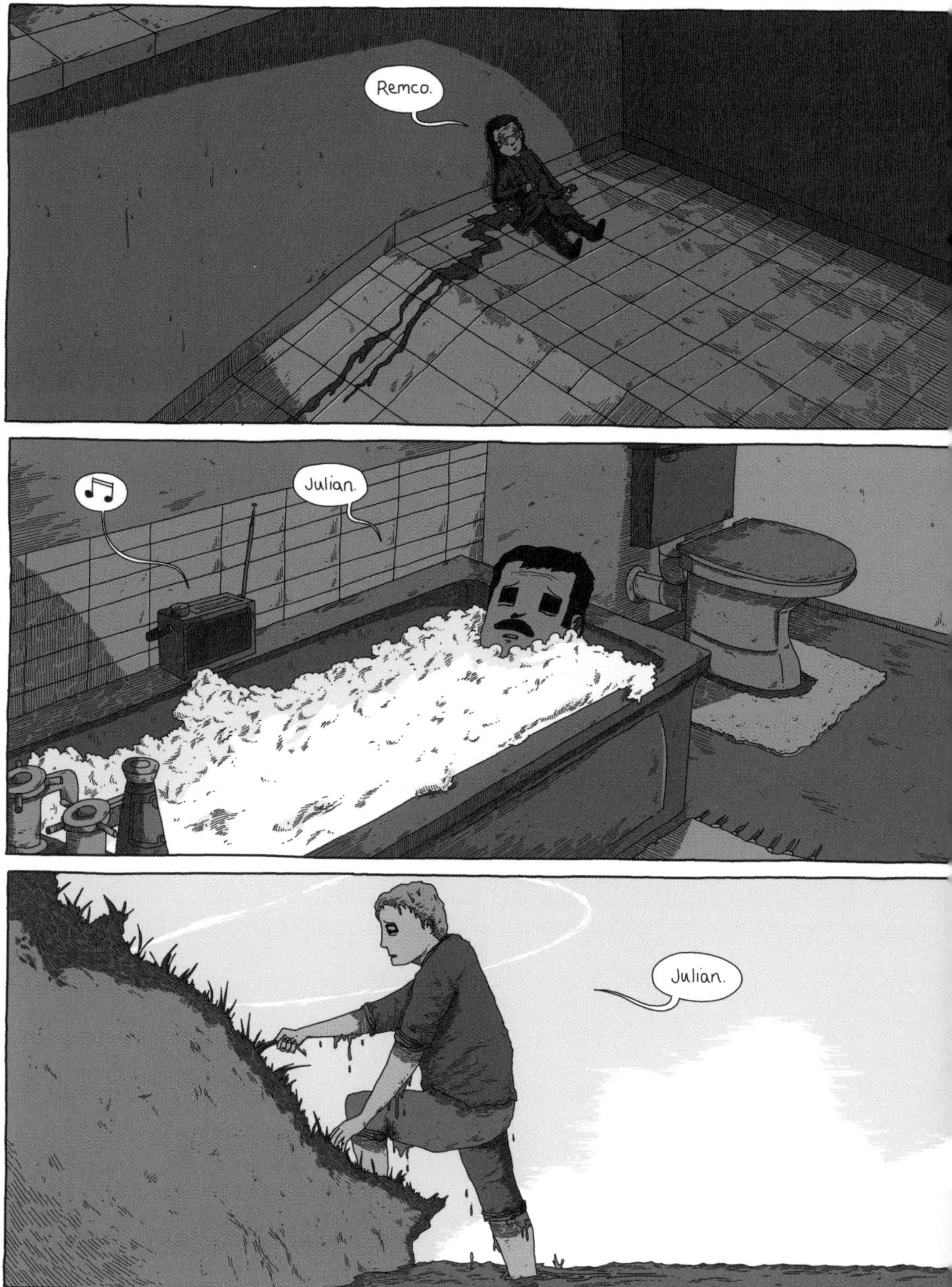
Remco.
♫
Julian.
Julian.

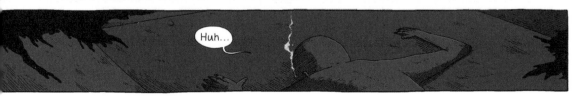

Huh...

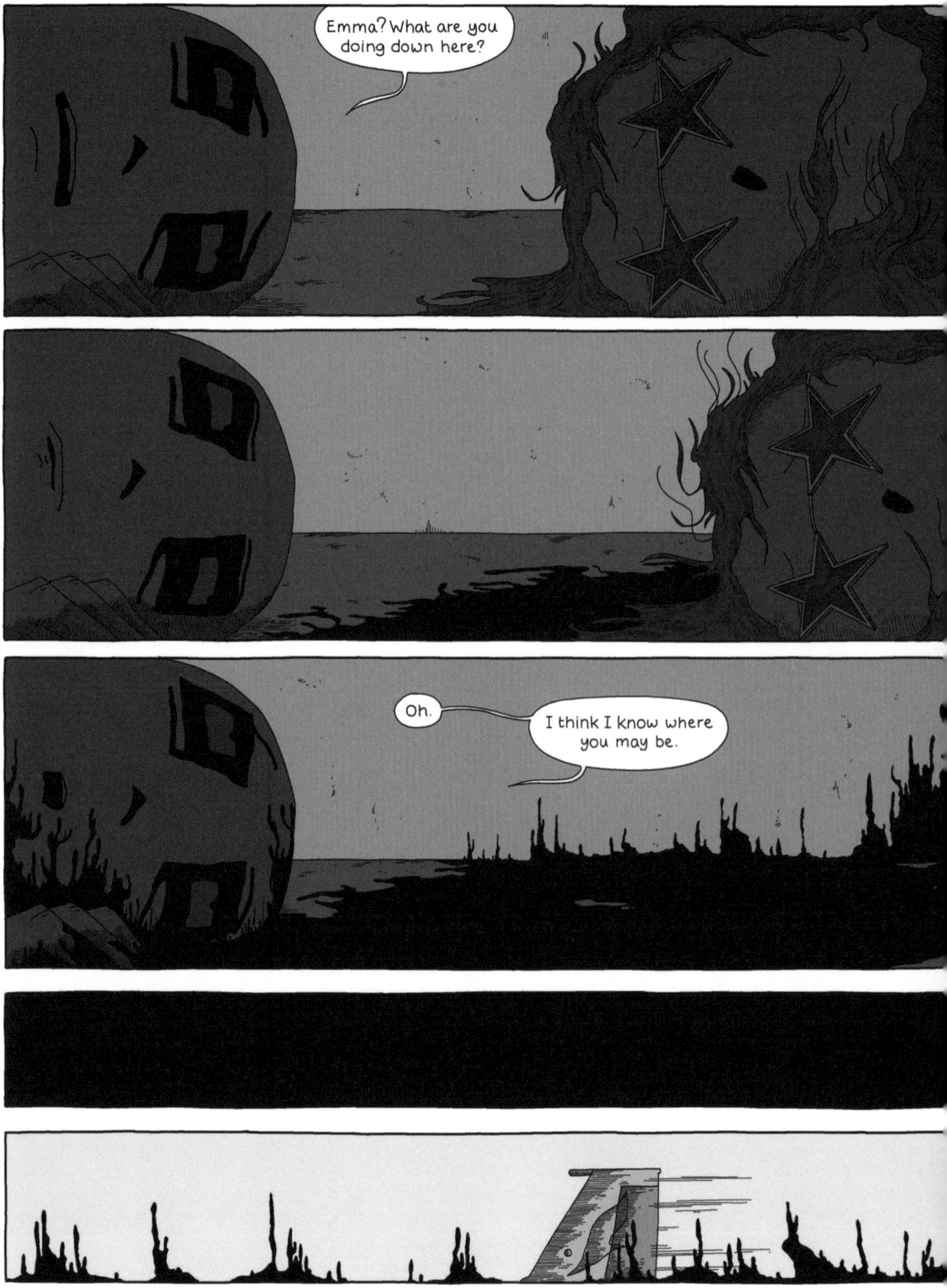
Emma? What are you doing down here?
Oh.
I think I know where you may be.

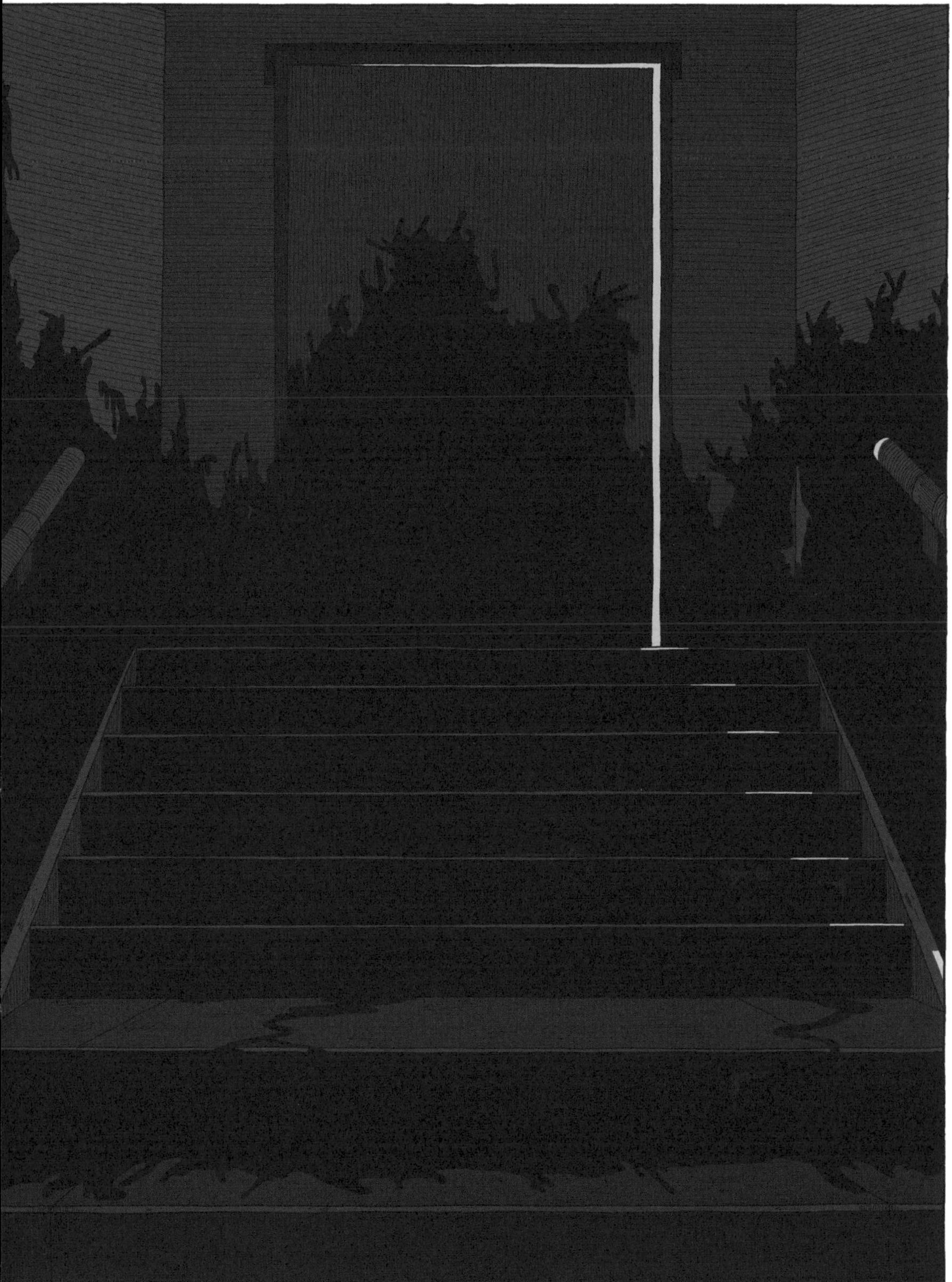

Huh?

I'm back. With my hat on.

Odd.

Also...

...why am I sinking? And why is the hotel...

...over there looking all weird and broken?

Something's not...

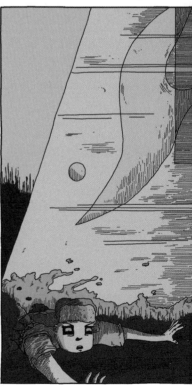

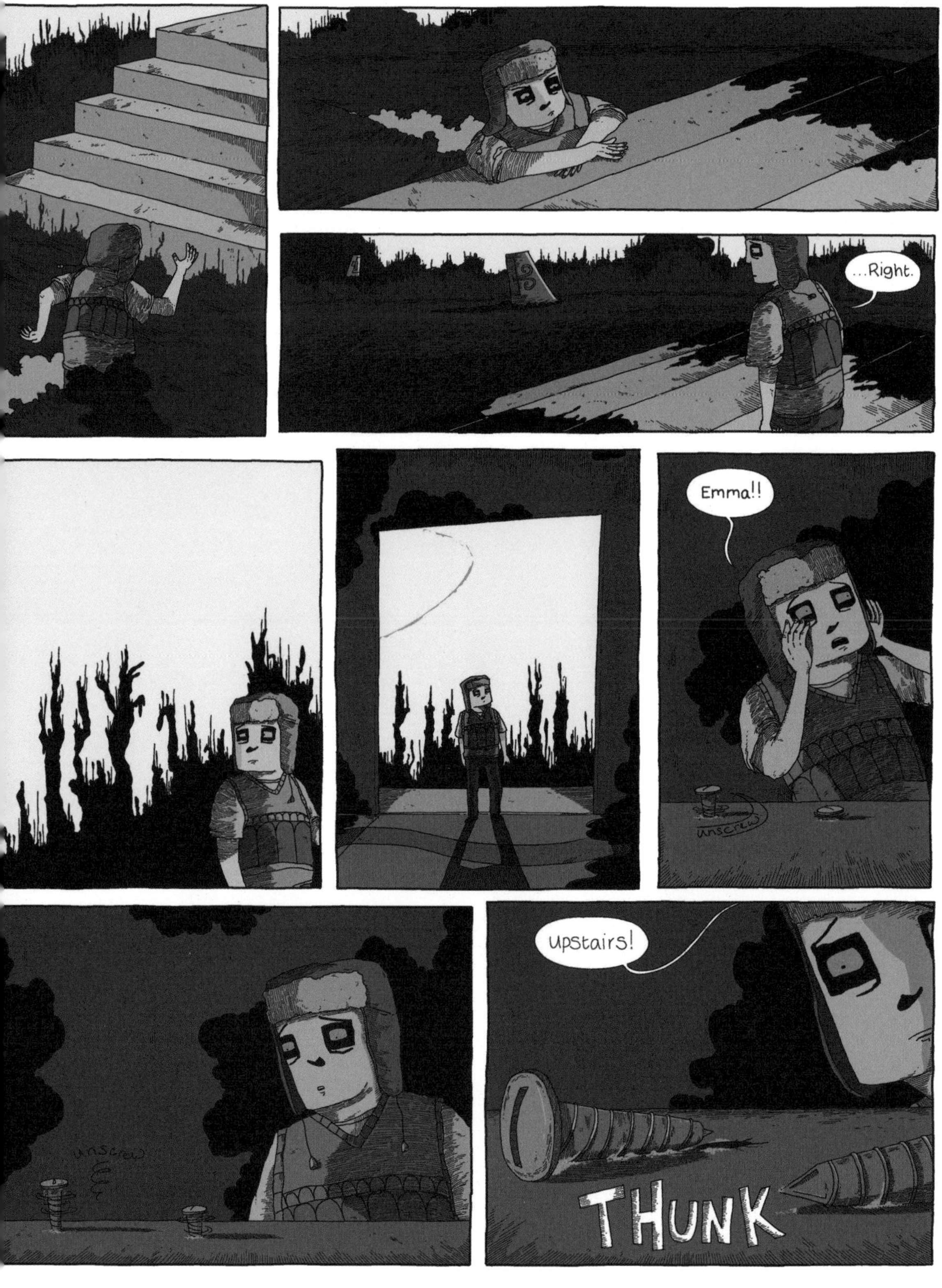
...Right.
Emma!!
unscrew
unscrew
upstairs!
THUNK

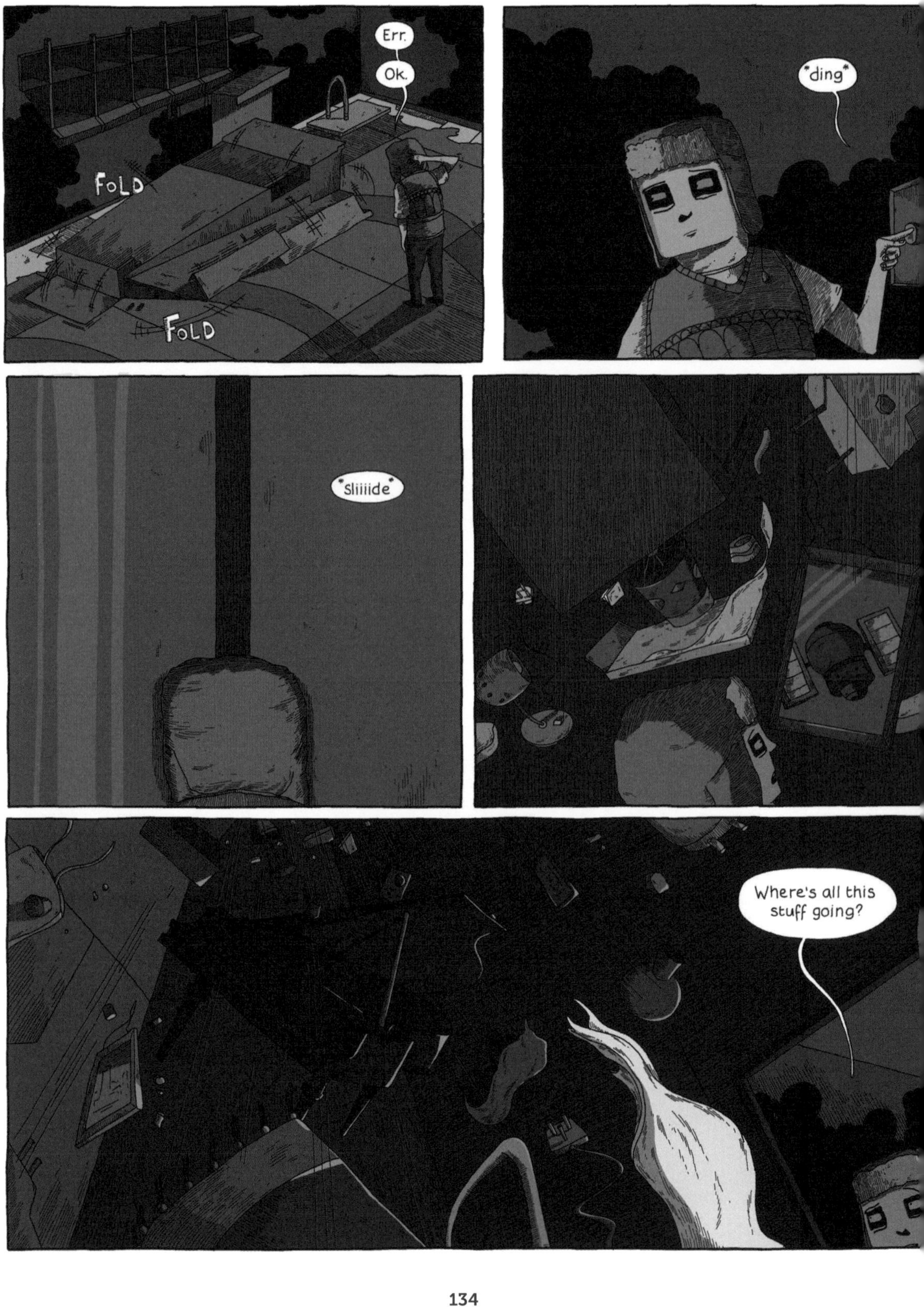
Err.
Ok.
FOLD
FOLD
ding
sliiiide
Where's all this stuff going?

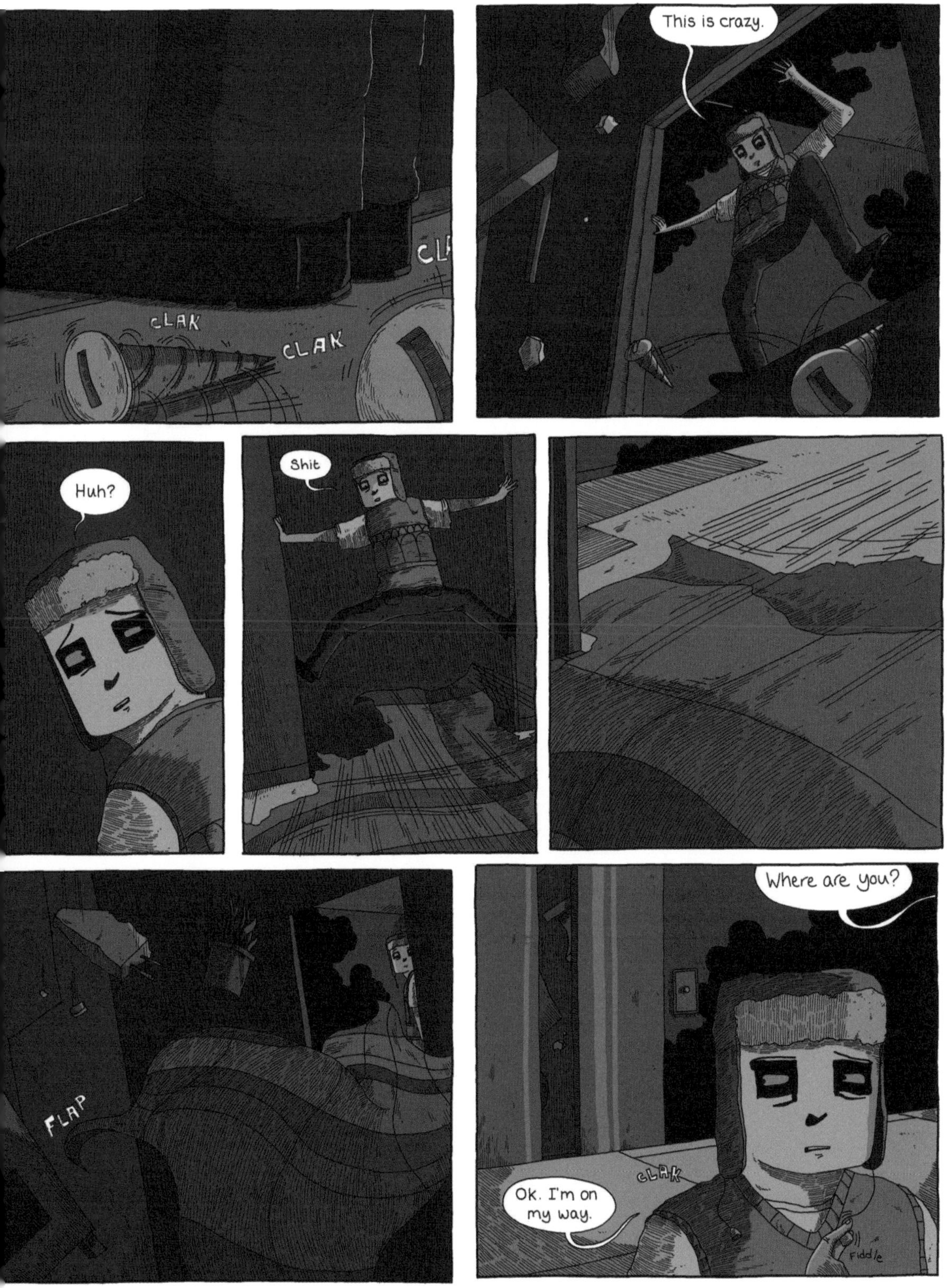

CLA
CLAK
CLAK
This is crazy.
Huh?
Shit
Where are you?
CLAK
Ok. I'm on my way.
Fiddle

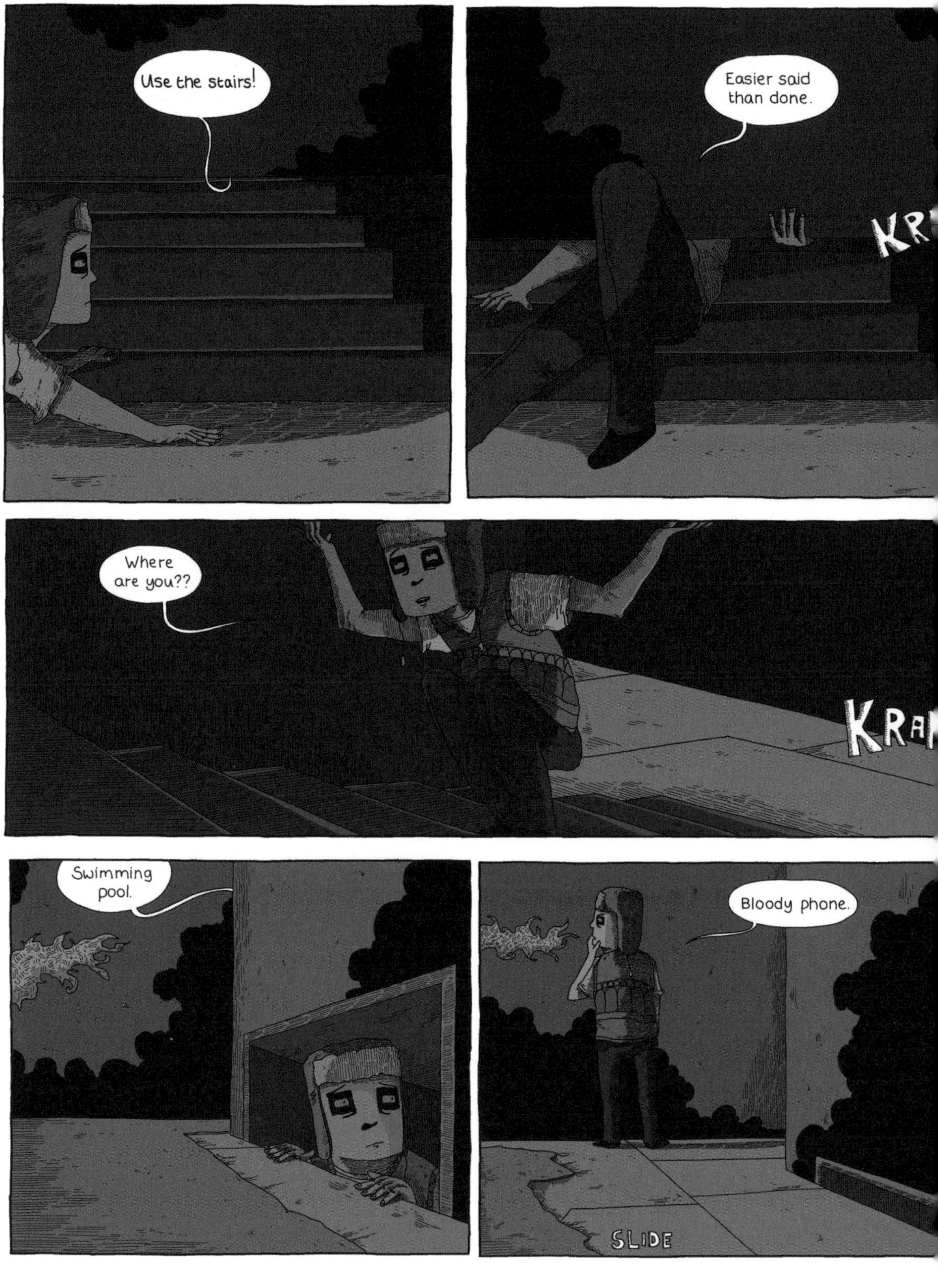
Use the stairs!
Easier said than done.
KR
Where are you??
KRA
Swimming pool.
Bloody phone.
SLIDE

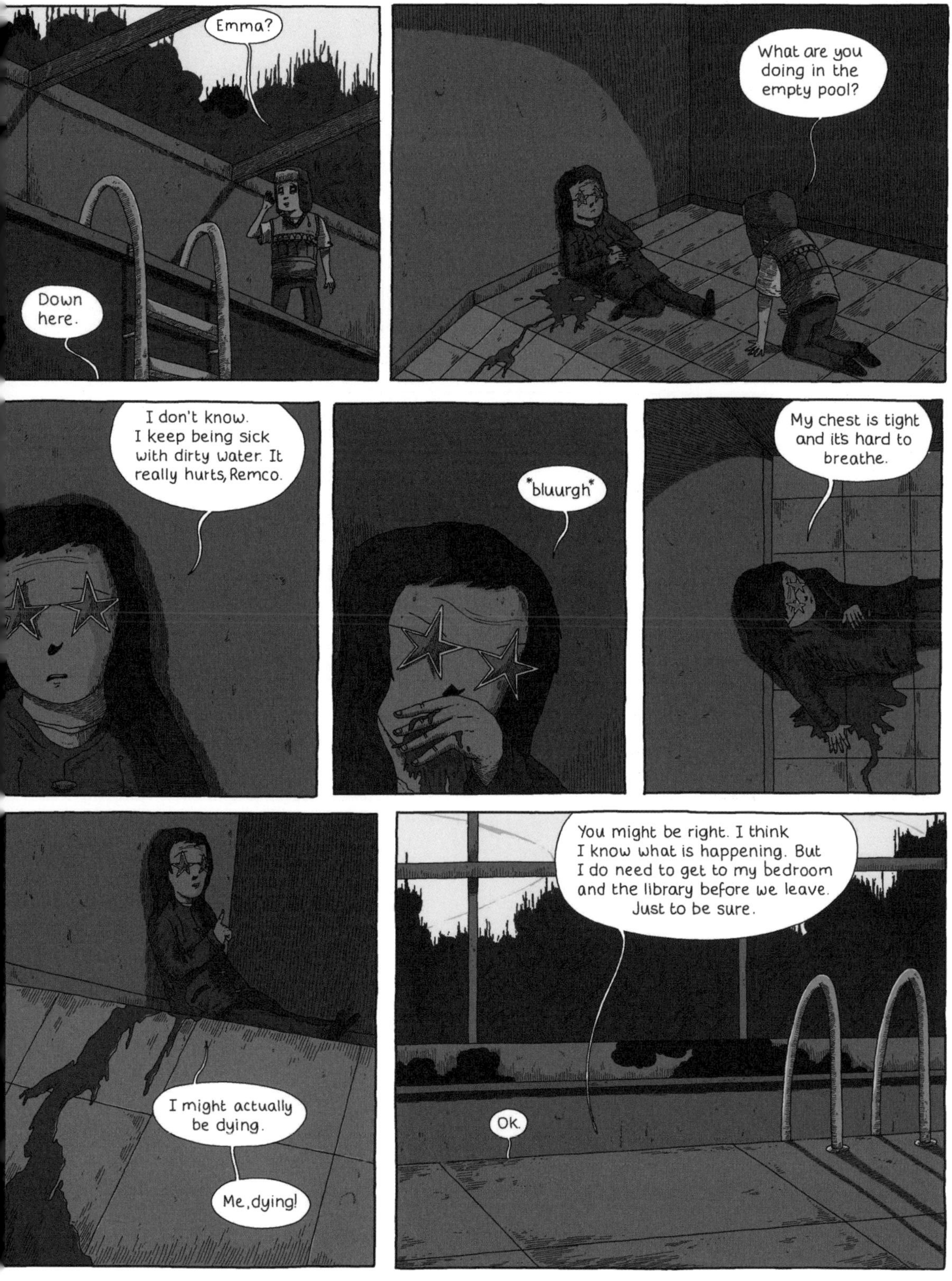
Emma?
Down here.
What are you doing in the empty pool?
I don't know. I keep being sick with dirty water. It really hurts, Remco.
bluurgh
My chest is tight and it's hard to breathe.
I might actually be dying.
Me, dying!
You might be right. I think I know what is happening. But I do need to get to my bedroom and the library before we leave. Just to be sure.
Ok.

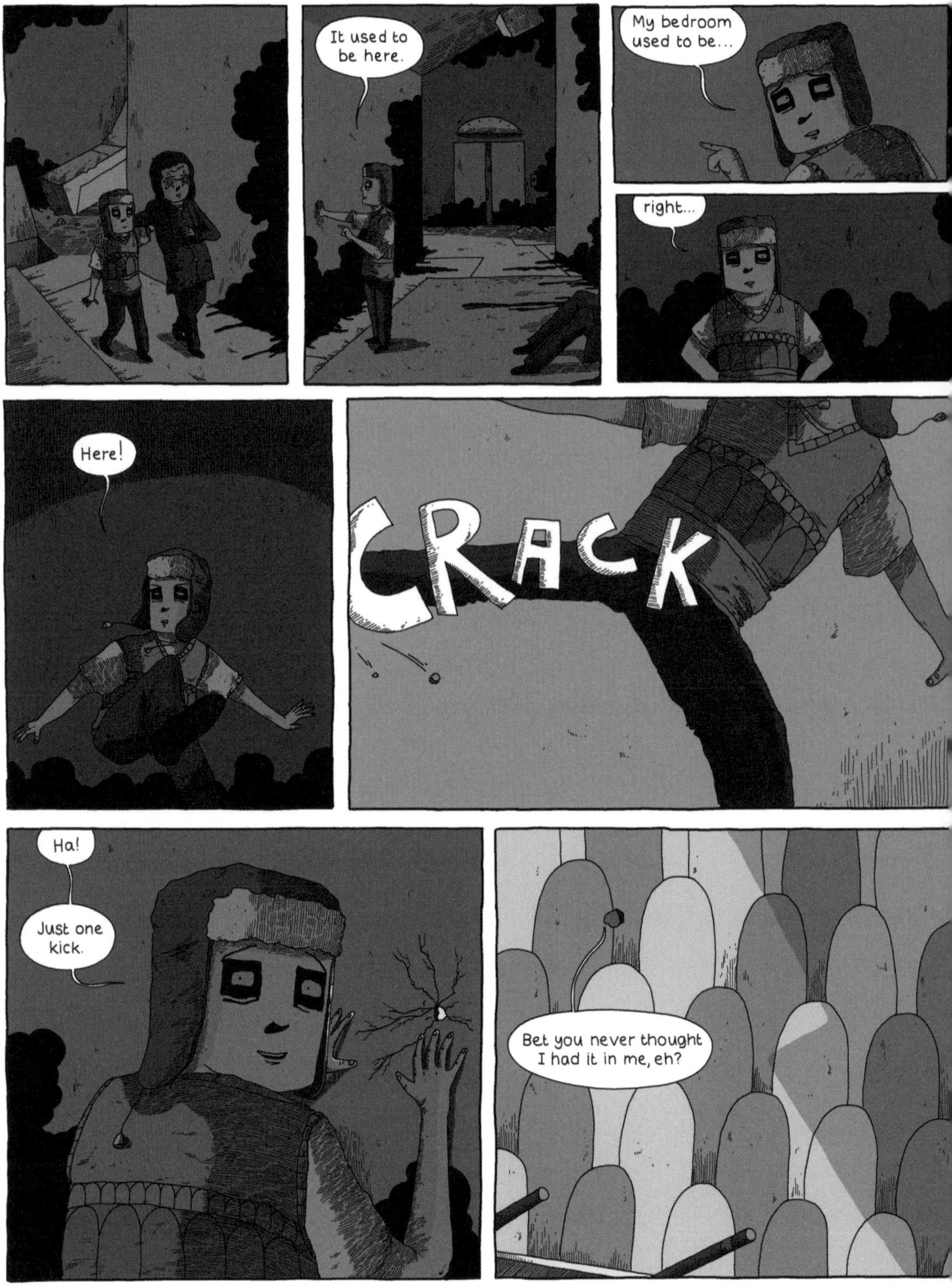
It used to be here.
My bedroom used to be...
right...
Here!
CRACK
Ha!
Just one kick.
Bet you never thought I had it in me, eh?

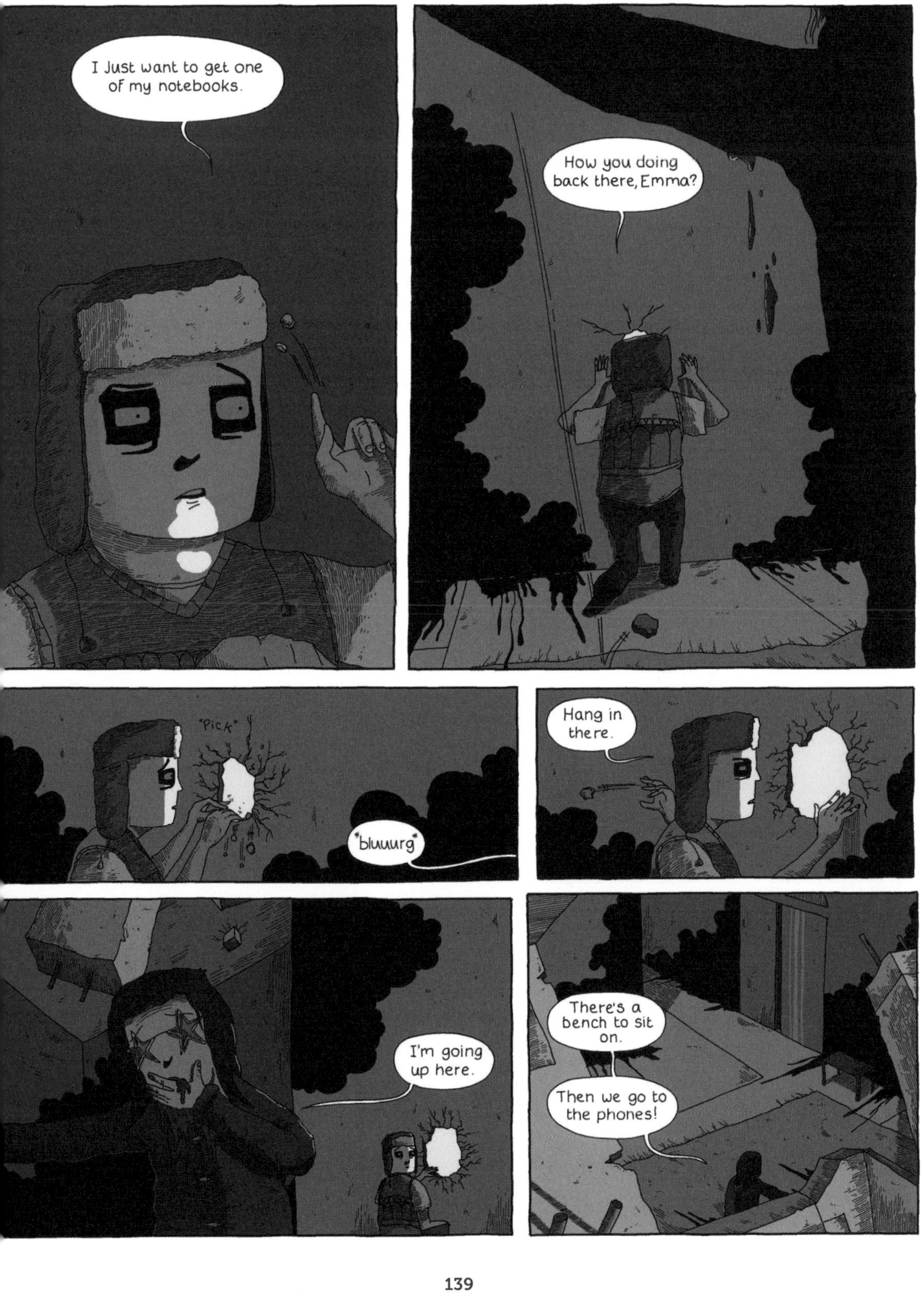
I Just want to get one of my notebooks.
How you doing back there, Emma?
"Pick"
bluuurg
Hang in there.
I'm going up here.
There's a bench to sit on.
Then we go to the phones!

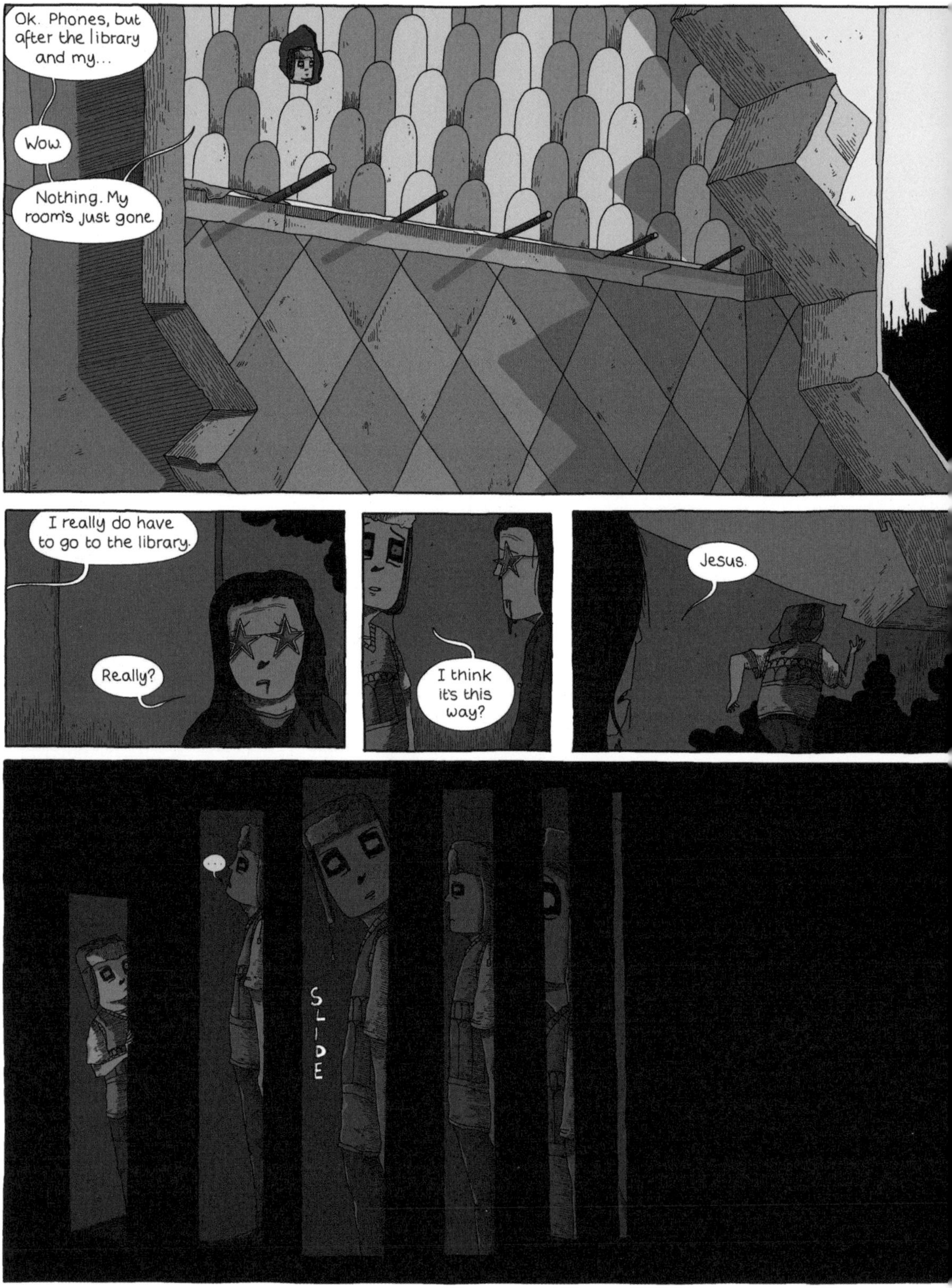
Ok. Phones, but after the library and my...
Wow.
Nothing. My room's just gone.
I really do have to go to the library.
Really?
I think it's this way?
Jesus.
...
SLIDE

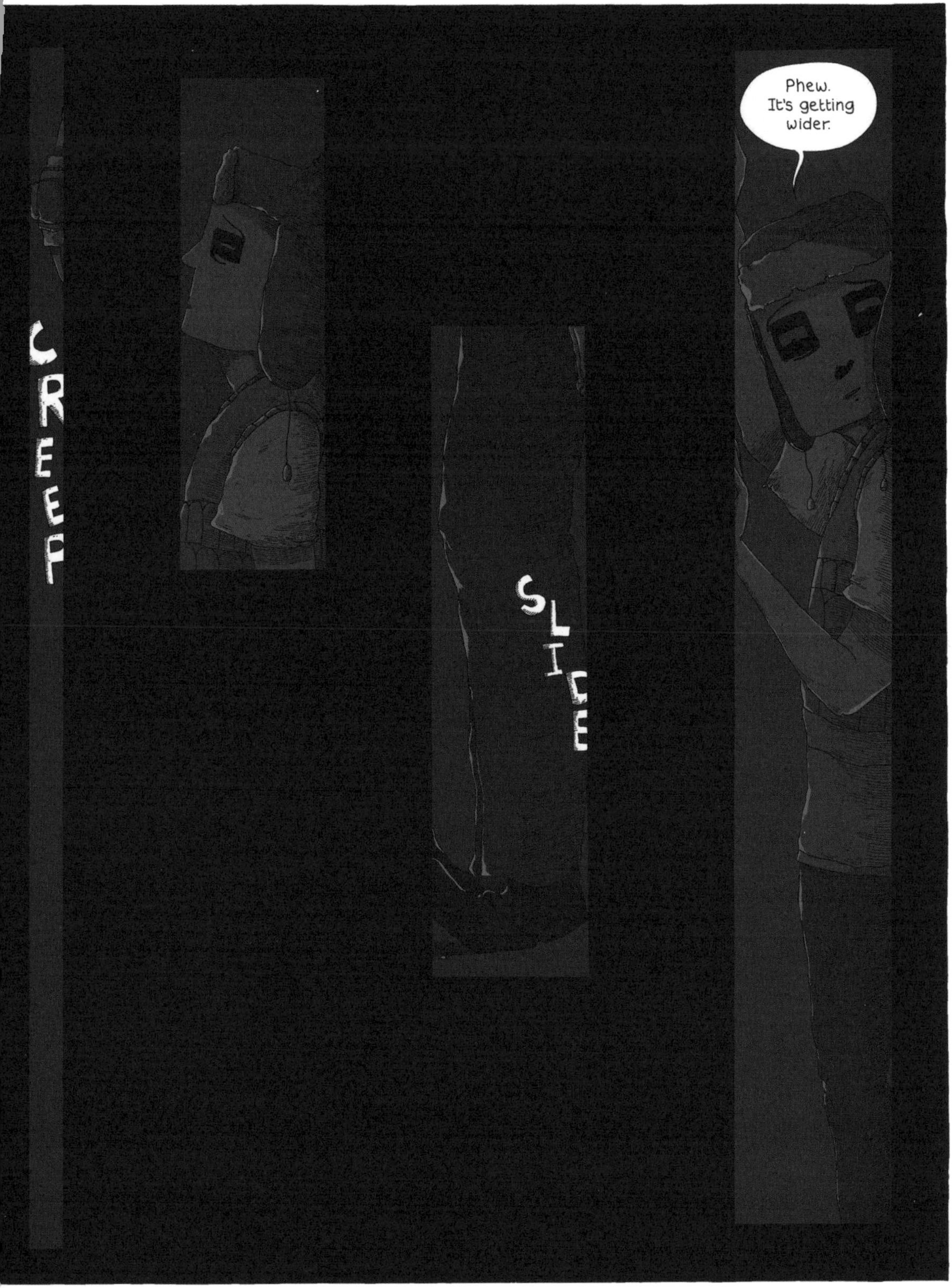

CREEP
SLIDE
Phew.
It's getting
wider.

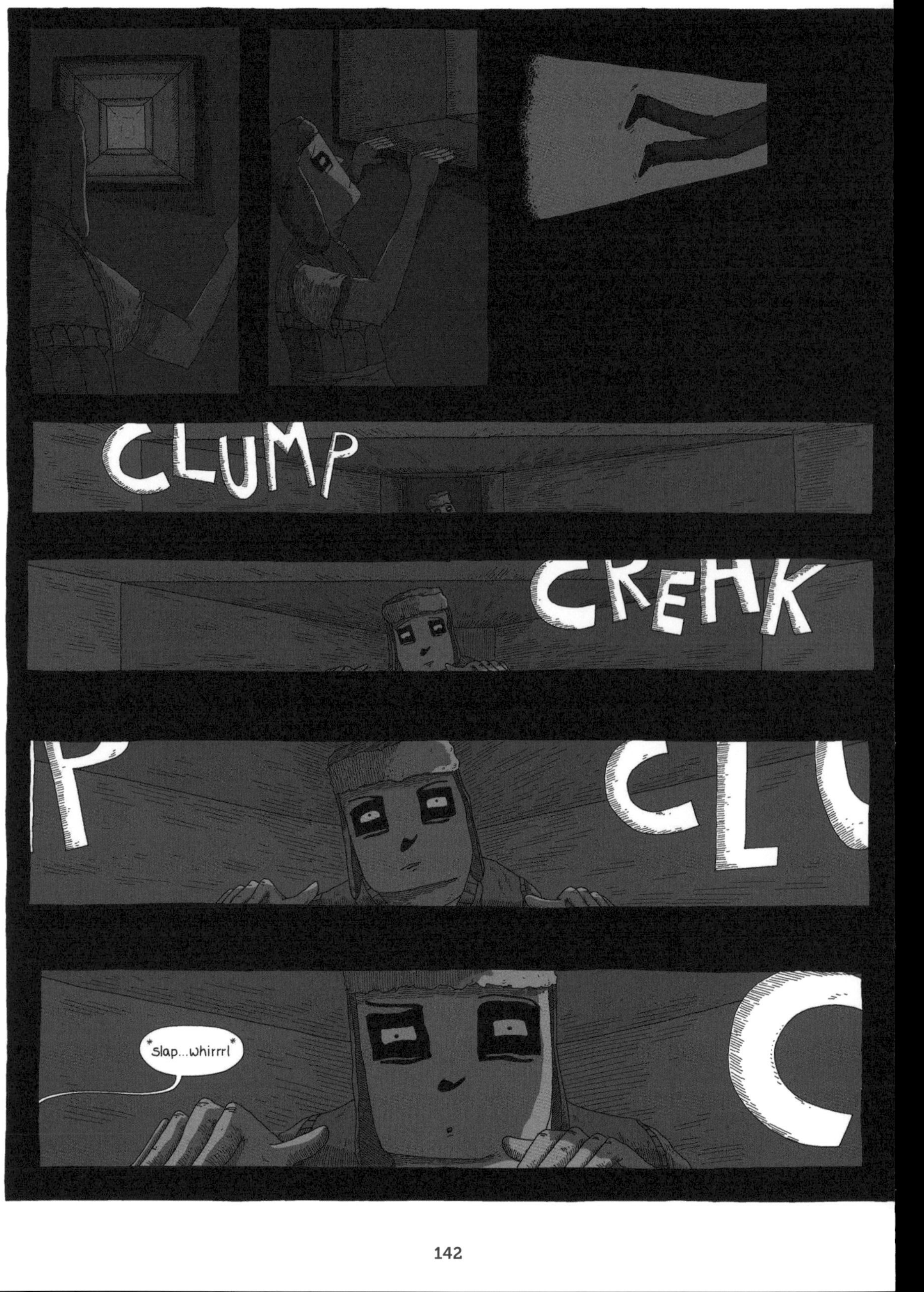
CLUMP
CREAK
P
CLU
slap...whirrrl
C

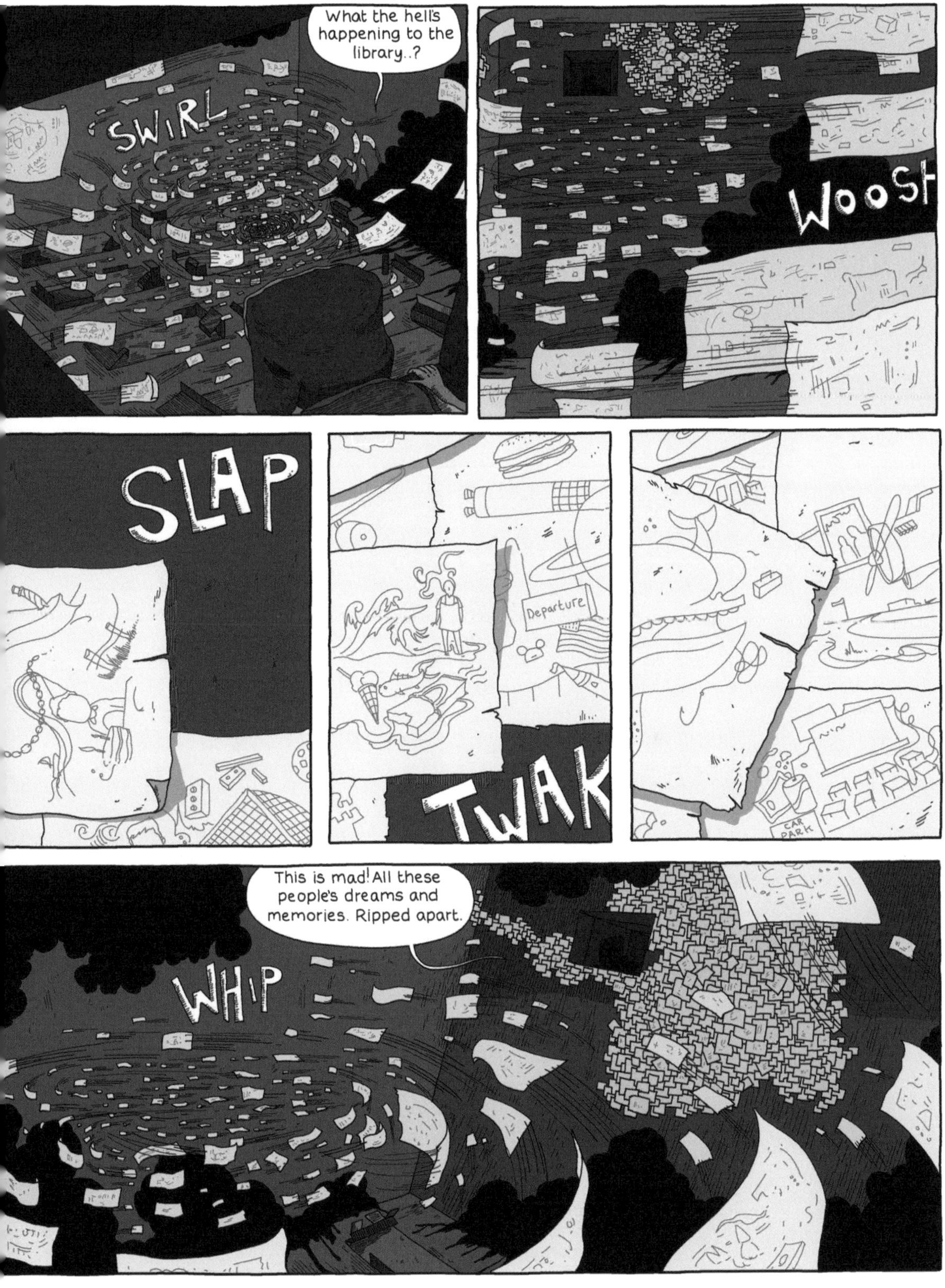
What the hell's happening to the library..?
SWIRL
WOOSH
SLAP
Departure
TWAK
CAR PARK
This is mad! All these people's dreams and memories. Ripped apart.
WHIP

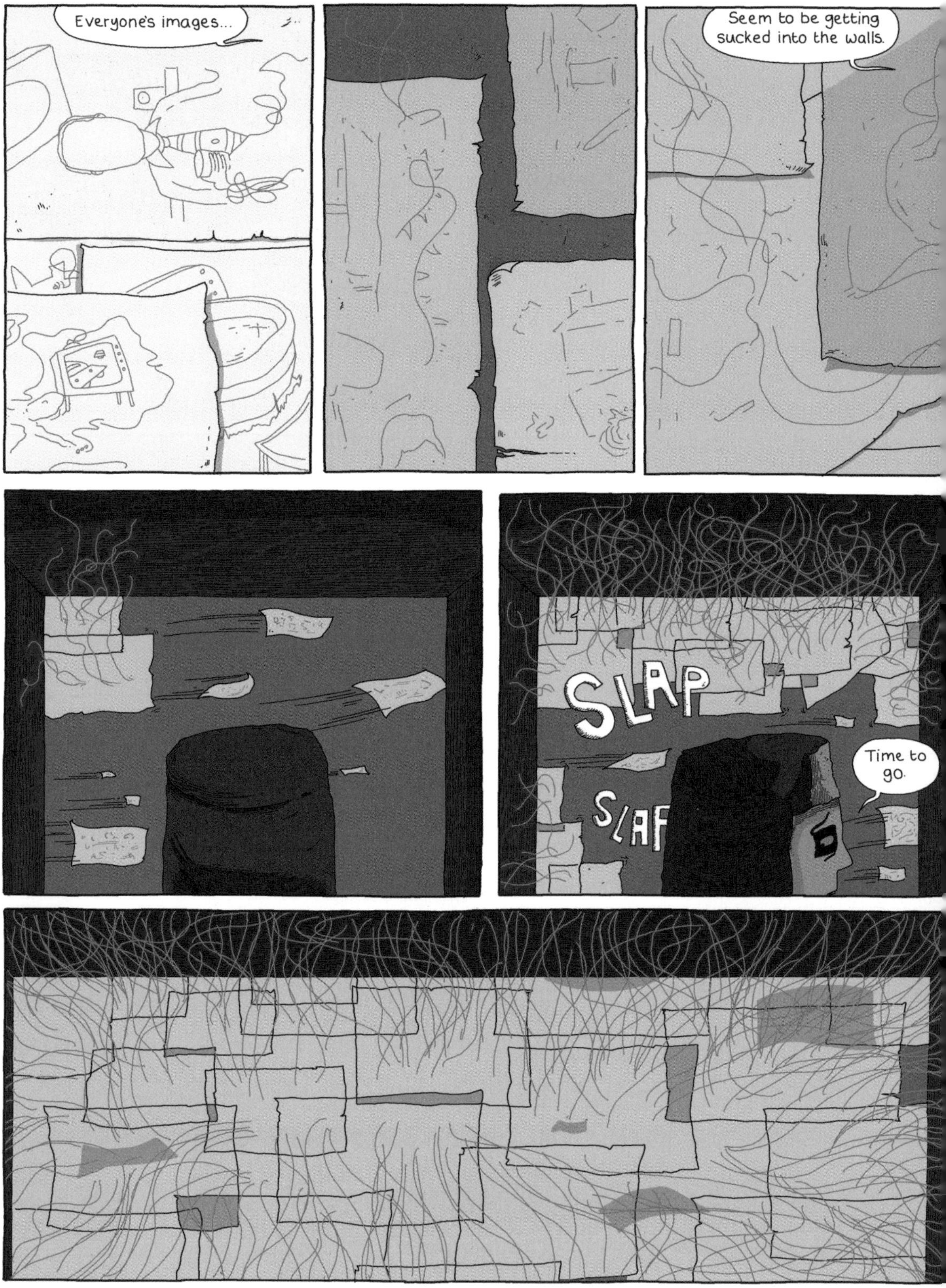
Everyone's images...
Seem to be getting sucked into the walls.
SLAP
SLAP
Time to go.

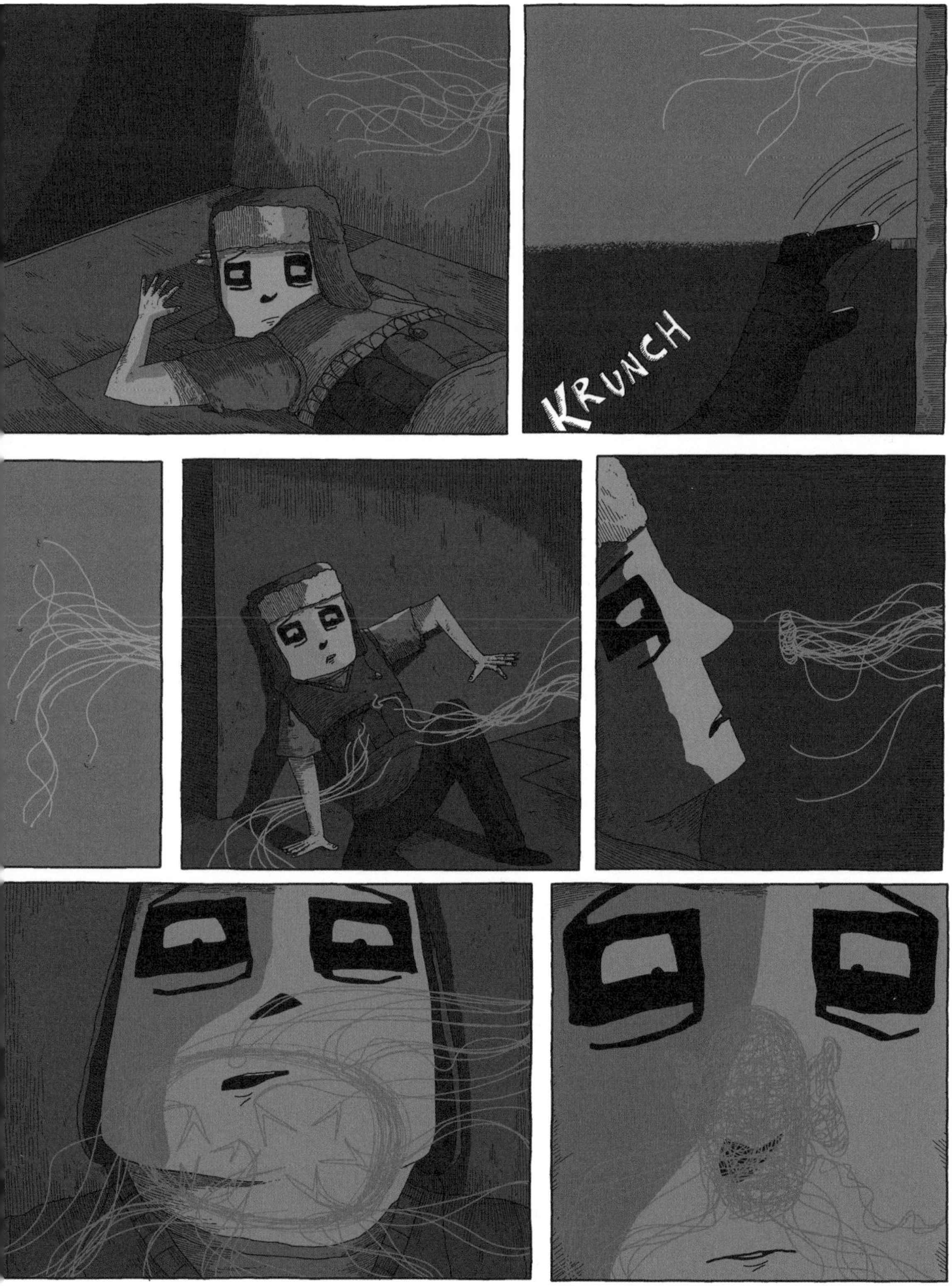
KRUNCH

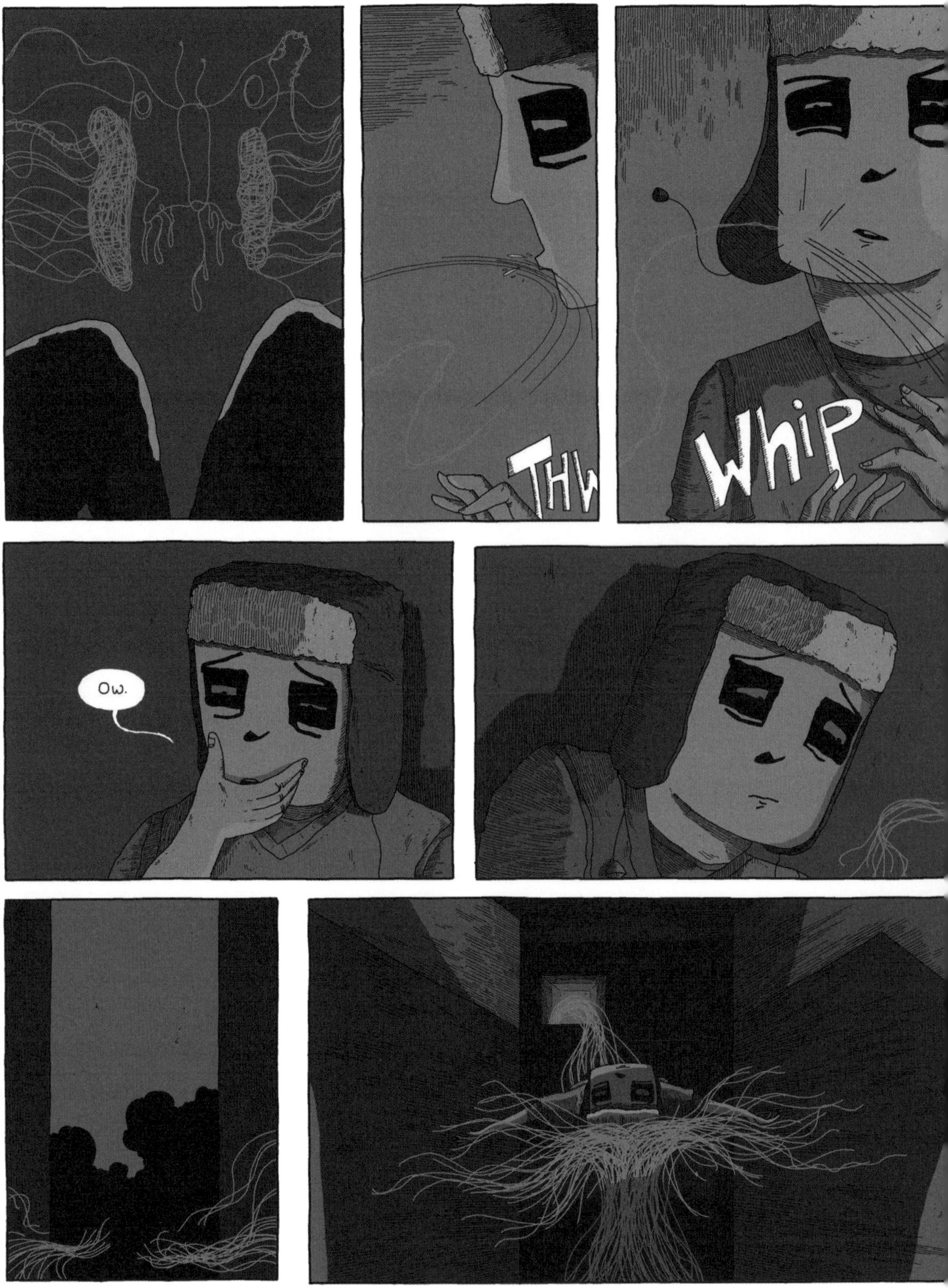
THW
WHIP
Ow.

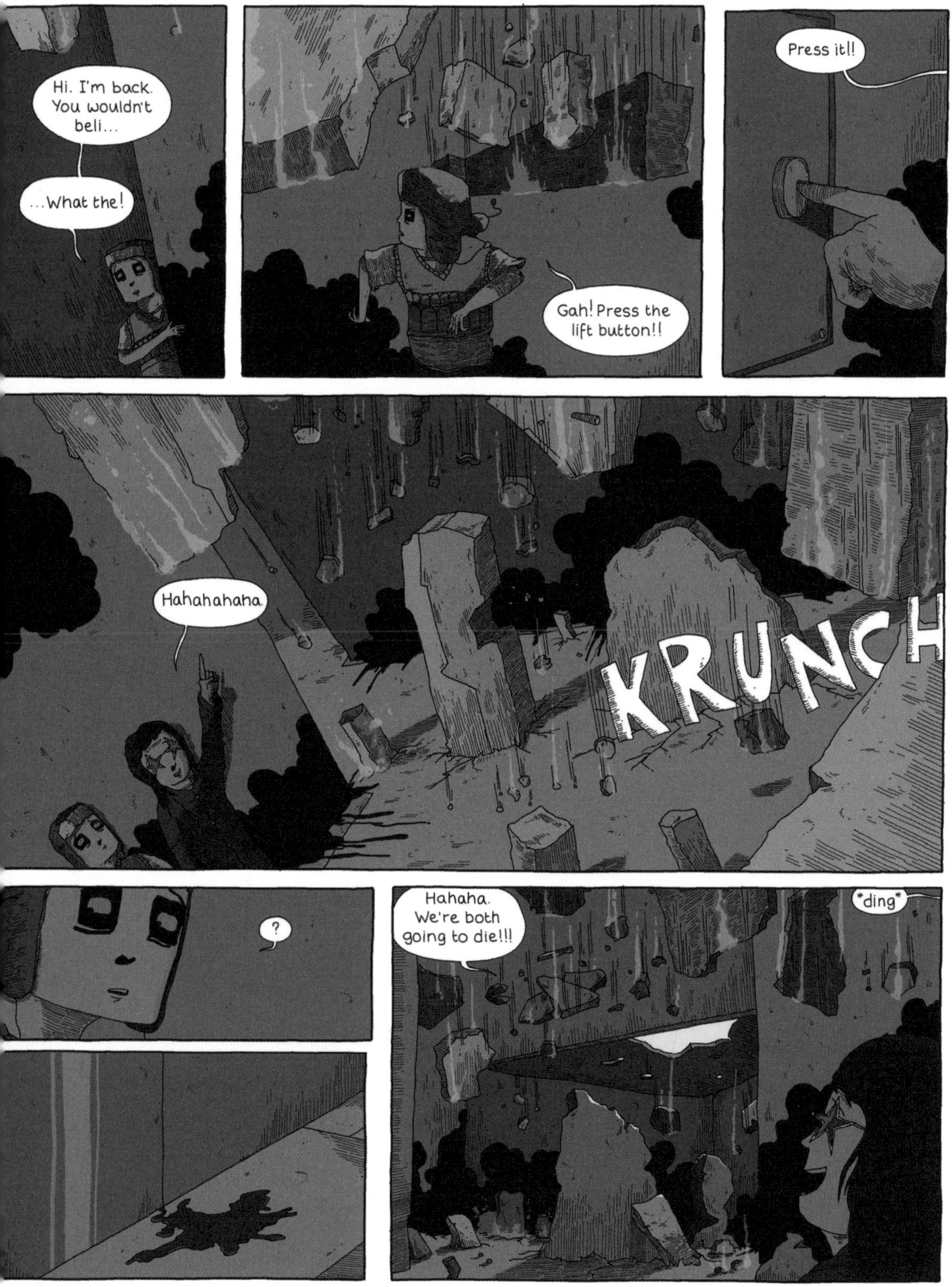
Hi. I'm back. You wouldn't beli...
...What the!
Gah! Press the lift button!!
Press it!!
Hahahahaha.
KRUNCH
?
Hahaha. We're both going to die!!!
ding

Emma. We both need to try and get out. I can find you! I think you've been sent back already...it's just no one has found you.

Figures.

This place wants us gone. And if I'm still here when it goes...that's it for me. You need to find me, Remco.

God, I feel awful.

ding

What's that gurgling noise?

I don't know.

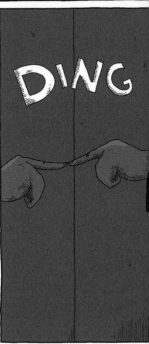

DING

148

"squeeze"

Oh. Shit.

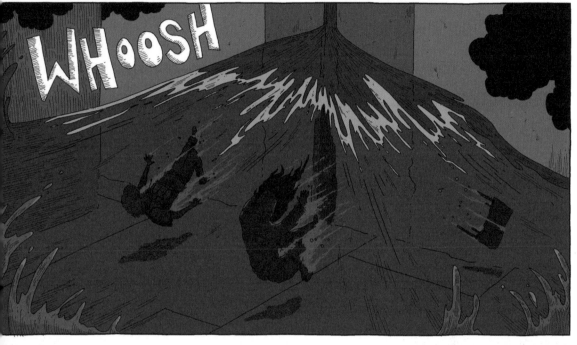

WHOOSH

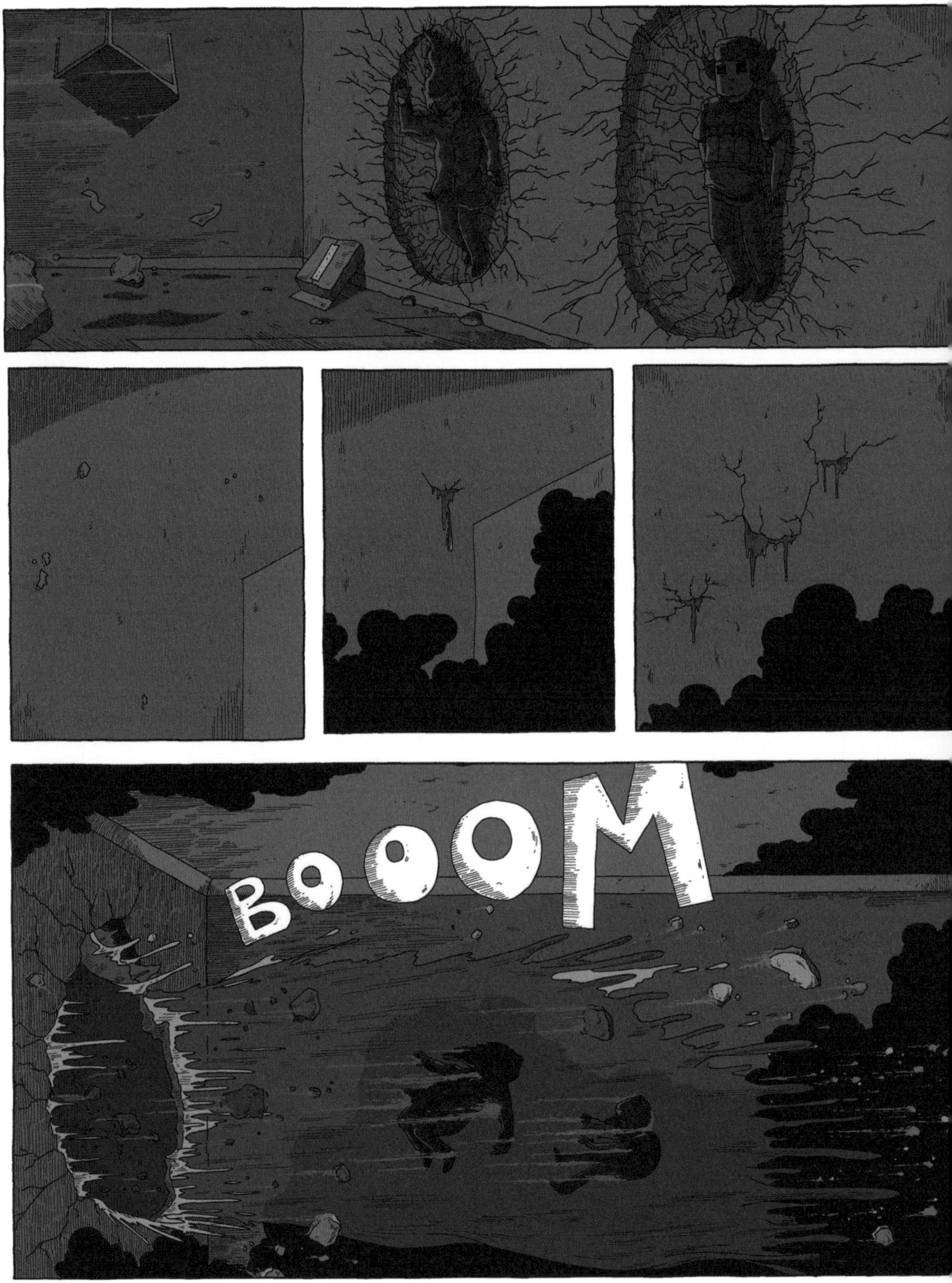
BOOOM

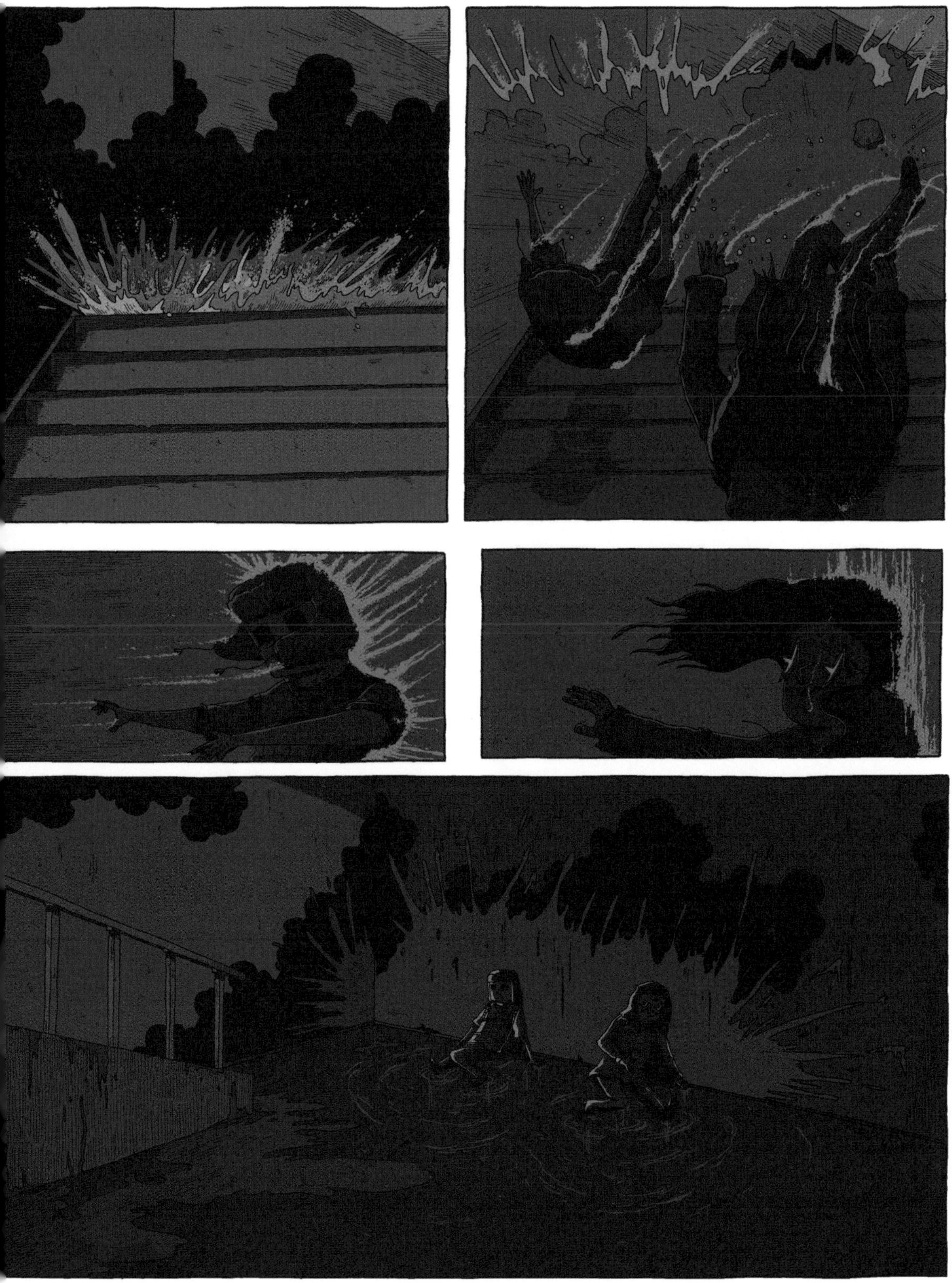

PFFT

Hahahahahaha.

Hahaha.
This is crazy.
You are crazy.

Answer the
bloody pho—

Urrgh!

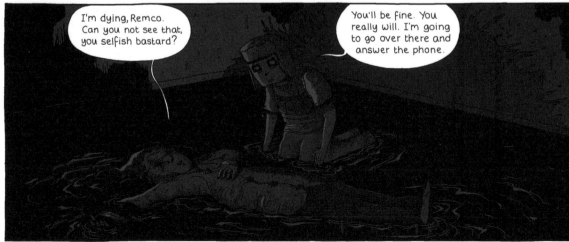

I'm dying, Remco.
Can you not see that,
you selfish bastard?

You'll be fine. You
really will. I'm going
to go over there and
answer the phone.

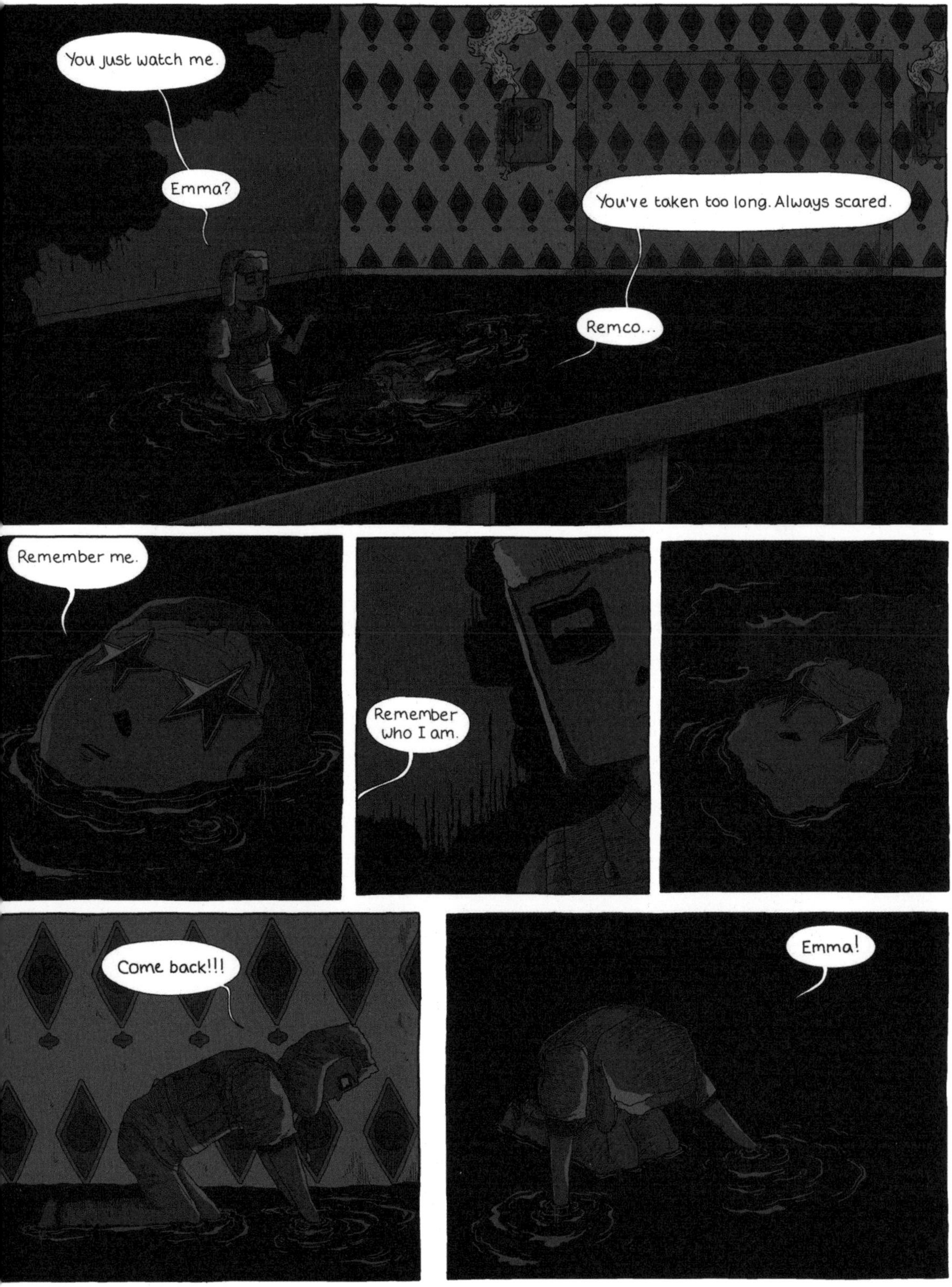
You just watch me.
Emma?
You've taken too long. Always scared.
Remco...
Remember me.
Remember who I am.
Come back!!!
Emma!

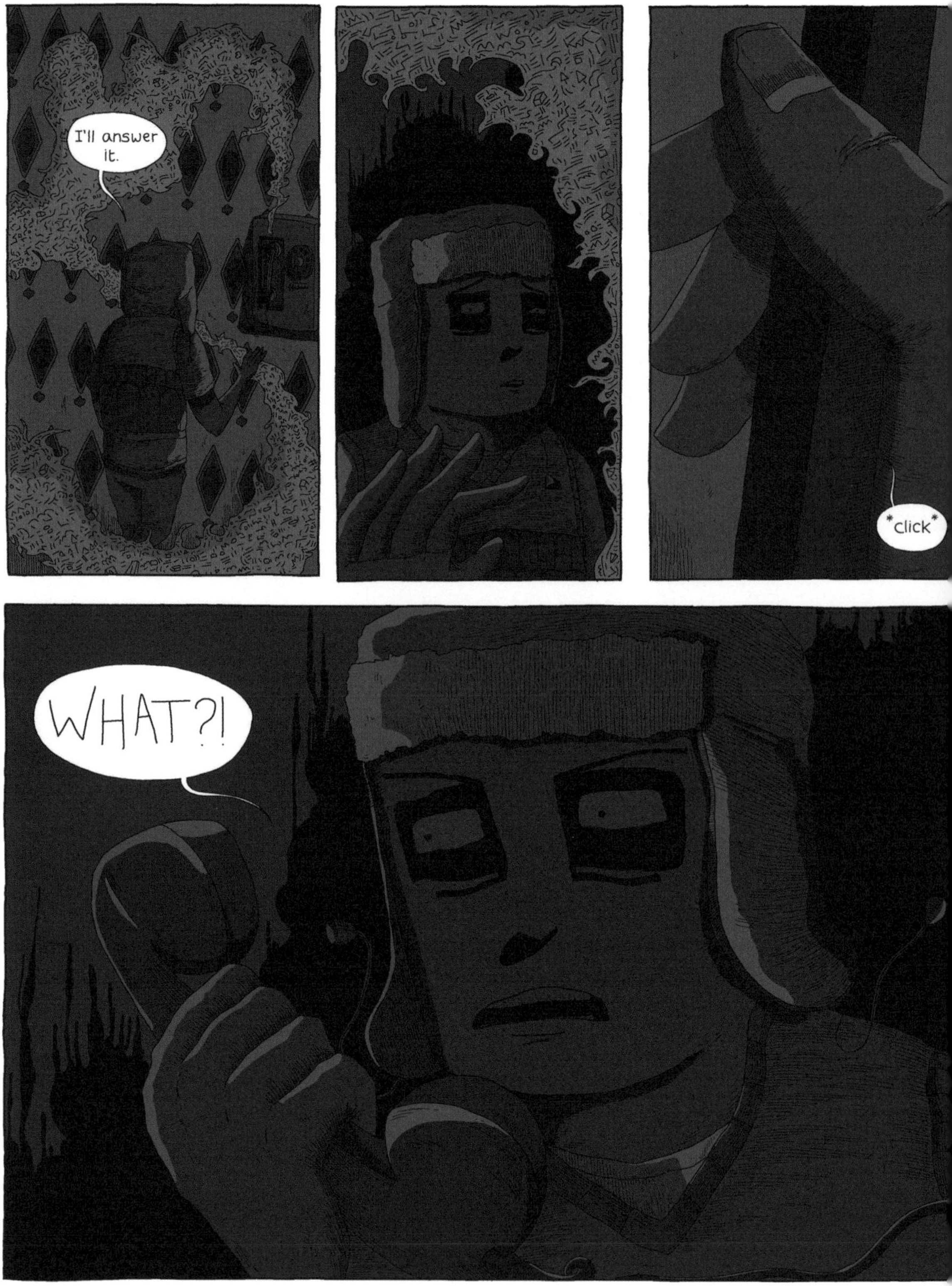
I'll answer it.
click
WHAT?!

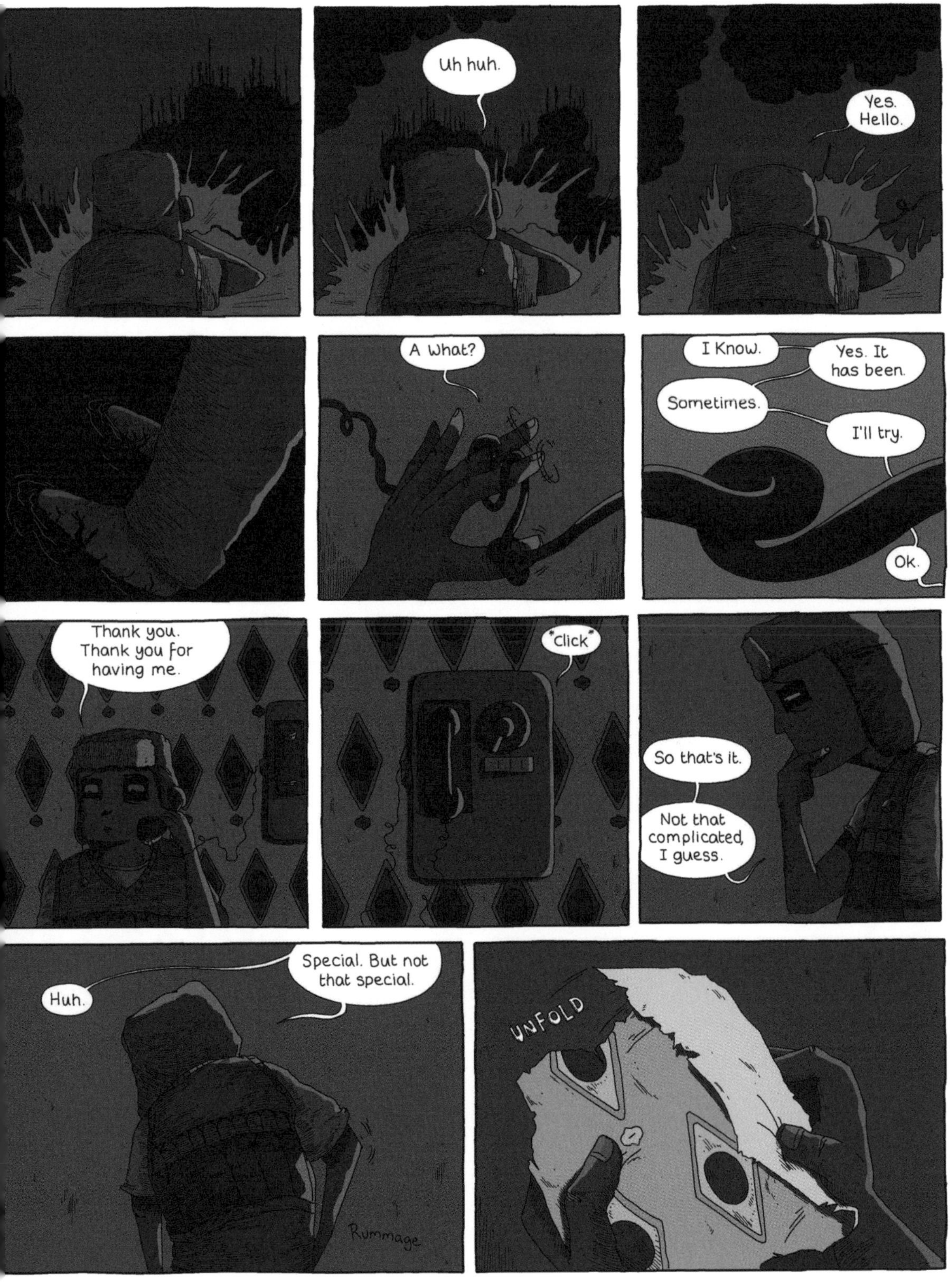
Uh huh.
Yes. Hello.
A What?
I Know.
Yes. It has been.
Sometimes.
I'll try.
Ok.
Thank you. Thank you for having me.
Click
So that's it.
Not that complicated, I guess.
Huh.
Special. But not that special.
Rummage
UNFOLD

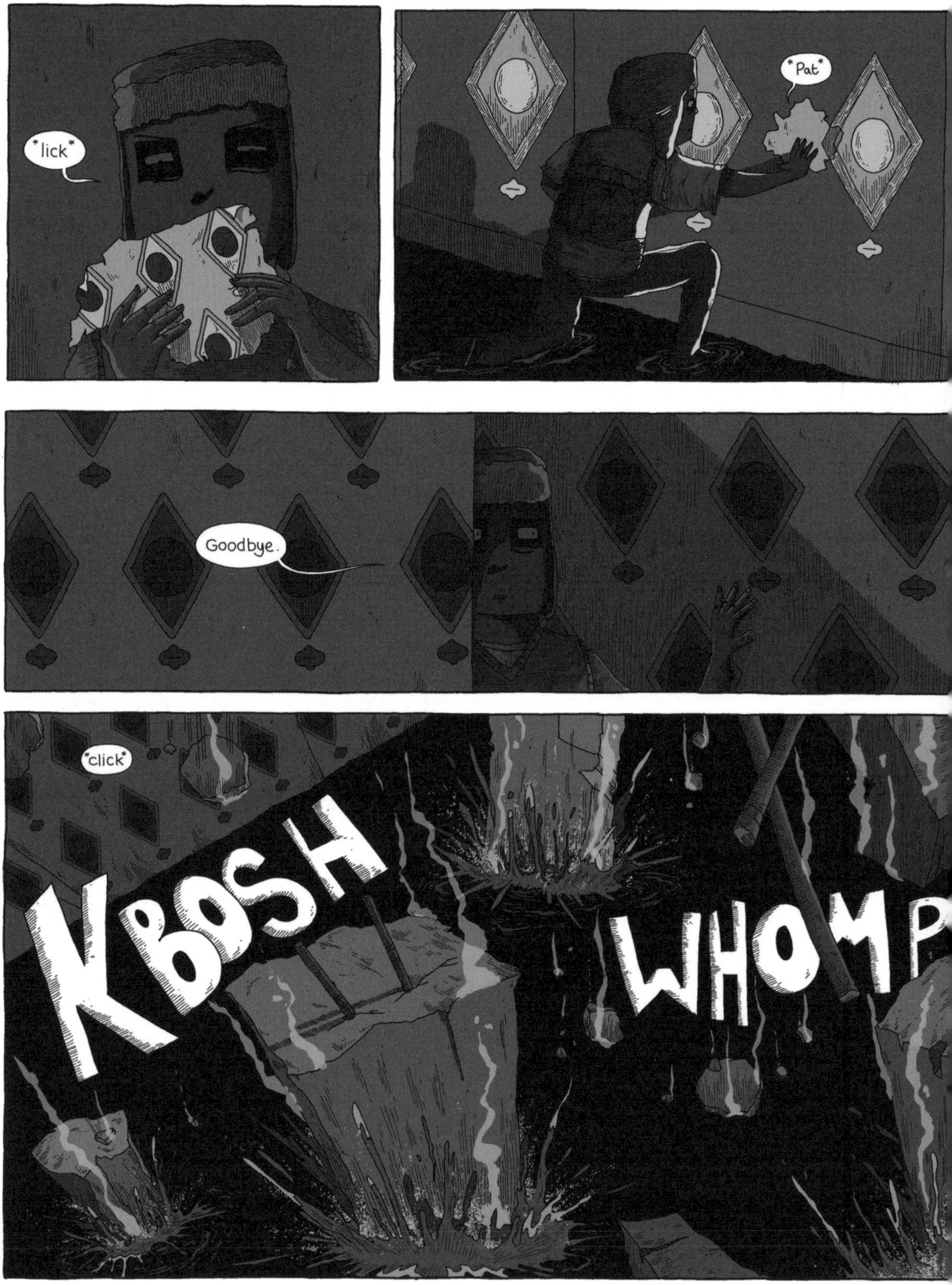
lick
Pat
Goodbye.
click
KBOSH
WHOMP

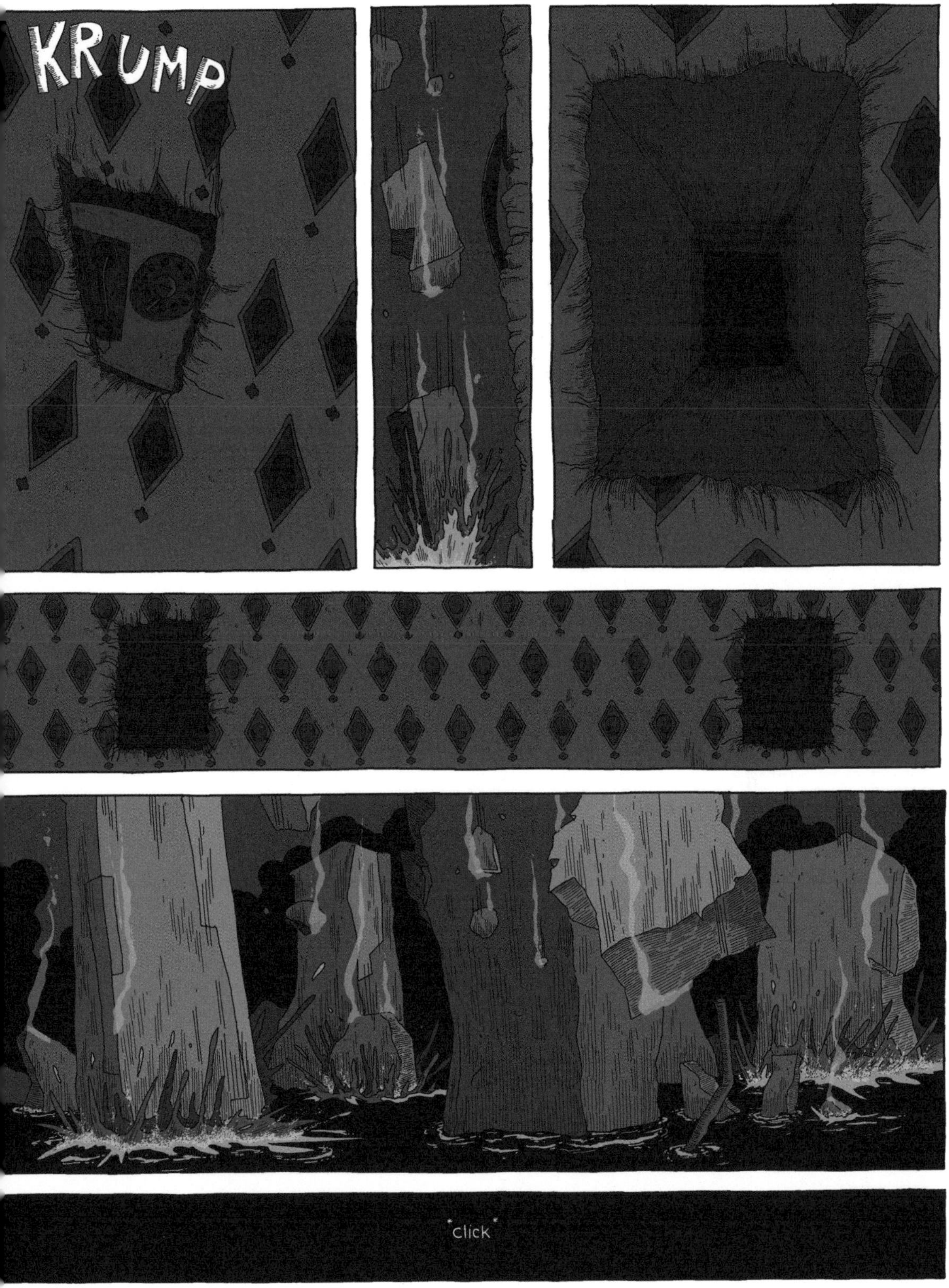
KRUMP
click

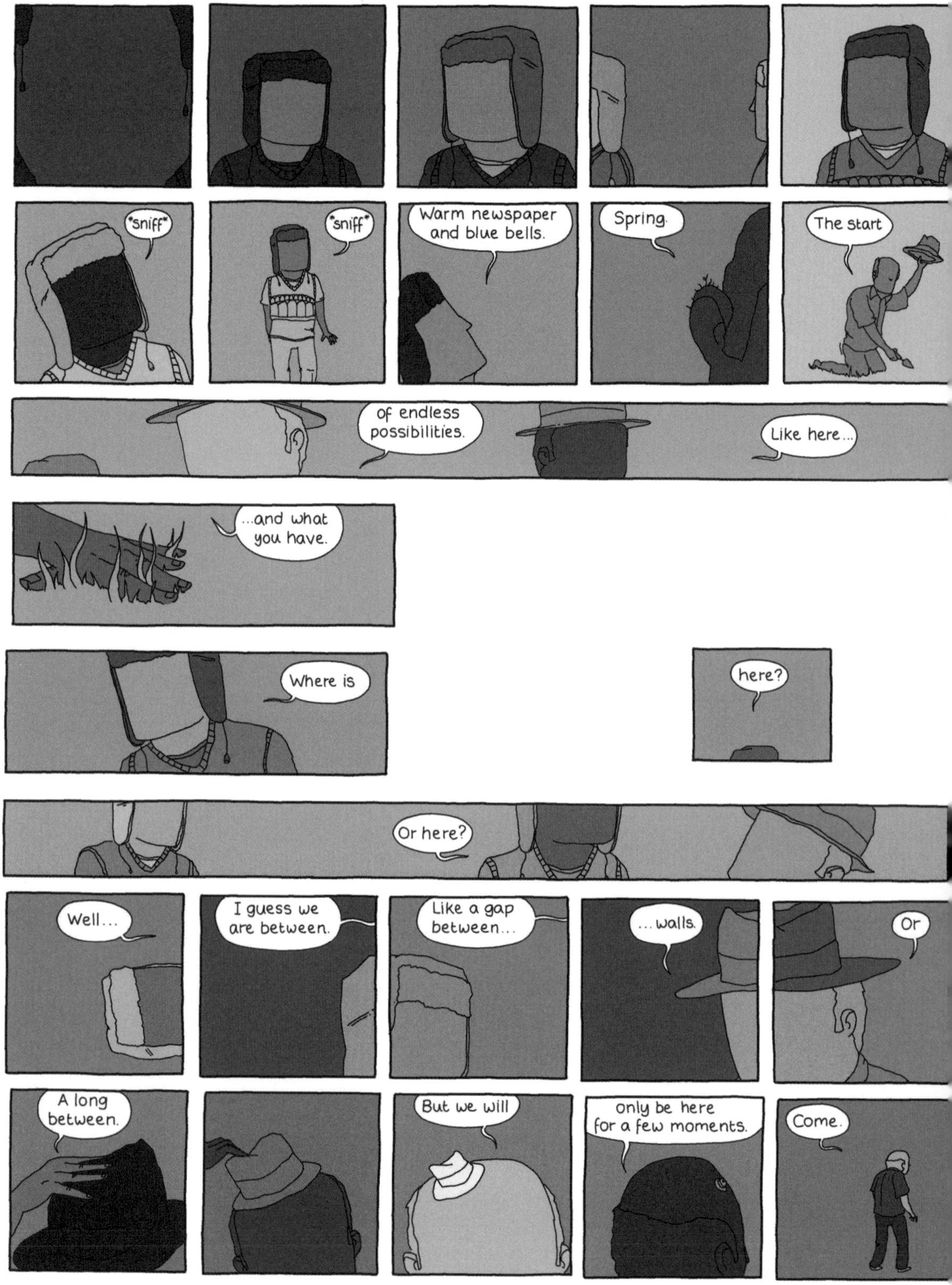
sniff
sniff
Warm newspaper and blue bells.
Spring.
The start
of endless possibilities.
Like here...
...and what you have.
Where is
here?
Or here?
Well...
I guess we are between.
Like a gap between...
...walls.
Or
A long between.
But we will
only be here for a few moments.
Come.

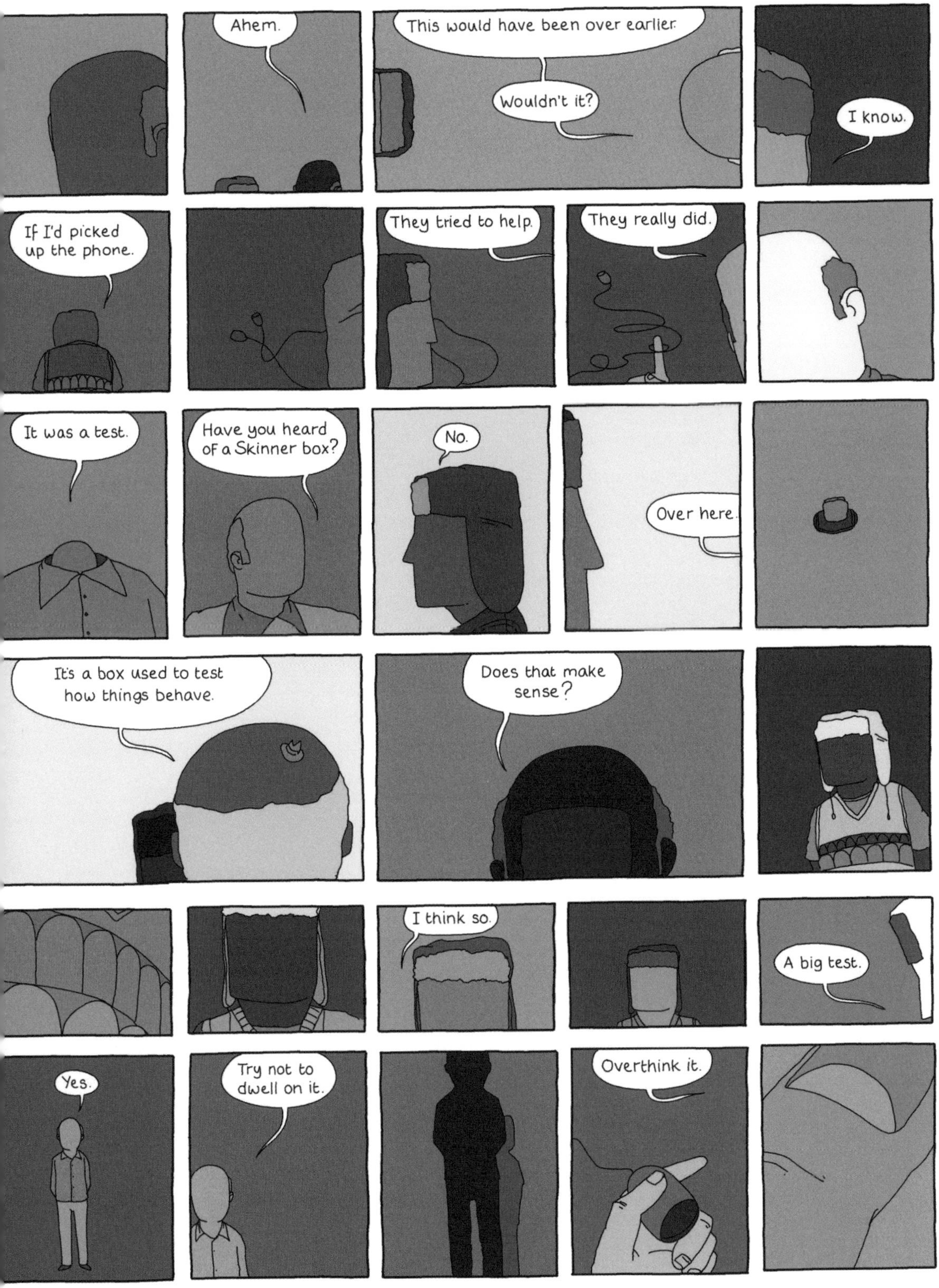
Ahem.
This would have been over earlier.
Wouldn't it?
I know.
If I'd picked up the phone.
They tried to help.
They really did.
It was a test.
Have you heard of a Skinner box?
No.
Over here.
It's a box used to test how things behave.
Does that make sense?
I think so.
A big test.
Yes.
Try not to dwell on it.
Overthink it.

Don't worry.
I didn't kill you, Grandad.
I know.
It was just bad timing,
I'm sorry you had to see it.
And I should never had asked you to do those things.
I'm glad you didn't.
Soon you will go back. And soon I will too.
You know how if you pass someone...
...on a train going the other way. You see each other for a second.
Something like that is happening here.
Oh. Ok.
I'm not dead.
But you are?
That's right.
We'd better
be quick.
Train's a-movin'.
Sniff
Take care.
It's going
to be fine.
I'm with you.
But you must...
Take the first step.

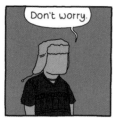

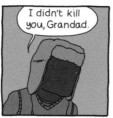

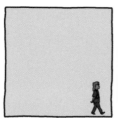

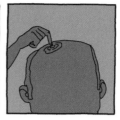

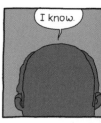

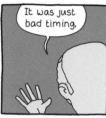

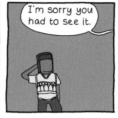

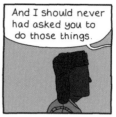

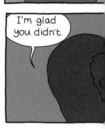

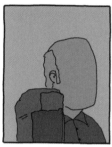

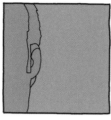

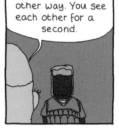

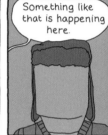

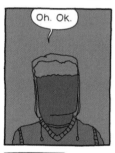

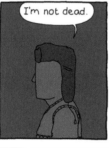

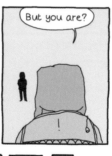

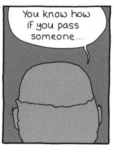

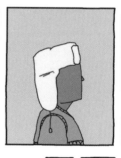

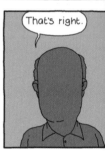

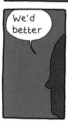

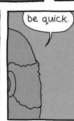

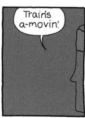

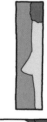

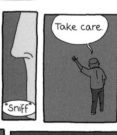

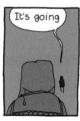

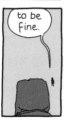

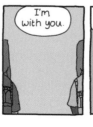

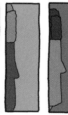

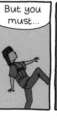

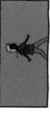

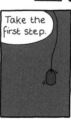

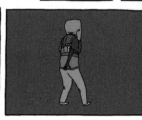

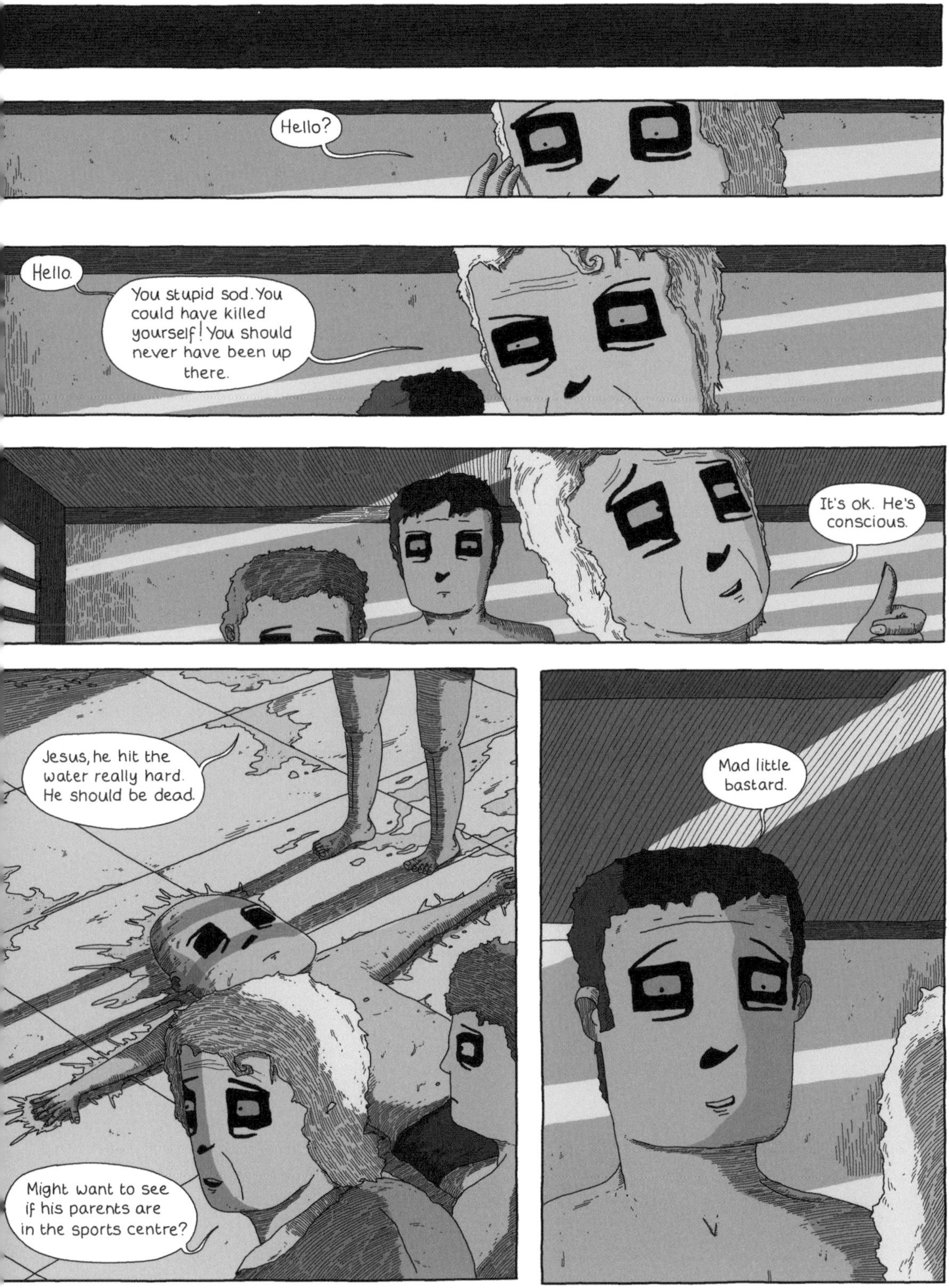
Hello?
Hello.
You stupid sod. You could have killed yourself! You should never have been up there.
It's ok. He's conscious.
Jesus, he hit the water really hard. He should be dead.
Might want to see if his parents are in the sports centre?
Mad little bastard.

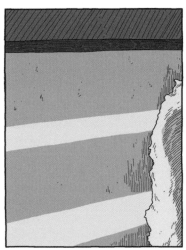

Here.

Have a nice cup of tea.

Where's

Err. I made a bit of an executive decision while you...

He needs to get out and about more. We can't fence him in. I can't fence him in. I know that.

But not the woods.

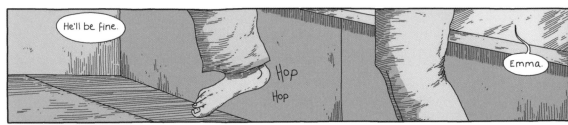

He'll be fine.

Hop

Hop

Emma.

TANG

Cherry

COLA

162

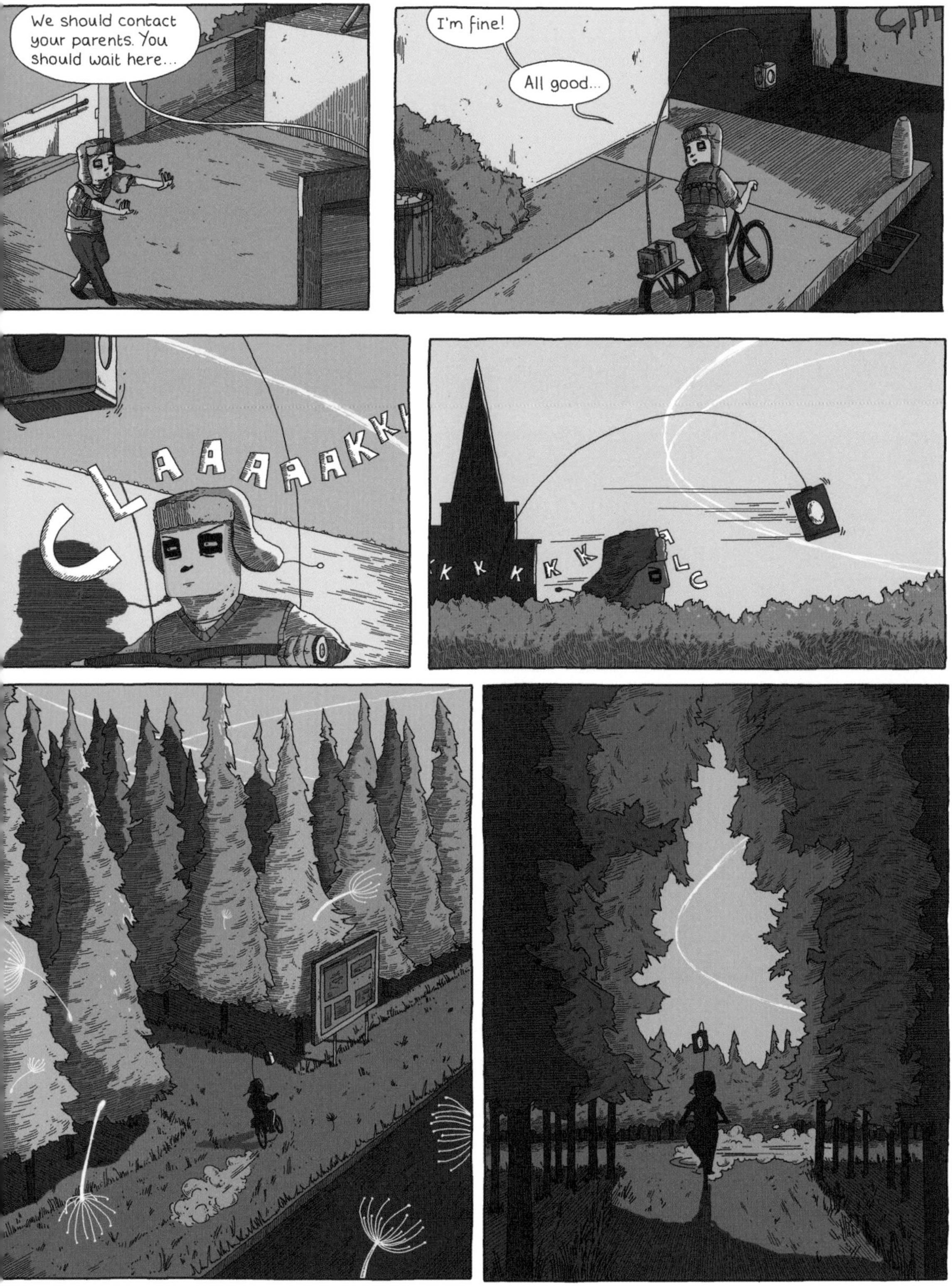
We should contact your parents. You should wait here...
I'm fine!
All good...
CLAAAAAKK
K K K K K
A L C

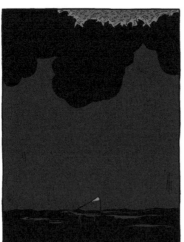

BLURRGI

C'mon, you bloody noisy sod. I'm here for you now.

CLICK

Ha.

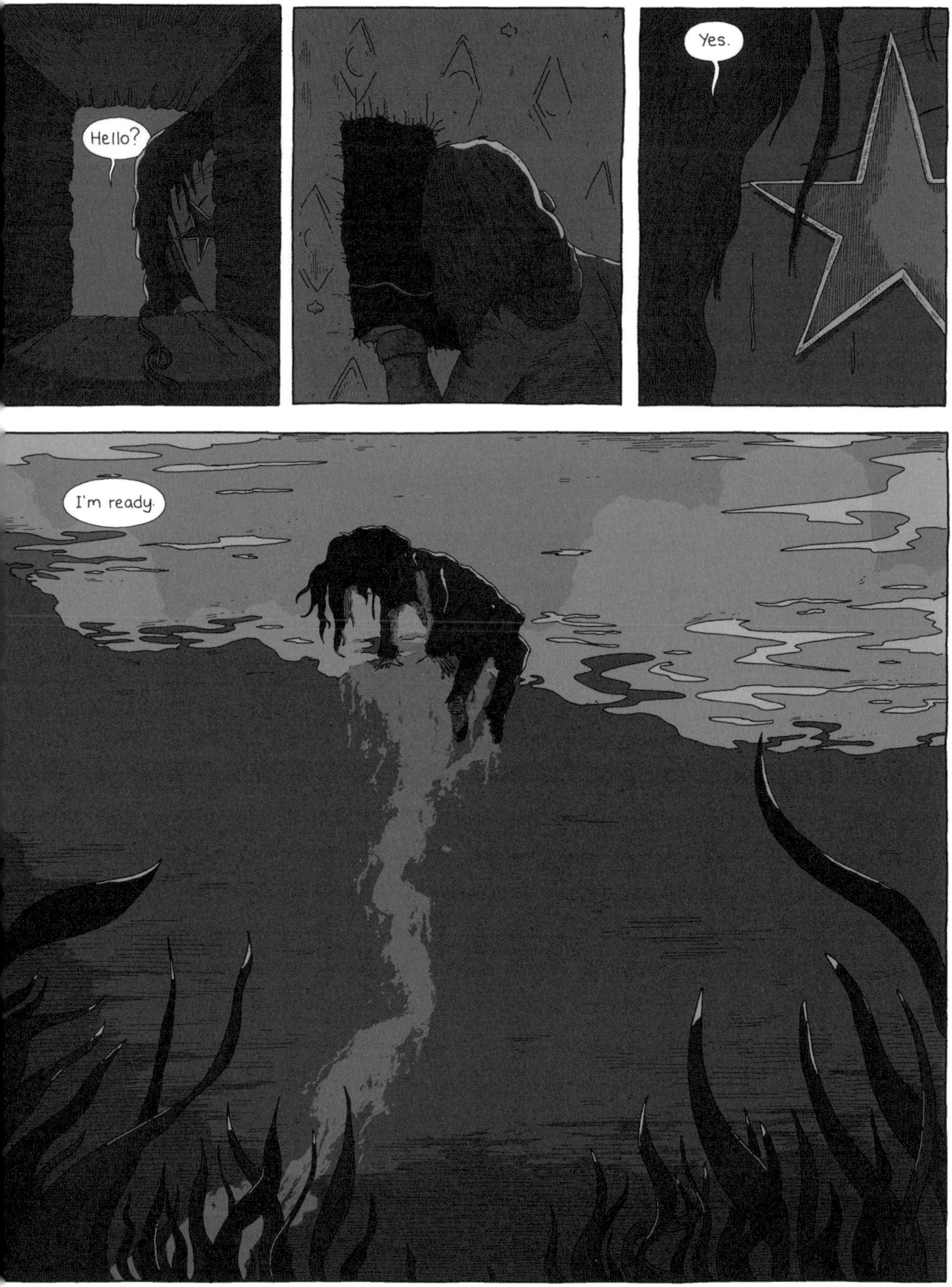
Hello?
Yes.
I'm ready.

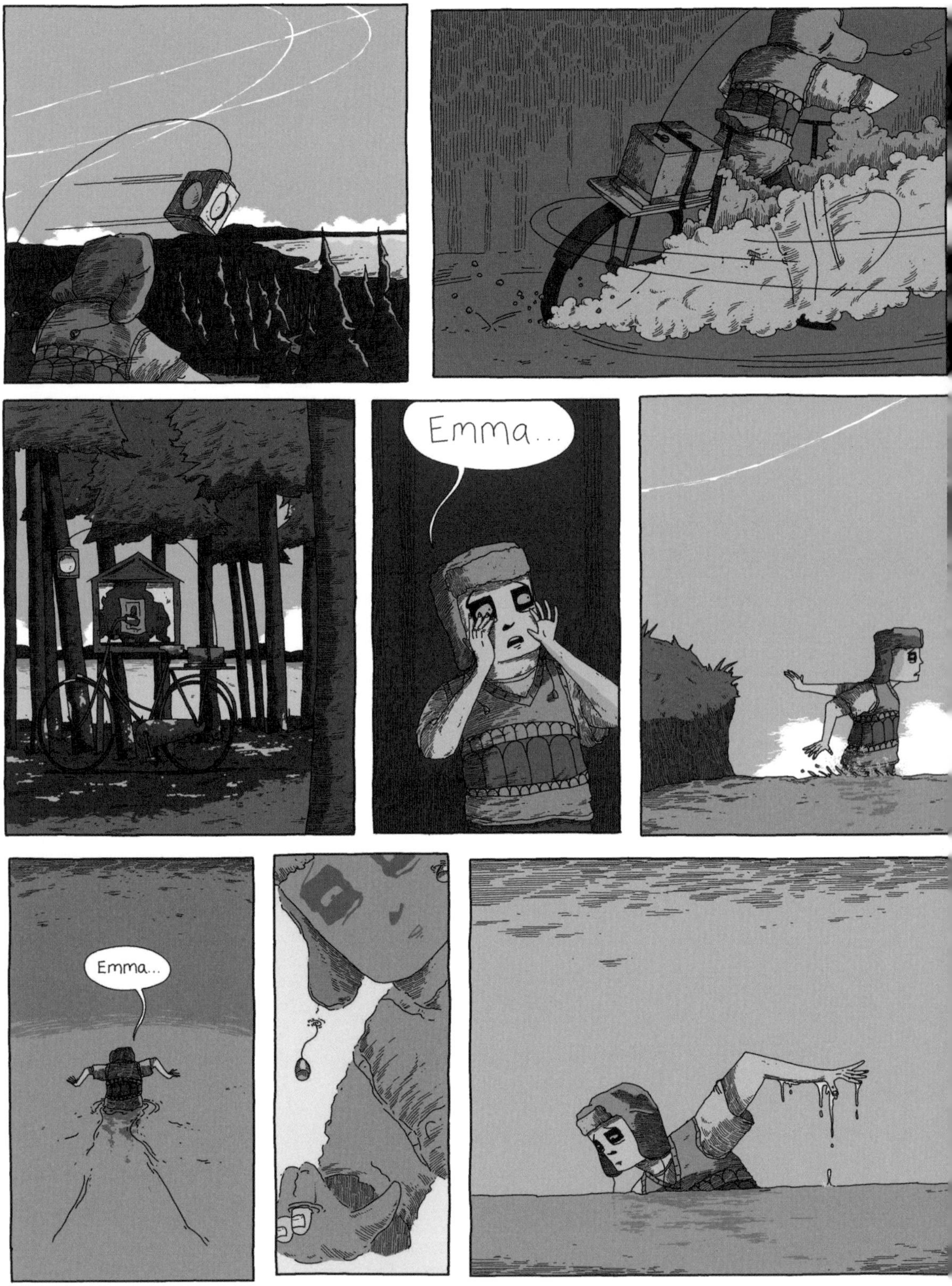
Emma...
Emma...

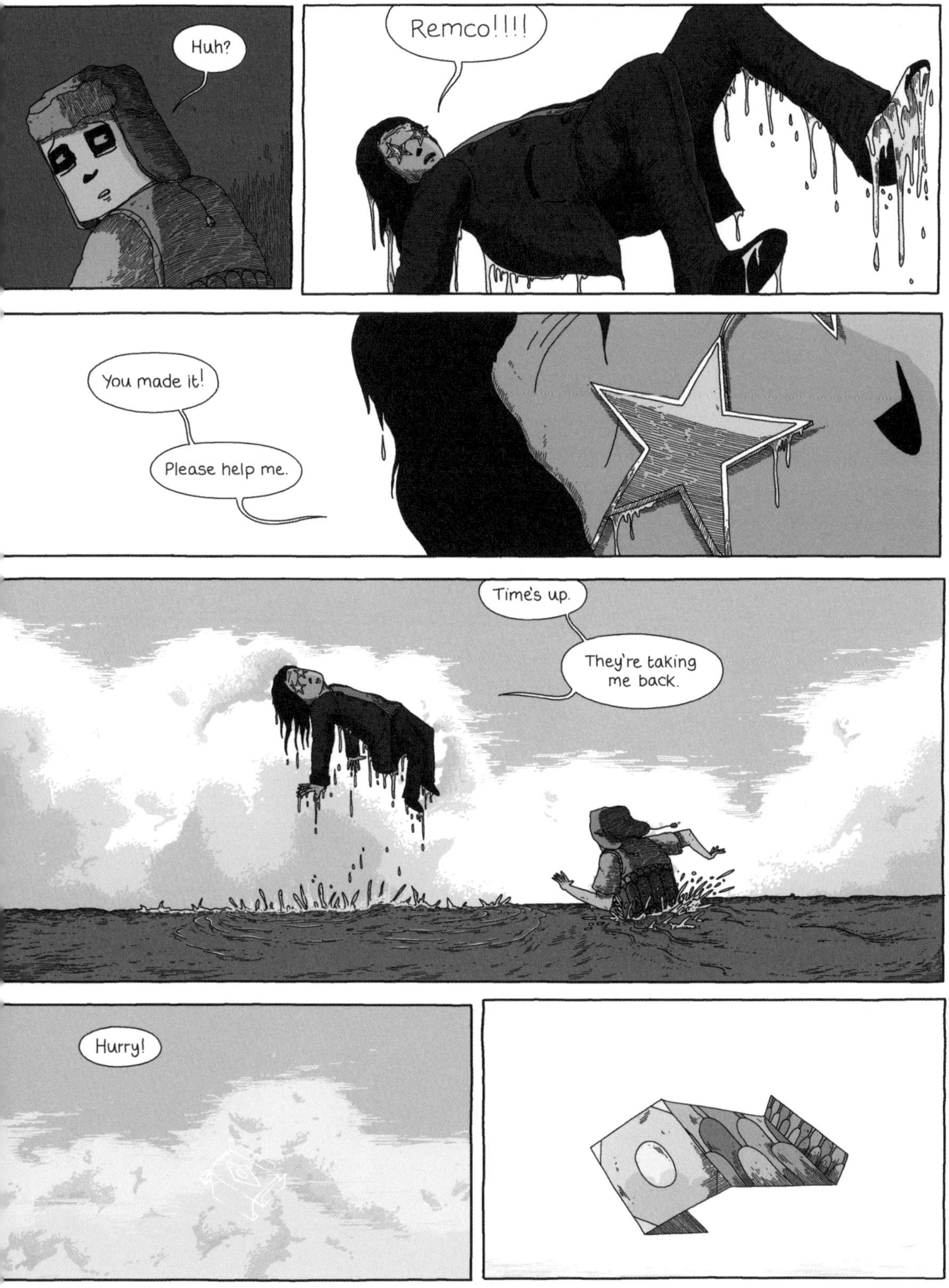
Huh?
Remco!!!!
You made it!
Please help me.
Time's up.
They're taking me back.
Hurry!

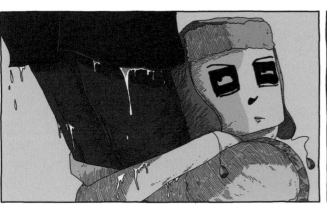

Got you!

Remco...thank you.

For coming to find me.

Emma, listen... my real n–

Err...

. . .

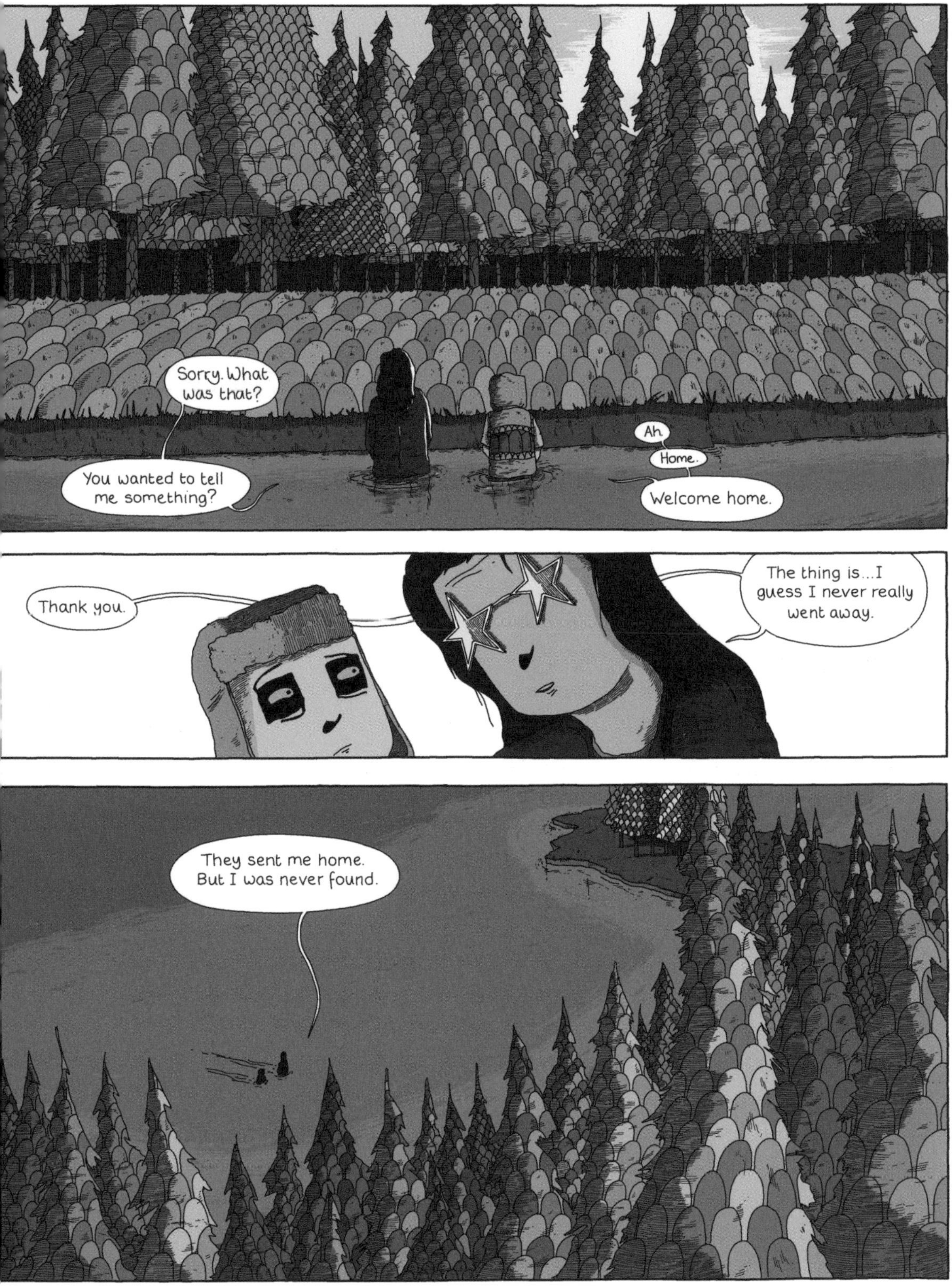
Sorry. What was that?
You wanted to tell me something?
Ah.
Home.
Welcome home.
Thank you.
The thing is...I guess I never really went away.
They sent me home. But I was never found.

Think we'll ever go back up there..?

Hmm.

Ready to go?

Sure. How about a backie on your bike?

The world awaits.

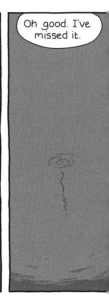

Oh good. I've missed it.

East Sussex
England
2017

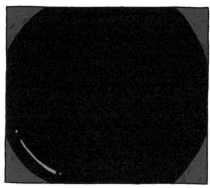

Things, as they tend to do, have changed since then. I've not seen Emma or used the name Remco for many years...it feels unreal. Like someone else's life.

But I still pretend I'm not me when I get nervous, I just don't use the name.

If my sentences go up at the end? I'm doing it.

Remco was merely a name I saw by chance in my local library while looking for books on UFO's as a kid, trying to make sense of what I'd seen. If I remember correctly it's a Nordic name, derived from Remme, one of the ravens that went between the gods and humans.

It appealed to my youthful ego.

I hope wherever Emma is, she's happy.

"clak"

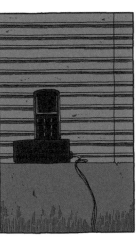

Now, I sleep soundly next to my wife by the English Channel...

...and in those still nights, I find myself thinking of that huge object less frequently now.

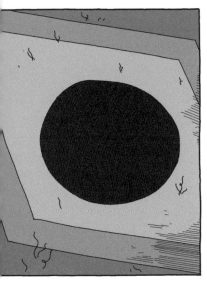

It changed everything. And I know I was lucky to have seen it.

Lucky...

...but not special.

Thank you

Sarah Faith. Linda & John. Diane & Rory Snookes.
Juliette & Stephen Wall. Steve Hughes. Krent Able.
Jennifer Hayden. Chris Staros. Leigh Walton.
Gilberto Lazcano. Alexander Boyagis. Shaun Tan.

And a special thank you to Steve 'badtwin' Turner.

Julian Hanshaw won the Observer/Comica short story award in 2008.
His graphic novels include the Prix-Europa-winning *The Art of Pho*
and *I'm Never Coming Back*. Julian also contributed to *Hoax: Psychosis
Blues*. His most recent graphic novel, *Tim Ginger*, was shortlisted
for the British Comic Awards and the LA Times Book Prize.

He lives on the south coast of the UK with his wife.

@HanshawJulian